CW00727030

Business and the State in Africa

The dominant developmental approach in Africa over the past twenty years has been to advocate the role of markets and the private sector in restoring economic growth. Recent thinking has also stressed the need for "ownership" of economic reform by the populations of developing countries, particularly the business community. This book studies the business–government interactions of four African countries: Ghana, Zambia, South Africa, and Mauritius. Employing a historical institutionalist approach, Antoinette Handley considers why and how business in South Africa and Mauritius has developed the capacity to constructively contest the making of economic policy while, conversely, business in Zambia and Ghana has struggled to develop any autonomous political capacity. Paying close attention to the mutually constitutive interactions between business and the state, Handley considers the role of timing and how ethnicized and racialized identities can affect these interactions in profound and consequential ways.

ANTOINETTE HANDLEY is Assistant Professor in the Department of Political Science at the University of Toronto. Her research interests include policy-making and economic reform in developing countries, business–government relations, and HIV/AIDS and the political economies of Africa. She has published articles in the *Journal of Modern African Studies*, *Current History*, and the *Canadian Journal of African Studies*.

Business and the State in Africa

Economic Policy-Making in the Neo-Liberal Era

ANTOINETTE HANDLEY
University of Toronto

CAMBRIDGE
UNIVERSITY PRESS

CAMBRIDGE UNIVERSITY PRESS
Cambridge, New York, Melbourne, Madrid, Cape Town, Singapore, São Paulo, Delhi

Cambridge University Press
The Edinburgh Building, Cambridge CB2 8RU, UK

Published in the United States of America by Cambridge University Press, New York

www.cambridge.org
Information on this title: www.cambridge.org/9780521713719

First published 2008

Printed in the United Kingdom at the University Press, Cambridge

A catalogue record for this publication is available from the British Library

Library of Congress Cataloguing in Publication Data
Handley, Antoinette.
  Business and the state in Africa: economic policy-making in the neo-liberal era /
  Antoinette Handley.
      p.   cm.
  Includes bibliographical references and index.
  ISBN 978-0-521-88605-5 (hbk) – ISBN 978-0-521-71371-9 (pbk.)
  1. Industrial policy–Africa   2. Business enterprises–Africa.   3. Africa–Economic
  policy.   I. Title.
  HD3616.A36 2008
  338.96–dc22
  2008011872

ISBN 978-0-521-88605-5 hardback
ISBN 978-0-521-71371-9 paperback

Contents

Figures

Acknowledgments

While I was working at the South African Institute of International Affairs in Johannesburg, South Africa, the Institute's then-director, Greg Mills, challenged me to think harder about the relationship between business and government in Africa. Many years have passed since then, over the course of which I learned a great deal and acquired many other debts, both intellectual and personal, but this first setting is most responsible for the genesis of this book. At Princeton University this germ of an idea took shape and I in turn was shaped into a political scientist. Jeff Herbst guided the project as it developed further and his perspicacity, intellectual rigor, and friendship challenged and motivated me throughout. Kent Eaton and Atul Kohli were similarly stimulating and generous teachers. In particular, Atul shaped my thinking on the historical development of institutions in important ways. Now a teacher myself, I must acknowledge my students, especially those in my seminar on African political economies, for what they have in turn taught me.

As a graduate student at Princeton, my work was supported by the Fulbright Program, the Center of International Studies, Council of Regional Studies, the Graduate School Princeton, and the MacArthur Foundation. Many of my early ideas were honed in discussion with fellow Woodrow Wilson Scholars at Princeton University and the Fellowship also supported me financially. The Irving Louis Horowitz Foundation for Social Policy and the Institute for the Study of World Politics provided crucial additional support. The University of Toronto subsequently provided a generous and convivial research environment via the Connaught Start Up and New Faculty funding programs, in addition to much appreciated teaching leave that facilitated additional field research.

At the University of Toronto, this project was shaped by dialogues facilitated by that long corridor in Sidney Smith Hall. Joe Carens provided wise counsel at every stage of the project, as did Richard

Simeon. Dick Sandbrook generously read numerous versions of almost every chapter of the book; although he will disagree with much of what I have to say, his remedial hand is everywhere to be seen. My colleagues Lou Pauly and Joe Wong both made time to read an entire early draft of the manuscript, as did Peter Lewis of Johns Hopkins, along with Bruce Berman (Queens University) and Sylvia Maxfield (Simmons) who kindly participated in a manuscript workshop organized by my department. I have benefited from the support of the talented community of Africanists at the University of Toronto, especially Dickson Eyoh, Sean Hawkins, Michael Lambek, Wambui Mwangi, Nakanyike Musisi, Richard Stren, and Richard Sandbrook.

It is a great pleasure to acknowledge those who taught me so much while I was doing fieldwork, in particular the interviewees who spoke with me so frankly about business–government relations in their countries. Many of them are named in what follows; many more remain unlisted. I thank also the librarians and staff at the University of Ghana in Legon, Ghana; the University of Zambia and the Institute for Economic and Social Research, both in Lusaka, Zambia; the University of the Witwatersrand and the South African Institute of International Affairs, both in Johannesburg, South Africa; and the University of Mauritius, Reduit. They keep their libraries accessible and conducive to research under what are often exceptionally difficult circumstances.

For their specific input into this project, I would like to acknowledge Johann Fedderke, Steven Friedman, Merle Lipton and Stefan Malherbe. Espelencia Baptiste, Girindre Beeharry, Kate Kuper, Melissa Levin, Giuliana Lund, Laurence Piper, Christian Sellars and Thomas Tieku commented on early drafts of chapters, greatly improving them. Dear friends and respected colleagues Sigrid Adriaenssens, James Akpo, Francis Antonie, Jeff Boulton, the late Theo Bull, Kathy Bunka, Hannah Green, David Gordon, Judi Hudson, Sally Jacques, Laurence Kuper, Earl Ofori-Atta, Bhizima Phiri, Spencer Rahman, Guy Scott, Naunihal Singh, and Neil van Heerden were tremendously helpful local sources of support, pointing me toward important contacts. Nic van de Walle and Muna Ndulo invited me to present some of these ideas at Cornell's Institute for African Development where I enjoyed a tremendously stimulating set of discussions.

Many thanks to my editor John Haslam for having shepherded this book through the review process with such courtesy and efficiency.

The suggestions of two anonymous CUP readers greatly improved the manuscript; any remaining errors or gracelessness are however mine alone. Pippa Lange's keen editorial eye over many years has made my writing easier to read, ironing out the harshest infelicities, and my readers may wish to join me in thanking her for that. Likewise, heartfelt thanks to Melissa Levin for her note-taking, eagle-eyed proofreading and keen political insights, and to Renan Levine for help with the tables. I thank the *Journal for Modern African Studies* (43, no. 2, 2005) and *Canadian Journal for African Studies* (41, no. 1, 2007) for granting copyright permission to use material first published in those journals.

Finally, many thanks to friends and family, in South Africa and elsewhere, who have put up with me all through the writing of this book. Giulio Boccaletti, Josh Greene, and Andrea Heberlein provided valued friendship and intellectual counsel as did Amanda Dickins who inspires me always with the verve and wit of her own writing. Special thanks to Sean for his unceasing love and support, and his great wisdom about how long it really takes to write a book. Thanks too to my wonderful family, especially my mother, for a lifetime of love. This book is dedicated to my late father, who answered many of my very first questions in life about politics.

Abbreviations

AAC	Anglo American Corporation
AGC	Ashanti Goldfields Company
AGI	Association of Ghana Industries
AHI	Afrikaanse Handelsinstituut
AHRIM	Association des Hôteliers et Restaurateurs de l'île Maurice
ANC	African National Congress
BAF	Business Assistance Fund
BEE	Black Economic Empowerment
BMF	Black Management Forum
BSA	Business South Africa
CBM	Consultative Business Movement
CEO	Chief Executive Officer
CIBA	Council of Independent Business Associations
CMB	Cocoa Marketing Board
CODESA	Conference for a Democratic South Africa
COSATU	Congress of South African Trade Unions
CPP	Congress People's Party
EAZ	Economics Association of Zambia
EPZ	Export Processing Zone
ERC	Economic Review Committee
ERP	Economic Recovery Programme
EU	European Union
FAGE	Federation of Associations of Ghanaian Exporters
FCI	Federated Chambers of Industry
FDI	Foreign Direct Investment
GDP	Gross Domestic Product
GEA	Ghana Employers' Association
GFA	*Growth for All: An Economic Strategy for South Africa*
GNCC/I	Ghana National Chambers of Commerce and Industry

GNPC   Ghana National Petroleum Company
IDC   Industrial Development Corporation
IFI   International Financial Institution
IMF   International Monetary Fund
INDECO   Industrial Development Corporation (Zambia)
ISI   Import Substitution Industrialization
JEC   Joint Economic Council
JSE   Johannesburg Stock Exchange
LP   Labour Party
MCCI   Mauritius Chamber of Commerce and Industry
MD   Managing Director
MEF   Mauritius Employers' Federation
MERG   Macro-Economic Research Group
MMD   Movement for Multi-Party Democracy
MMM   Mouvement Militant Mauricien
MP   Member of Parliament
MSM   Mouvement Socialiste Militant
MSPA   Mauritius Sugar Producers Association
NAFCOC   National African Federated Chambers of Commerce
NDC   National Democratic Congress
NEDLAC   National Economic Development and Labour Council
NEF   National Economic Forum
NP   National Party
NPP   New Patriotic Party
OECD   Organisation for Economic Co-operation and
          Development
PEF   Private Enterprise Foundation
PMSD   Parti Mauricien Social Démocrate
PMXD   Parti Mauricien Xavier Duval
PNDC   Provisional National Defence Council
PSAG   Private Sector Advisory Group
RDP   Reconstruction and Development Programme
SACOB   South African Chamber of Business
SACP   South African Communist Party
SAF   South Africa Foundation
SAP   Structural Adjustment Programme
SIT   Sugar Investment Trust
SOE   State-Owned Enterprise

UDF	United Democratic Front
UGCC	United Gold Coast Convention
UGFC	United Ghana Farmers' Council
UNIP	United National Independence Party
VAT	Value-Added Tax
ZACCI	Zambia Association of Chambers of Commerce and Industry
ZAM	Zambia Association of Manufacturers
ZCCM	Zambia Consolidated Copper Mines
ZESCO	Zambia Electricity Supply Commission
ZIC	Zambia Investment Centre
ZIMCO	Zambia Industrial and Mining Corporation
ZNFU	Zambia National Farmers' Union
ZPA	Zambia Privatisation Agency

Introduction: the African business class and development

It now seems to me less important that the domestic bourgeoisie should be efficient – technically, financially or otherwise – as capitalists, as individual accumulators, than they should be competent politically as a class: that they should, as a class, recognise the requirements of capital accumulation for capital as a whole and be able to see to it that these requirements are met.[1]

In the late summer of 1981, in a hot and sticky Washington DC, staff members of the World Bank were strategizing how best to release a report entitled *Accelerated Development in Sub-Saharan Africa*.[2] Some were nervous about how the report might be received – and rightly so.[3] The content of those 200-odd pages proved highly controversial. They would also be enormously consequential, reshaping the role of the state in economies across the developing world for decades to come. In sub-Saharan Africa,[4] the impact of the report would be directly felt through policies of structural adjustment that linked access to development finance to a neo-liberal set of economic policies. Africa's growth prospects, the report argued, had been curtailed by the overreach of the state; what was needed instead was a greater role for unfettered market forces and for the private sector. The report represented nothing less than an agenda to revolutionize the respective roles of the public and private sectors in African economies. The attempt to implement that agenda, however, produced uneven results.

---

[1] Colin Leys, "Learning from the Kenya Debate," in *Political Development and the New Realism in Sub-Saharan Africa*, ed. David E. Apter and Carl G. Rosberg (Charlottesville, VA: University Press of Virginia, 1994), 230.

[2] Known, for short, as the Berg Report.

[3] Devesh Kapur, John P. Lewis, and Richard Webb, *The World Bank: Its First Half Century*, 2 vols., vol. 1 (Washington, DC: Brookings Institution Press, 1997), 717.

[4] Henceforth, I will use Africa as shorthand for sub-saharan Africa.

This book focuses on what are, from one perspective at least, a counterintuitive set of policy-making outcomes arising out of those efforts: During the neo-liberal era, the World Bank pressed African states to accord a greater role in the running of the economy and in economic policy-making to the private sector. At the start of the 1990s, the governments of both Ghana and Zambia were regarded as two of the most radical neo-liberal reformers in Africa and both expressed – and even displayed – some commitment to consulting business in the making of economic policy. By the end of that decade, however, the impact of the business community as a whole on economic policy-making in those two countries was negligible.

By contrast, at the beginning of the 1990s, neither the new government in South Africa nor Mauritius appeared likely supporters of neo-liberalism, and the World Bank enjoyed little policy leverage in either country. Moreover, in both instances, the state had little reason to regard business as a policy-making partner but instead regarded business with a considerable degree of hostility. Nonetheless, by the end of the decade, in these two countries business did have a significant and sustained impact on economic policy-making.

How do we explain these strikingly divergent results? My answer is that outcomes in South Africa and Mauritius differed from those in Ghana and Zambia for reasons that had little to do with the World Bank. Rather, policy-making in the former cases was shaped by the existence of strong institutions on both sides. Both business and government displayed high levels of capacity to engage in a robust and sustained set of exchanges concerning policy; to wit, business–government interaction fostered a process of constructive contestation in South Africa and Mauritius. In Ghana and Zambia, by contrast, the process more closely resembled neo-patrimonial collusion. In such a situation, where both the state and the local business community lack capacity, the state will win out, and where the state in question is neo-patrimonial, policy-making will probably be highly personalized.

Constructive contestation of policy is unlikely to occur where business is so weak that the state can act as it chooses nor where business is so strong that the state simply rolls over and serves business interests. Rather, it requires energetic policy contestation between two relatively well-matched protagonists, and that each player is both structurally powerful enough and organizationally efficient enough that its views must be taken seriously in resolving on any course of action. Policy processes are strengthened when the state is forced to engage in considered, inclusive consultation with important social actors – such as business.

Crucially then, it is not just the state but business too that must have a significant level of political capacity. Of course, the characters of these two actors are closely connected: how business looks and behaves depends in large part on the state, and the reverse is true too although perhaps less so. Nonetheless, the quality of policy-making in any given moment will ultimately depend on the nature of the state, the nature of business, and the consequent relationship between these two sets of actors.

The phrase "constructive contestation" implies a number of features about this policy-making relationship.[5] First of all, it signifies that it was a genuine process of *contestation*. In South Africa and Mauritius, business and government often had very different ideas about what optimal economic policies were, and their engagements over the content of that policy were not always entirely friendly. Indeed relations between business and government were at times marked by mutual suspicion and some coolness. This is in contrast with Ghana and Zambia where elements of the business community were instead very close to government – perhaps too close – and their interactions were often conducted on a highly personal basis.

The second element of the interaction is also important, however, namely that the policy interactions were *constructive*, i.e. it is not just that government's interactions with business were beneficial for the policy-making process but also that they were constructive in an architectural sense, viz. that they had the quality of actively constructing a particular kind of business community. In observable (if often unintended) ways, the states of Mauritius and South Africa fortified the ability of organized business to develop and defend a distinct set of interests. Moreover, while the state often mistrusted and disliked business, the interactions between the state and business were regularized and took place through institutionalized mechanisms. By contrast, in Ghana and Zambia, while the few businesspeople who enjoyed the favor of the state met with their political connections behind closed doors, the rest of the business community enjoyed little

---

[5] These ideas were developed also in discussions with Joe Carens and Amanda Dickins.

systematic access to policymakers. This resulted in the fracturing of the business community and the striking of individual bargains – a process that was unlikely to produce policy that was in the public interest or to foster the development of a powerful business class. My cases demonstrate then that not only are the character of state and business respectively important but also that states may be stronger (more developmentally effective) when they are weaker (constrained in policy-making).

There is another important respect in which an apparent weakness may in fact constitute a source of strength viz. with respect to ethnic divisions, often regarded as unambiguously detrimental to economic prospects. In particular circumstances these divisions may actually strengthen the capacity of business to serve as a robust policy partner. In Mauritius and South Africa, racialized and ethnicized cleavages effectively generated a kind of power-sharing arrangement, splitting power between two separate economic and political spheres. Public and private actors were thus forced to balance against each other, and their interaction was charged with a small but healthy dose of opposition. Such a process may well be in the interests of economic growth and the society as a whole. By contrast, elsewhere on the continent where there were few political imperatives for the separation of political and economic power, the workings of the neo-patrimonial state instead resulted in a fusion of political and economic elites, and policy-making strayed far from anything resembling the broader public interests, converging instead on the very particular needs of that small circle of overlapping elites.

These dynamics may well be true of many kinds of policy-making in many different parts of the world. I focus on *economic* policy-making because of its significance for broader economic outcomes and I argue that, all things being equal, a policy-making process characterized by constructive contestation is more likely to produce policy that serves the interests of a wider slice of the population than one of neo-patrimonial collusion. And I focus on *Africa* because its states continue to pose many of the sharpest challenges to those concerned with economic development.

Some might interpret my focus on the role of business in economic policy-making as indicating sympathy for the interests of business above all others in policy-making. This is to misunderstand the very nature of constructive contestation. If business were able to dominate economic policy it would be bad news for both the economy and the population. Rather, on a continent where it is all too easy for a small group of state-based elites to make policy in their own specific interests, it is preferable if the state, at the very least, is forced to negotiate and engage with one other set of organized and institutionalized interests, namely business. Ideally of course, one would wish to see the state consulting also other key social sectors – but this book is concerned with business in particular because of the role that it can play in economic development.

The subject of this book may also provoke broader questions about whether a market-based or capitalist route is best for African states. As important as this issue is, that is not the primary focus of this text. Rather, given that the dominant international milieu within which African economies currently operate is a capitalist one; that history has presented us with few happy examples of non-capitalist routes to economic development; and that neither of these two propositions seems likely to change anytime soon, my concern is with how best to make such a system work to the benefit of all. This challenge is especially difficult in a region of the world where the state seems remarkably ill-equipped to play a developmental role.

Constructive contestation – or neo-patrimonial collusion?

It is at least as true in Africa as it is elsewhere that the nature of business and of the economic environment within which it operates is shaped to a significant extent by the state. Granovetter uses the notion of embeddedness to demonstrate how personal networks and social institutions generate the milieu within which firms operate. This milieu can be positive, where developmental states generate trust, or it can be malign, where neo-patrimonial states encourage malfeasance.[6]

Of course, to argue that the market is mediated by the state is not novel. A distinguished line of thinkers that includes Polanyi, Gerschenkron, and Hirschman has long argued that the state is deeply implicated in the business of capitalist economic development.[7] As

---

[6] Mark Granovetter, "Economic Action and Social Structure: The Problem of Embeddedness," *American Journal of Sociology* 91, no. 3 (1985): 498.

[7] Alexander Gerschenkron, *Economic Backwardness in Historical Perspective, a Book of Essays* (Cambridge, MA: Belknap Press of Harvard University Press,

Weber taught us, a variety of capitalisms are "politically oriented"[8] –
but the generality of this assertion obscures as much as it reveals.
Politically oriented capitalists may flourish in many kinds of state–
business relationships, from the felicitous developmental state, to
varieties of corporatism, crony capitalism, and neo-patrimonialism.

How are we then to distinguish among these forms of capitalism?
In the same way that Evans developed a typology of the state's interaction with the market,[9] we need a typology in turn of the market's
interaction with the state. In the tradition of historical institutiona-
lism,[10] this book employs a focused, comparative analysis of the
relationship between business and government, highlighting three
junctures which are critical for the formulation and development of
business and of that relationship: colonialism, independence, and the
neo-liberal reform era. In each of these three eras, the private sector
emerges from and/or is "embedded" in an environment which is shaped
by the state – to widely differing degrees. In South Africa and Mauritius, business enjoys some breathing room, a sphere of economic
activity in which the business community can develop a discrete sense
of its own interests. By contrast, for Ghanaian and Zambian business,
their dominant mode of operation and incentives is driven by the state.
In all cases, however, the state faces its own incentives and constraints,
and the choices that political elites make in response to these are
enormously consequential in sculpting the political economy.

The state of the state

Let us begin then with the state itself. When I use the term "state,"
I am concerned not with the entire administrative and political

---

1962), Albert O. Hirschman, *The Strategy of Economic Development* (New
Haven, CT: Yale University Press, 1961), Karl Polanyi, *The Great
Transformation* (Boston, MA: Beacon Press, 1944).

[8] Max Weber, *Economy and Society: An Outline of Interpretive Sociology*, ed.
Guenther Roth and Claus Wittich, 3 vols., vol. 1 (New York: Bedminster Press,
1968), 165.

[9] Peter B. Evans, "Predatory, Developmental and Other Apparatuses:
Comparative Political Economy Perspectives on the Third World State,"
Sociological Forum 4, no. 4 (1989), Peter B. Evans, *Embedded Autonomy:
States and Industrial Transformation* (Princeton, NJ: Princeton University
Press, 1995).

[10] Peter A. Hall and Rosemary C. R. Taylor, "Political Science and the Three New
Institutionalisms," *Political Studies* 44 (1996).

structure of the state but with those sectors of the state that exert the greatest influence over economic policy-making.[11] These include the cabinet, those top-ranking politicians who deal with matters of economic policy, and high-level civil servants in the appropriate ministries (such as finance, trade, and industry). This group can be distinguished from, but often overlap with, the political elite. The political elite include those commentators, advisors, analysts, and family members who are not necessarily formally associated with the state, but who exercise decisive influence over key policymakers within the state.

State capacity has received a great deal of academic attention over the past twenty years.[12] For our purposes, the understanding of state capacity articulated by Hobson and Weiss is probably most helpful viz. "the ability to mobilize and coordinate society's resources in such a way as to augment the overall investible surplus (and ultimately raise living standards)."[13] In addition to the penetrative and extractive dimensions of state power, these authors stress – as I do – the importance of *negotiated* power, arguing that "state strength increases with the effective embedding of autonomy."[14]

A wide range of analysts agree that the capacity of African states to develop their economies has generally been low.[15] Nonetheless, the African state has been particularly important in shaping African

---

[11] In particular, I refer to the national government. Arguably, in South Africa at least, a rather different set of business–government relations pertains at the provincial level as opposed to the national level; specifically, provincial-level interactions might present greater coincidence of neo-patrimonial and ethnicized connections. (Many thanks to Melissa Levin for this observation.) This is an important qualification that deserves a fuller treatment than is possible here.

[12] Michael Mann, "The Autonomous Power of the State: Its Origins, Mechanisms and Results," in *Political Geography: A Reader*, ed. J. Agnew (London: Arnold, 1997), Theda Skocpol, "Bringing the State Back In: Strategies of Analysis in Current Research," in *Bringing the State Back In*, ed. Peter B. Evans, Dietrich Rueschemeyer, and Theda Skocpol (Cambridge University Press, 1985), Linda Weiss and John M. Hobson, *States and Economic Development: A Comparative Historical Analysis* (Cambridge: Polity Press, 1995).

[13] Weiss and Hobson, *States and Economic Development*, 4.   [14] Ibid., 7.

[15] The list is potentially very long. It includes Goran Hyden, *Beyond Ujamaa in Tanzania: Underdevelopment and an Uncaptured Peasantry* (London: Heinemann, 1980), Atul Kohli, *State-Directed Development: Political Power and Industrialization in the Global Periphery* (Cambridge University Press, 2004), Crawford Young, *African Colonial State in Comparative Perspective* (New Haven, CT: Yale University Press, 1994).

business communities – for two reasons. First, decolonization in the late 1950s and early 1960s coincided with the heyday of development economics when there was wide support for the view that Third World countries could catch up with the developed world if their governments substituted for the failings of private capital markets. This complements the Gerschenkronian expectation that the later the process of industrialization, the more the state would have to intervene to organize and invest capital.[16]

Newly independent African states thus came of age in an international context that warmly approved state-led and import substitution industrialization (ISI) development models. Most inherited very weak, small indigenous business communities but, in terms of the conventional wisdom of the day, this was regarded as no great obstacle. Governments employed a range of strategies to develop their economies. The constellation of social cleavages in each territory and how these mapped onto struggles over economic and political power would determine exactly how these instruments were employed and to what effect.[17] The result was often to place a large amount of discretion over the functioning of the market in the hands of a few state-based actors.

Second, the African state was unusually influential on the formation of the African business class not only because of this late, late-industrialization context, but also because of its particular character, viz. neo-patrimonial. Because I am concerned with how the neo-patrimonial state fashions the "rules of the game" for business too, I find Nicolas van de Walle's definition of neo-patrimonialism most useful:[18]

---

[16] Gerschenkron, *Economic Backwardness in Historical Perspective*. For a masterful treatment of this idea, see John Iliffe, *The Emergence of African Capitalism* (Minneapolis, MN: University of Minneapolis Press, 1983). Baran and Kurth also argue that it is important to consider the timing of a particular country's industrialization for the kind of economic development that follows. Paul Baran, *The Political Economy of Growth* (New York: Monthly Review Press, 1957), James R. Kurth, "The Political Consequences of the Product Cycle: Industrial History and Political Outcomes," *International Organization* 33, no. 1 (1979).

[17] See, for example, Nicola Swainson, "Indigenous Capitalism in Postcolonial Kenya," in *The African Bourgeoisie*, ed. Paul M. Lubeck (Boulder, CO: Lynne Rienner, 1987).

[18] Nicolas van de Walle, *African Economies and the Politics of Permanent Crisis 1979–1999* (Cambridge University Press, 2001), 51–2.

Outwardly the state has all the trappings of a Weberian rational-legal system, with a clear distinction between the public and the private realm, with written laws and a constitutional order. However, this official order is constantly subverted by a patrimonial logic, in which officeholders almost systematically appropriate public resources for their own uses and political authority is largely based on clientelist practices, including patronage, various forms of rent-seeking and prebendalism.

Van de Walle is talking explicitly here about the state, but that state actively structures the economic context for social actors. Subversion of institutional authority and self-interested behavior is thus not unique to state officials but equally may describe how politically connected businesspeople behave in a neo-patrimonial political economy. In such a context, the distinction between the public and private realm – and the public and private sectors – may virtually disappear. Indeed, where the state is highly neo-patrimonial, it seeks to draw the business and economic elite further into an incestuous relationship with itself – and this pressure can be enormously hard to withstand.

Neo-patrimonialism is thus not restricted to the state nor is it a given condition; it arises out of ongoing tussles between leading political and economic actors. The social cleavages that may carve up political and economic power – or fuse them – play into these struggles and are similarly dynamic. Nonetheless, history matters for the institutions and for the milieu that it generates, and some factors will make neo-patrimonialism more likely. Chief among these is the extent to which the state succeeds in monopolizing the decision-making terrain.

The first question then to consider at any given moment is whether the role and power of the state is being buttressed at the expense of other political and economic actors. Here it is not just the level of intervention by the state that is important, but the character of that intervention too. What kinds of functions, responsibilities, and powers does the state assume? In particular, is the intervention in the economy developmental or neo-patrimonial?

One of the key determinants of the state's character operates via its revenue stream: Can the state safeguard its economic interests merely by controlling the leading sub-sector, or does it have to negotiate with a wider range of disparate economic actors? Are there incentives in place that might induce a state to diversify the economy? Finally, are there external sources of funding (such as international development aid), which allow the state to ignore domestic economic actors? All of these factors will determine the extent to which the state negotiates policy decisions with other local actors.

The nature of business

I use the terms "business" or "the business community" as a proxy for the private sector, and the term "market" to indicate the arena of economic exchange within which that sector acts. Because I am interested in national-level policy negotiations, I focus predominantly on the indigenous business community.[19] This is to be distinguished from the "economic elite," those key individuals and families who comprise the topmost economic stratum of their society. Such people are situated most often within the business sector but also include those occupied in large-scale agriculture and those associated with international capital. The economic elite thus overlap but are not strictly coterminous with the business sector.

While acknowledging the importance of state capacity to economic development, this book advances our understanding of a frequently neglected dimension of that discussion viz. the capacity of business. The markers of business capacity differ from those for the state, but contribute likewise to the mobilization of societal resources in a way that adds to, rather than merely consumes, available surpluses.

Perhaps the most obvious prerequisite for business capacity is structural power in the Marxist sense, i.e. the power that comes from the private sector's economic weight in the economy. One of the clearest predictors of a business community with real political capacity is the existence of an "independent economic base" for the private sector.[20] If business is sufficiently prosperous to fund its own organization without recourse to the state or external donors, it is in a

---

[19] Some may object to my characterization of South Africa's white business community as indigenous. In the late nineteenth century, the South African business community included a large number of expatriate and specifically British businesspeople. However, as suggested by the moniker "settler," many of these businesspeople subsequently settled in South Africa, made it their permanent home, and became, for legal and political purposes, South African citizens.

[20] Analogous to Barrington Moore's notion of what is necessary for a bourgeois revolution. Barrington Moore, *Social Origins of Dictatorship and Democracy: Lord and Peasant in the Making of the Modern World* (Boston, MA: Beacon Press, 1966), xv.

far stronger position to negotiate with the state. This will reflect in large measure how influential the private sector – as opposed to the public sector – is in the national economy. As a rule, the more businesspeople rely on the functioning of the markets for their profitability, the greater their capacity (both as accumulators and political actors) will be.[21] This requires that, in its everyday functioning, business does not depend for its success on political fealty to the ruling party.

The structural power that business enjoys in the economy both facilitates and is enhanced by organizational effectiveness, in particular the degree to which it has developed a high level of institutional efficiency. Here we should consider such factors as the extent to which the administration and activities of organized business are institutionalized and considered legitimate. We should focus on business' capacity to respond to policies, to project these responses publicly, and to strategize its lobbying of policymakers. With respect to the latter, we must distinguish between business influence which is exercised via formal, transparent, and legitimate institutions, and the behind-the-scenes, personalized influence sometimes enjoyed by individual businesspeople. These two forms of influence have very different content and outcomes. The first builds the capacity of the organized business community. The latter has the tendency to further weaken and divide businesspeople from each other.

Further, a business community should not only include a diversity of interests within its own ranks, but have the capacity to effectively manage that diversity. Crucial here is the ability of businesspeople to see themselves as part of a larger grouping (what Marxists might term "class consciousness"), but they should also possess the organizational capacity to generate and collate pan-business positions, and to pursue them, i.e. the ability to cohere as a set of political actors. A key component of political capacity is thus the ability of an institution to resolve conflicts, not only with other parties, but within its own ranks too, and to develop a baseline set of policies that serve the interests of business more broadly. How difficult this task is depends on the structure of both business itself and of the economy. If the economy is

[21] This is the direct corollary of Catherine Boone's argument concerning the political autonomy of rural elites. Catherine Boone, *Political Topographies of the African State: Territorial Authority and Institutional Choice* (Cambridge University Press, 2003), 23.

dominated by one large sub-sector whose interests are at odds with those of the rest of the business community and which could be co-opted or taken over by the state, this could weaken the capacity of business. This is not to suggest that business organizations need always represent each single member perfectly. In Mauritius and South Africa, it is evident that some sectors of the business community won a greater share of the policy "voice" than others. What was important, however, was that there was a process of internal contestation of policy too, to mirror business' own external contestation of the state.

Finally, a minimal level of autonomy for business (autonomy from the state in particular) is also an important component of business capacity in Africa.[22] Atul Kohli has written that a key feature of a developmentally effective modern state is "a well-established public arena that is both normatively and organizationally distinguishable from private interests and pursuits."[23] One might invert his object and subject and argue that, similarly, a developmentally effective business community operates within a well-established *private* arena that is both normatively and organizationally distinguishable from the interests and pursuits of the state and the ruling party. For the purposes of this study, I define an autonomous business community as one which conceives of its economic and political interests as identifiable and distinct (from those of other groups in society, including the state), and is organized in pursuit of those interests.

In a region where the norm more closely approximates a fusion of political and economic elites, some autonomy is a necessary but not sufficient component of business capacity. Because the state looms large in much of Africa and frequently assumes a neo-patrimonial aspect, it is crucial that business interests secure some "space" within which they can develop a distinct sense of their own interests. I should stress, however, that the concept of autonomy only makes sense in a relational context.[24] Autonomy is not solipsism.[25] More concretely

---

[22] Here I depart from Weiss and Hobson who argue that "strong states cultivate collaborative strategies with civil society." In a neo-patrimonial context, collaboration all too easily slips into collusion. Weiss and Hobson, *States and Economic Development*, 5.

[23] Kohli, *State-Directed Development*, 9.

[24] Feminist theorists have made a similar observation about the autonomy of individuals. Cf. Jennifer Nedelsky, "Reconceiving Autonomy," *Yale Journal of Law and Feminism* 1 (1989).

[25] Personal communication with Amanda Dickins.

stated, the nature of business and the kind of autonomy it enjoys is profoundly shaped by its relationship with the state and the nature of that state.

Autonomy, moreover, is only one variable that must be considered alongside other, more qualitative judgments about the nature of business–government interactions. After all, in and of itself, a low level of autonomy for business – say, where the state in question is more developmentally inclined – might still produce better policy-making outcomes than a scenario in which business has an equivalent level of autonomy but the state's neo-patrimonial tendencies are more pronounced. Indeed, autonomy is closely linked to the nature of the state in the sense that a highly neo-patrimonial state is unlikely to permit significant levels of political autonomy for business. Nonetheless, business autonomy is not inconsequential: it is striking that the business communities of South Africa and Mauritius evince significantly higher levels of autonomy than their counterparts in Ghana and Zambia (or indeed in most other African countries) which have very little capacity to constructively contest policy.

There are then four related characteristics to monitor with respect to the private sector: is the private sector growing more powerful within the economy, and, in its own organization, becoming more institutionalized, more diverse[26] and more autonomous? Four affirmative responses would likely significantly increase the sector's capacity and willingness to engage the state on crucial policy questions. Business would be increasingly empowered, both as a significant economic actor in its own right and as a litigant party in policy disputes, to shape the course of decision making. Moreover, business practices and modes of organization would be directed on and driven largely by developments in the economic sphere.

By contrast, to the extent that they directly engage the state, entrepreneurs operating in a neo-patrimonial context do so in strikingly different ways. In such societies, entrepreneurs must contend with a lack of predictability, insecure property rights, little or no contract enforcement, and prices for basic inputs that are largely determined by government. Understandably, businesspeople are loath to invest hard-earned capital in ventures that may be risky or only

---

[26] By diverse I mean with reference to the sub-sectors of the economy that business is based in, size of the firm, and domestic or export orientation.

produce returns over the long term. The result is low levels of private investment in fixed productive assets. Instead, those with capital may invest in currency speculation or export/import businesses, seeking to exploit arbitrage opportunities. Others may choose to keep their assets liquid, to invest in property or to expatriate their savings to foreign banks. All of these are rational accumulation strategies in an insecure economic context. Unfortunately, they do not contribute to a broad, diverse, and sustainable industrialization process; nor do they contest – but rather collude in – the political allocation of economic opportunity. It is crucial then to examine how social cleavages, built around factors such as race, class, ethnicity, and political partisanship, affect this economic milieu.

Public–private sector interactions

We ignore at our peril how the *interaction* between business and the state may sculpt each of those two parties, and ultimately transform policy-making outcomes. Neo-liberals, for example, while acutely aware of the power of the state to create and pursue rent-seeking opportunities in an economy tend to lionize the forces of the market and the private sector. Their analysis ignores the interaction between these two sets of actors and how they may fuse and come to be almost indistinguishable from each other.

We need to understand, therefore, the relationship between business and the state, and the kind of economic environment that this establishes. I have already argued that, relative to other parts of the world, Africa's private sectors are exceptionally close to their states. I have also pointed out that it is important to consider not just how close a business community is to the state, but the character of that state too. The relevant question here then is not whether there is any interaction or overlap between business and government. Inevitably there is some, even in liberal, highly industrialized economies. The real question concerns the quality of the two sets of actors, and the nature of their interaction. Here it is vital to distinguish between the fertile ground of embedded autonomy and the "developmental bog"[27] of neo-patrimonial fusion. The state looms large in all of this and serves to

[27] Paul D. Hutchcroft, *Booty Capitalism: The Politics of Banking in the Philippines* (Ithaca, NY: Cornell University Press, 1998).

determine the dominant political and economic incentives. In order to understand the dynamics of this interaction, we must consider when and how business and the state emerge and develop.

The origins and development of the African business class

The current literature on Africa is ill-equipped to answer specific questions about the nature of the indigenous business class or how it might have emerged. An early generation of developmental theorists argued that in developing economies market forces alone were insufficient to accelerate development, and the state would therefore have to intervene. This championing of the state had at least two consequences: a burgeoning literature on the Third World (and African) state and a variety of state-based development strategies. One such example was the "governed market" strategy which worked relatively well in East Asia where there was a very particular kind of state.[28] High levels of state involvement were, however, a resounding failure in much of Africa and provoked questions about the capacity of African states to lead development. A number of respected observers of Africa subsequently argued that African states are flawed in numerous ways and hence unable to fulfill their developmental role on the continent.[29] Accordingly, the policy focus shifted back to the African market.

In the 1980s, neo-liberals, for example, advocated the almost complete withdrawal of the state from any attempts at African development on the grounds that that state was ineluctably flawed and that only the forces of the market could restore sustainable growth. However, while studies of the failed African state abound, there is not an equivalent body of work on the "market." Africa's private sector is understudied in the academic literature, particularly when one considers its supposed centrality to economic development.[30] The bitter but largely

---

[28] Robert Wade, *Governing the Market: Economic Theory and the Role of Government in East Asian Industrialization* (Princeton, NJ: Princeton University Press, 1990).

[29] For example Robert H. Bates, *Markets and States in Tropical Africa: The Political Basis of Agricultural Policies* (Berkeley, CA: University of California Press, 1981), Richard Sandbrook and Judith Barker, *The Politics of Africa's Economic Stagnation* (Cambridge University Press, 1985).

[30] Hopkins remarks that "[i]ndigenous entrepreneurs have occupied a relatively modest place in the literature." A. G. Hopkins, "Big Business in African Studies," *Journal of African History* 28, no. 1 (1987): 126, 127 and 135.

unresolved battle over Kenya's indigenous capitalist class in the 1970s aside,[31] the subject is also under-theorized. This book therefore addresses an important and under-served topic.

A word about case selection: There is no doubt, in terms at least of the way their business communities look and behave, that South Africa and Mauritius appear exceptional in sub-Saharan Africa.[32] Some might object that this makes them less interesting or useful for considering the nature of the business class in Africa. On the contrary, it is precisely this feature that makes them crucial cases to consider alongside Ghana and Zambia, arguably more "typical" in this respect. If we are to understand why so many African business communities suffer from a severe lack of political capacity, we need also to understand why, in these two instances, politically effective business communities *were* able to emerge. In short, they provide the necessary variation on the dependent variable. At the same time, I do recognize that the distinguishing features of these cases are embedded in a larger history and that, as such, it is not possible to extract clear policy implications from South Africa and Mauritius and apply them unproblematically to vastly dissimilar cases. Nonetheless, a careful historical analysis can provide essential clues about how political processes and class formation diverge in our different cases.

Recent exceptions include Deborah Brautigam, Lise Rakner, and Scott Duncan Taylor, "Business Associations and Growth Coalitions in Sub-Saharan Africa," *Journal of Modern African Studies* 40, no. 4 (2002), Marcel Fafchamps, *Market Institutions in Sub-Saharan Africa: Theory and Evidence* (Cambridge, MA: The MIT Press, 2004), Alusine Jalloh and Toyin Falola, eds., *Black Business and Economic Power* (Rochester, NY: University of Rochester Press, 2002), Lise Rakner, "The Pluralist Paradox: The Decline of Economic Interest Groups in Zambia in the 1990s," *Development and Change* 32 (2001).

[31] Raphael Kaplinsky, "Capitalist Accumulation in the Periphery – the Kenyan Case Re-Examined," *Review of African Political Economy* 7, no. 17 (1980), Leys, "Learning from the Kenya Debate," Colin Leys, *Underdevelopment in Kenya: The Political Economy of Neo-Colonialism* (Berkeley, CA: University of California Press, 1974).

[32] I say "appear" because these are African states and they are, accordingly, studied as such. For persuasive arguments to this end, cf. Deborah Brautigam, "Institutions, Economic Reform and Democratic Consolidation in Mauritius," *Comparative Politics* 30, no. 1 (1997), Mahmoud Mamdani, *Citizen and Subject: Contemporary Africa and the Legacy of Late Colonialism* (Princeton, NJ: Princeton University Press, 1996), Richard Sandbrook, "Origins of the Democratic, Developmental State: Interrogating Mauritius," *Canadian Journal of African Studies* 39, no. 3 (2005).

A distinguished line of scholars argues that we should look to the sub-sector that dominates the economy to explain the character and functioning of the major political-economic institutions.[33] My case selection allows us to test this explanation too: Zambia and South Africa are both mining-based economies, while Ghana and Mauritius are more agricultural-based. I conclude, however, that, in the end, the sub-sectoral argument cannot adequately explain the outcomes that we see.

Finally, it might also be argued that a simpler explanation for the different policy-making outcomes is that Mauritius and South Africa had a higher level of economic development than Ghana and Zambia. I will deal with this argument more fully in the Conclusion. For now, however, I would like to address an analytically prior question arising from this objection: i.e. why is it that the business communities of South Africa and Mauritius are so much larger and stronger than those of Ghana and Zambia? I demonstrate that the institutional paths and relationships that inform business capacity in the neo-liberal era were laid down historically in two earlier critical junctures, colonialism and independence, and were enormously consequential for the nature and quality of the business community that resulted.

Over the course of my research, I spent five to nine weeks at a time in each of the four case study countries between 2001 and 2004, returning in some cases two or three times. During that time, I conducted hundreds of interviews, principally with businesspeople and policymakers. I spoke also with a range of informed observers, including journalists, diplomats, academics, and those working at policy and financial institutions. Many of these are cited directly in my study. (A small number of my sources requested confidentiality.) In addition, I consulted the policy documents and budget statements of the relevant government ministries and business associations, as well as reviewing newspaper and other archives, and the pertinent secondary literature.

Before moving on, it might be useful for the reader who is unfamiliar with these four countries to consider comparatively the following broad range of indicators (see Table 1). They confirm that both Zambia

[33] Terry Lynn Karl, *The Paradox of Plenty: Oil Booms and Petro-States* (Berkeley, CA: University of California Press, 1997), Michael D. Shafer, *Winners and Losers: How Sectors Shape the Developmental Prospects of States* (Ithaca, NY: Cornell University Press, 1994).

Table 1. *Select economic and political indicators for case study countries*

		Zambia	Ghana	Mauritius	South Africa
Freedom House	1990/1	Partly free	Not free	Free	Partly free
Score	2000/1	Partly free	Free	Free	Free
Corruption Perceptions Index	1998	3.5	3.3	5.0	5.2
1 = totally corrupt; 10 = corruption free	2000	3.4	3.5	4.7	5.0
Life expectancy	1990	46 years	56 years	69 years	62 years
at birth, total	2000	38 years	57 years	72 years	48 years
Per capita GDP (constant	1990	$361	$211	$2,535	$3,152
2000 US$)	2000	$303	$250	$3,766	$3,020

Sources: Freedom House, *Country Ratings* (website); available from www.freedom house.org (accessed 2007); Transparency International, Corruption Perceptions Index (website); available from www.transparency.org (accessed 2007); 1990 figures not available; World Bank Group, World Development Indicators (website); available from http://devdata.worldbank.org/dataonline/ (accessed 2007).

and Ghana at the start of the 1990s were low-income countries with a relatively poor state of political and civil rights. Mauritius and South Africa by contrast scored a little higher in both these areas.

Economic policy is the outcome of bargaining between key political and economic actors. When explaining the outcome of that bargaining, we need to ask what the relative strengths of the key protagonists are: for our purposes, the state and business. Part of the answer to this question lies in proximate developments, which can be uncovered by tracing the policy-making process of the 1990s. However, many of the underlying dynamics are the product of a long history of engagement and encounter between elites competing for various kinds of power and resources. Context is often omitted from the comparativist lexicon, and this comes at a cost. What is required is a comparative methodology that pays attention both to the specificity of individual cases and to their relevance to each other. In each instance we need to know what the historic origins of the business community are and how these have affected its development since.

The formation of a business class with real political capacity is a complex process that cannot be reduced to one or two variables. Nonetheless, my four cases generate a number of richly suggestive hypotheses. First, they suggest that there are clearly identifiable moments, "critical junctures,"[34] which result in the development of a capable indigenous business class in some cases and not in others. At each such juncture two related dynamics interact: a) *ceteris paribus*, states, wherever possible, seek to centralize and consolidate their power; and b) their ability to do so is constrained when social cleavages facilitate the emergence and consolidation of an autonomous sphere of private sector activity.

These junctures are times of social and political ferment when there is a real prospect that the relationship between the public and private sectors will be transformed, moments of potential "opening" where the roles and powers of core social institutions are under review. Such a juncture could be the result of external interventions, such as colonial occupation or the pressure exerted on economic policy-making by international financial institutions (IFIs) in the neo-liberal era.[35] It could also result from domestic challenges, for example when control of the state is secured by a new set of political players, as with the attainment of independence or democracy.

This book examines three of the most critical junctures that shaped the relationship between the public and private sectors. The first, the colonial era, was important because it established the relationship between an imposed state structure, indigenous political elites, and both expatriate and indigenous economic elites. At more or less the same moment that African societies were subjected to the colonial state form, their encounter with capitalism was also intensified.

---

[34] Cf. Stephen Krasner, "Approaches to the State: Alternative Conceptions and Historical Dynamics," *Comparative Politics* 16, no. 2 (1984).

[35] This is not to suggest that there were no critical junctures for any of the four cases prior to colonialism. See, for example, Jean-Francois Bayart, "Africa in the World: A History of Extraversion," *African Affairs* 99 (2000). Colonialism is by no means the definitive "starting point" of the encounter with capitalism – but it is perhaps the first point which can be systematically compared across all four cases. Moreover, the encounter with capitalism accelerates and intensifies in the colonial period.

The second juncture was the immediate post-independence era, the 1960s and 1970s, in which the state commonly embarked on a concerted effort to restructure its own economic and political role, and to reorder economic activity in that society. This, rather than the colonial era, was the critical moment for most of Africa's indigenous business classes, many of whom were born nearly simultaneously with – or shortly after – independence. Indeed, in a number of instances, a significant part of the indigenous business class was "birthed" by that newly anointed political class.

Finally, as already alluded to, the neo-liberal era is a critical juncture because it was a period of sustained international (and in some instances domestic) pressure for fundamental changes in the role of the public and private sectors in the economy. These three then were foundational moments in which the balance between state and market might have been tipped one way or another.

As argued above, the independence era was the most significant in terms of laying down a set of institutional pathways; it was at this point that our cases really began to split away from each other, so that by the era of neo-liberalism, the four cases already had very different institutional and structural endowments. This is not to assert a rigid path determinism. Once a path has been laid down, it may still be refused. The path will, however, make certain directions easier to follow than others and, as Kohli argues, institutions will likely endure "beyond the forces that have brought them into being."[36]

Timing matters for the development of these institutions, in at least two senses. First, timing matters as a sequencing issue: when and how did the private and public sectors first emerge in relation to each other, and what was their relative strength and character? It matters whether it is business or the state that emerges and consolidates the foundations for its political capacity first. In particular, if the state is able to consolidate itself well before the emergence of a sizable and economically powerful indigenous private sector, this can strengthen the hand of that state in subsequent interactions with business.

Timing matters in a second sense, already alluded to: the ideological and policy flavor of the era in which the local business community emerges will shape the nature of the state and its intervention in the economy and hence will determine the kind of "market" in which

---

[36] Kohli, *State-Directed Development*, 16.

business interests will have to function. Received wisdom about what the appropriate level and nature of the state's interventions in the economy are has shifted dramatically over the course of the past century and a half, sometimes favoring a high level of state intervention and at other points emphasizing instead the role of the private sector. It matters therefore whether a business community first emerged in the late nineteenth century or in the mid-twentieth century.

In many instances, like Zambia and to a lesser extent Ghana, Africa's highly centralized, newly independent states actively and directly engineered the birth of a new generation of African industries, firms, and state-owned-enterprises.[37] The origins of the managerial and business class were thus intimately connected with the state, from the moment of political independence.[38] Given these relatively recent – and coincident – origins, it is small wonder that, in many African countries, markets and the actors who animate them are still so closely tied to the state.

It is not just about various kinds of timing, however. The dynamics of timing are vitalized by social cleavages which may motivate state behavior in a direction that is either destructive of or helpful to the creation of a politically capacitated business community. Not all social cleavages are politically relevant to the relationship between business and government. However, my specific country cases suggest a counterintuitive role for ethnic identifications. Where the ethnic identification of the business class differs from that of the political class, this can serve to separate out a country's political and economic elites, not only in terms of the specific individuals who comprise each community, but also in terms of their logics, modes of social organization, and how they understand their economic and political interests. It is important to say, however, that ethnicity *per se* is not the crucial feature of this dynamic; nor is it unchanging over time. Rather, its significance is as a mechanism that serves to separate out the interests and functioning of the political and economic elites respectively.

[37] Sayre P. Schatz, *Nigerian Capitalism* (Berkeley, CA: University of California Press, 1977).

[38] Of course, there is a history of production and commercial activity across the subcontinent that long predates both independence and colonialism. This account, however, focuses on the classes associated with capitalist production and industrialization.

Neither should we assume that there is anything fixed or immutable about the nature of the state or the political economy that it fosters. A little regional perspective serves to make the point here. In his writing on Thai entrepreneurs in the 1960s, Fred Riggs painted a grim developmental picture. He argued that careers in government there provided "the greatest opportunities for combining high income with security, prestige and power." The private sector was a last resort for those who could not gain access to government and, once in the private sector, it was still necessary for businesspeople to engage with the state and, in particular, to contribute "financially to the private income of protectors and patrons in the government."[39] This gave rise not to productive, accumulative capitalism but to a destructive kind of rent capitalism. According to Riggs, ISI in Thailand was "an unmitigated failure from the viewpoint of industrial development, a giant pork barrel into which politicians and their friends, newly dubbed entrepreneurs, dipped their fingers"[40] – all of which sounds a lot like neo-patrimonial Africa.

Riggs was pessimistic about the developmental potential of this model, but he was ultimately proven wrong. A more assertive and politically effective business class has emerged in Thailand. In addition, there has been a slight downgrading of the prestige and earning power of the bureaucracy. The relationship between business and government in Thailand today resembles more closely the developmental compact found elsewhere in East Asia than the neo-patrimonial bargain struck in much of Africa. There may thus be conditions under which rent-seeking can evolve into something that more closely resembles productive capitalism. We will return to this tantalizing possibility in the Conclusion.

Structure of the book

The methodological orientation of this book is inherently comparative. Only by looking for similarities and differences within a reasonably diverse yet pertinent set of cases can we hope to adequately

[39] Fred Riggs, *Thailand: The Modernisation of a Bureaucratic Polity* (Honolulu, HI: East West Center Press, 1966). Cited in Ruth McVey, "The Materialization of the Southeast Asian Entrepreneur," in *Southeast Asian Capitalists*, ed. Ruth McVey (Ithaca, NY: Cornell Southeast Asia Program, 1992).
[40] McVey, "The Materialization of the Southeast Asian Entrepreneur," 11.

assess the significance of state and business capacity and of their interaction in generating broader processes of economic development. Parts one and two follow and are organized around a comparison of the four cases.

Part one begins with the "exceptional" cases and considers why it is that in South Africa and Mauritius strong, well-institutionalized business communities could constructively contest economic policy-making. In chapter 1, I consider the historical emergence of a sphere of private commercial activity in South Africa. Central to this was the way in which ethnicity separated out economic and political power in South Africa, with English-speaking white South Africans coming to dominate the economy and white Afrikaners seizing control of the state (black South Africans were marginalized from both spheres). Chapter 2 picks up the story in the 1990s, when the triumph of democracy shifted control of the state to the numerically preponderant black community, while white businesspeople retained significant control over the country's economic wealth. The chapter traces the ongoing influence of that small but powerful white economic elite despite compelling reasons for the state to favor a less business-friendly set of policies and speculates about how recent attempts to broaden economic ownership may shape both business and the state.

Mauritius presents a complementary case. While different from South Africa in many respects, it is similar to the extent that a racial minority has long controlled the economy while a different and larger racial group, hostile to that minority, controlled the state. Again, however, the outcomes were surprisingly constructive. Chapter 3 tells the story from the earliest days of human occupation of Mauritius on into the neo-liberal era.

Part two examines the historical and policy processes that produced very different outcomes in Ghana and Zambia. In chapter 4, I consider the historic role of the colonial and independent states in shaping Ghana's emerging political economy. Arguably, Asante could have served as the site for the development of a home-grown business class. Instead, the state proved dominant in creating and shaping a state-dependent economic elite, from colonialism and on into independence. The incentives and modes of operating laid down here triumphed too in the neo-liberal era, despite the attempt to reform policy-making, as laid out in chapter 5. The chapter concludes by noting more recent and potentially positive developments under a new government.

Chapter 6 presents the complementary case of Zambia, again from the colonial era to the neo-liberal age, tracing how opportunities for local entrepreneurship in that country too were effectively smothered by the persistence of politically dependent acquisition centered on access to the state.

The Conclusion revisits the four cases, comparing and contrasting their most important features. It considers how existing patterns might shift before concluding with a consideration of cases from other parts of the developing world and the implications of the findings of this study.

Having begun this Introduction with Leys, it seems fitting to turn to him once again as we close. He poses what is, for me, the central issue: "How far has the class that has the greatest interest in surmounting and resolving the problems confronting capitalist development in Kenya [or elsewhere in Africa] identified these problems or shown itself able to tackle them?"[41] He refers, of course, to the business sector.

It may be that the answer to this question is at once bleaker and more hopeful than we commonly perceive. The "state versus market" debate may leave Africanists feeling hopeless, for the truth is that both the state and the market in Africa are severely flawed. Neither the state nor the market in Africa closely resembles the classical models, be they liberal or Marxist. As this Introduction has argued, business in Africa is often plagued by an unhealthily close relationship with the state. The good news may be that this tendency is not unique to Africa. In Asia, Latin America, the former Soviet Union, and even in the advanced countries of the OECD, the relationship between political and economic actors is made up of two-way traffic. Complete independence is not necessarily the best condition for cultivating a developmental project.[42] While Africa represents the extreme end of an autonomy continuum, a low level of state-society autonomy is not unknown nor is it necessarily damning.

In addition, as the four country studies will demonstrate, there is nothing inevitable or permanent about the fusion of economic and political elites. Certainly not all African businesspeople are in bed with the state. A significant number of African entrepreneurs closely

---

[41] Leys, "Learning from the Kenya Debate," 231.
[42] Evans, *Embedded Autonomy*, Wade, *Governing the Market*.

resemble Schumpeter's avatars: They work very hard, in a testing environment, to run their businesses in a way that is not dependent on the state. Further, not all African states are unremittingly neo-patrimonial. The four country cases display significant variation at the level of both state and society.

When Fred Riggs saw political elites moving onto the boards of Chinese-run companies in Thailand in the mid-twentieth century, he assumed that this "was simply the modern guise of the older relationship between pariah entrepreneur and political patron/protector/parasite."[43] As McVey reminds us, however, "[i]n retrospect ... it is clear that great shifts in business-political relationships and attitudes were in fact taking place. What Riggs saw as an economic slough of despond was in fact the beginning of Thailand's great leap forward."[44] In Latin America, too, business has in some cases emerged from its corporatist past. Indigenous political and economic elites can move from being "parasites" on development to serving as "promoters" of development.[45] These transformations raise the real possibility of change for Africa.

---

[43] McVey, "The Materialization of the Southeast Asian Entrepreneur," 22.
[44] Ibid. [45] Ibid.

PART ONE

Institutionalizing constructive contestation

1 | Ethnicity, race, and the development of the South African business class, 1870–1989[1]

It was not capitalism *per se* which was the enemy of the Afrikaner people ... but the control of the system by non-Afrikaners.[2]

Thomas Koelble argues that South Africa's "nationless state has produced two competing versions of modernity, one based on the precepts of the liberal ethos of universal human and individual rights, individual entitlement and autonomous citizenship. The other version of modernity is based on the assertion of group rights and ethnic solidarity."[3] Neither one of these two versions has been exclusively associated with any one ethnic or racial group – or indeed any one class – in South Africa. Rather, these competing versions have waxed and waned, been taken up and discarded, by a number of groups in response to broader political developments. While the policy needs of mining magnates dominated policy-making in the early twentieth century, political and economic power were divided on an explicitly ethnicized basis from the 1930s with the rise of a brand of Afrikaner nationalism that was hostile to the English-speaking mining magnates. The coincidence of ethnic

---

[1] Throughout this chapter and the next I will use racial terminology as it is used and understood in South Africa, namely "white" to indicate those South Africans who are predominantly European in origin, "black" or "African" to indicate those who are of indigenous or African ancestry, "Indian" to indicate those whose forebears hailed from South Asia, and "colored" to indicate those of mixed racial origin.

[2] Shula Marks and Stanley Trapido, "The Politics of Race, Class and Nationalism," in *The Politics of Race, Class and Nationalism in Twentieth Century South Africa*, ed. Shula Marks and Stanley Trapido (London: Longman, 1987), 18–19.

[3] Thomas A. Koelble, "Building a New Nation: Solidarity, Democracy and Nationhood in the Age of Circulatory Capitalism," in *What Holds Us Together: Social Cohesion in South Africa*, ed. David Chidester, Phillip Dexter, and Wilmot James (Cape Town, South Africa: Human Sciences Research Council Press, 2003), 157.

identifications and economic strata has, however, been enormously consequential.

Throughout the modern history of South Africa, English-speakers were advantaged by their association with British capital; they were the most skilled, educated, and urbanized group from the outset and this gave them a head start, economically speaking. The Afrikaners did, however, manage to win control of the state from at least the late 1940s and, for the next decade, systematically set out to use that control to win explicitly ethnicized economic gains.

The Afrikaner state – and the state-sponsored Afrikaner capitalist class that it created – did not enjoy uncontested policy-making freedom, however. Rather, over the course of the twentieth century, government constantly had to negotiate and compromise with already established business interests. The end result was that, by the late 1980s, Afrikaner business was successfully integrated into the pre-existing larger business community rather than, as in Ghana and Zambia, remaining within the suffocating realm of the state.

A second story runs parallel to this one, namely the rise of a broad-based and increasingly radicalized African nationalism that emerged in response to apartheid and to the racially stratified capitalist economy. The initial focus of the movement was on limiting the harm being done to black South Africans and gaining direct access to political power. Cold War dynamics, the parlous state of relations between black labor and white capital and the South African state's own virulent anti-communism pushed what would become the dominant voice of the black opposition, the African National Congress (ANC), into a soft-left camp on economic issues. Few in the black community were inclined to rely on the benignity of business or to consider gratefully the scant economic benefits that capitalism had delivered for them.

When viewed historically, the emergence of South Africa's business sector bears some surprising resemblances to that of Mauritius. In both cases, the country's economic class developed early on, out of the exploitation of a single natural resource, and was historically concentrated in an ethnic minority community, while a separate – sometimes hostile – ethnic group consolidated its hold on political power.

South Africa's white community was split almost equally between English-speakers and Afrikaners although the Afrikaners enjoyed a slight preponderance. The conventional wisdom was that the former enjoyed most economic power while the latter won political power through their dominance of the state.[4] While crude, this description was true for much of the country's history. Control of the economy by English-speakers dates back to the early part of the century when English-speaking entrepreneurs created and seized control of fledgling commercial and mining interests. This chapter will begin by examining the origins of South African capitalism and its ethnicized character. The rise of politicized Afrikaner nationalism and attempts by the state to prosecute a form of economic Afrikaner nationalism meant that the free-for-all economic liberalism of the "gold rush" economy was subsequently tempered by the development of a broader industrial and manufacturing sector and gave way to economic nationalism and a range of ISI-type strategies. These and other developments shaped the broader relationship between business and government, and the ANC's own view of business. I conclude with a review of the state of the economy and the landscape of business–government relations in the late 1980s.

The origins of South African capital

In contrast with what occurred in much of the rest of the continent,[5] an early form of surplus extraction through rent emerged in regions of South Africa even before the discovery of South Africa's mineral wealth, as black South Africans were dispossessed of their land by ever larger numbers of white settlers.[6] Thompson suggests that two distinct and ethnicized identifications emerged relatively fast within this white settler community:[7]

---

[4] Heribert Adam, "The South African Power Elite: A Survey of Ideological Commitment," in *South Africa: Sociological Perspectives*, ed. Heribert Adam (Oxford University Press, 1971), 73–4, Allister Sparks, *The Mind of South Africa* (London: Heinemann, 1990), 46–7.

[5] With the possible exception of the Highlands of Kenya and much of what became Zimbabwe.

[6] Mike Morris, "The Development of Capitalism in South Africa," in *South African Capitalism and Black Political Opposition*, ed. Martin J. Murray (Cambridge, MA: Schenkman, 1982), 44.

[7] Leonard Thompson, *A History of South Africa*, revised edn (Binghamton, NY: Yale University Press, 1995), 112.

Most of the descendants of the seventeenth and eighteenth century settlers identified themselves as Afrikaners, with their distinctive language, religious affiliation, historical consciousness and social network, whereas nearly all of the nineteenth century white immigrants (most of whom came from Britain), kept aloof from Afrikaners, despised their language and culture, and underestimated their achievements. Nearly all Afrikaners, moreover, continued to live and work in a rural environment, whereas most immigrants were townspeople.

The differences then between these two identifications were not just "ethnic" or cultural, but were rooted in different occupations and classes. Accordingly, their political significance would shift with changing class and occupation patterns as we shall see, but they do have some historical basis.

It was, however, the discovery of diamonds in 1870 at Kimberley in the Orange Free State, one of the Boer (Afrikaner) republics, that most dramatically galvanized the development of a capitalist class. This was particularly so as it was followed, just sixteen years later, with the discovery of significant gold deposits on the Witwatersrand area of the Transvaal, the other Boer republic.[8] Almost from the start, both Afrikaners and Africans were marginalized in these developments as "[o]wnership of the numerous and overlapping diamond claims was at an early stage concentrated in European hands."[9] Many of those who had profited from early investment in the diamond mines were well placed to move onto the goldfields as they opened up, and quickly won significant levels of ownership in what would become lucrative gold-mining companies. It was a messy process but over time a small number of firms came to achieve a disproportionate prominence in the industry.[10]

Part of the reason for this was that South African gold mining proved to be a highly capital-intensive process: the Witwatersrand deposits were characterized by low-grade ore, much of it buried deep underground; the extraction of this gold required significant levels of

---

[8] Martin J. Murray, "The Development of Capitalist Production Processes: The Mining Industry, the Demand for Labour and the Transformation of the Countryside 1870–1910," in *South African Capitalism and Black Political Opposition*, ed. Martin J. Murray (Cambridge, MA: Schenkman, 1982), 129.

[9] Stanley B. Greenberg, *Race and State in Capitalist Development: Comparative Perspectives* (Binghamton, NY: Yale University Press, 1980), 37.

[10] Murray, "The Development of Capitalist Production Processes," 128.

capital and technical expertise (as well as cheap labor – more on this later). The Kimberley magnates aside, there was not much local capital to be had; much of the requisite investment initially came from outside of the country.

The result was that South Africa's new gold-mining economy was dominated by *uitlanders* (foreigners), many of them British but also entrepreneurs from other parts of Europe. Foreigners dominated not only as miners and mine-owners, but they swiftly came too to dominate the service economy that grew up around the mines, i.e. as tradespeople servicing the mines. Crucially, no Afrikaner in the early 1890s held any financial interests in a mine.[11] Instead, most were still based in the rural areas. There were some Afrikaners who, along with Africans, had established small businesses in the cities.[12] Even here, however, neither group could compete effectively against the better capitalized, better educated, and more highly skilled British immigrants, so that "[b]y the mid-1890s, ... most Afrikaners and African enterprises were being crushed out of business by industrial enterprises run by the mining companies."[13] The result was a highly internationalized capitalist class, in the makeup of its local managers and magnates, in the origins of its investment, and in the markets for its minerals output.[14]

As Clark points out, the discovery of gold therefore had somewhat contradictory effects for the Afrikaners of the Transvaal: the economic growth that accompanied the discovery consolidated white rule and accelerated the marginalization of black South Africans from political and economic power. It also, however, established English-speaking dominance of key natural resources and laid the basis for an ethnically charged contest over economic power more broadly.[15]

The government of the Boer Republic of the Transvaal, led by Paul Kruger and supported predominantly by Afrikaners, was relatively

[11] Nancy L. Clark, *Manufacturing Apartheid: State Corporations in South Africa* (New Haven, CT: Yale University Press, 1994), 19.
[12] This is not to suggest that the economic or political status of white Afrikaners and black South Africans was in any real sense equivalent. While they were both marginalized in an economy dominated by English-speakers, the position of black South Africans was far more desperate and exploited than that of Afrikaners.
[13] Thompson, *A History of South Africa*, 121–2.
[14] Murray points out that in 1913, less than 15 percent of shares were held in South Africa. Murray, "The Development of Capitalist Production Processes," 129.
[15] Clark, *Manufacturing Apartheid*, 12.

hostile to the mining magnates. This government was effectively replaced, however, as a result of the South African war of 1899–1902, which the British won. British control was expanded – and British investors continued to "pour" money into South African mining.[16] Mining operations grew enormously so that, by the early twentieth century, gold made up two-thirds of the country's exports by value.[17] Agriculture was also increasingly organized along commercial and capitalist lines, with small-scale African commodity producers being displaced by much larger, commercial operations.[18] South Africa, it seemed, had made the critical transition from "surplus extraction through rent" from seized lands, to "capitalist exploitation through the sale of labour power (i.e. the large-scale mining of gold and diamonds)."[19]

In this struggle for control of the country's mineral (and economic) resources, foreign investors did not have it all their own way. Capital's need for assistance from the state, and the way in which many businesses came to be owned and controlled by settlers who regarded South Africa as their permanent home, meant that international capital had to lobby and contend with various sets of South African-based interests. In the early twentieth century, the broad outlines of economic policy were still relatively *laissez faire*, in accord with the preferences of the mining magnates, but during the period crucial for the consolidation of capitalism (between the 1890s and 1910) those magnates relied on "tremendous state assistance," in particular for filling their low-cost labor requirements.[20]

As Murray argues, three factors structured the South African gold-mining industry: first, the region's relatively low-grade ore; second, the fact that gold was a commodity that had to be sold at a price that was fixed internationally; and finally, the high overhead costs associated with the opening of new mines and the further development of existing mines.[21] These factors created a hard set of constraints within which the industry had to maintain profitability. The easiest place for the mines to cut costs was in labor[22] – but the problem was how to

---

[16] Ibid., 22.   [17] Ibid., 28.

[18] Murray, "The Development of Capitalist Production Processes," 238–9.

[19] Morris, "The Development of Capitalism in South Africa," 44.

[20] Murray, "The Development of Capitalist Production Processes," 131.

[21] Ibid., Alex Callinicos, *South Africa between Reform and Revolution* (Reading: Bookmarks, 1988), 10.

[22] Greenberg, *Race and State in Capitalist Development*.

convince that labor to work in dreadful conditions for paltry pay. This was accomplished by "forcibly tearing Africans from their means of subsistence on the land,"[23] and mining, along with commercial agriculture, benefited enormously from a brutal restructuring of black labor.

Alongside the dispossessed Africans, commercial agriculture left a large number of "poor whites" landless too. Most of these were Afrikaners and they made their way to the cities, looking for work, which was not always easy to find. As I have already described, the more skilled British immigrants dominated the better paying jobs (usually in manufacturing) and many of the poor Afrikaners had to make do with less remunerative, unskilled jobs on the mines. Not surprisingly then, Afrikaners were attracted to – and informed – the propaganda of the new National Party, which "stressed the oppression of Afrikaans speakers by British imperialists and English-speaking Jewish gold magnates."[24]

In 1910 four territories, the two Boer republics and the two British possessions of the Cape and Natal, were formally consolidated in the Union of South Africa. Little changed for the country's already well-established English-speaking business class "who dominated the twentieth century political economy of South Africa as they had the nineteenth."[25] The economic policies of the new national government, headed up by Louis Botha and his deputy Jan Smuts, were marked by their sympathy for the needs of the mining industry – not surprisingly, given the sector's overwhelming contribution to government revenue.[26] The highly influential Chamber of Mines was a very effective voice for its members, and, anxious to preserve the mines' ability to source their imports at the lowest cost possible, consistently opposed what it termed protectionism.[27] When Smuts succeeded

---

[23] Morris, "The Development of Capitalism in South Africa," 44.

[24] There was a high level of antisemitism and a great deal of skepticism about the benefits of capitalism in this strand of Afrikaner nationalism. Clark, *Manufacturing Apartheid*, 46.

[25] Marks and Trapido, "The Politics of Race, Class and Nationalism," 2–3.

[26] According to Clark, by the end of the war, minerals "accounted for nearly three-quarters of the country's exports, which in turn provided nearly half of South Africa's national income." Clark, *Manufacturing Apartheid*, 39.

[27] D. E. Kaplan, "The Politics of Industrial Protection in South Africa, 1910–1939," in *South African Capitalism and Black Political Opposition*, ed. Martin J. Murray (Cambridge, MA: Schenkman, 1982), 306.

Botha as premier these trends continued: South Africa still had no real industrial policy. Instead, the government remained anti-protectionist in outlook.[28]

Marks and Trapido argue that "the omnipresence of the imperial power" (Britain) privileged English-speaking settlers[29] – but these close ties were useful too for the broader economy. Foreign capital continued to be vital to the development of the mining industry. By the beginning of the First World War, Europeans had invested £350 million, a sum – as Clark points out – larger than the investment in all other African economies combined.[30] It seems likely that the prominence of English-speakers in the business community facilitated these flows.

Botha and Smuts were both Afrikaner leaders. Indeed, they had both been heroes in the wars fought against the British. Nonetheless, as national premiers they had no trouble articulating and addressing the needs of the leading sector of the economy, albeit a sector dominated by English-speakers. It should not be assumed therefore that all Afrikaners were hostile to the capitalist class or were poor or working class. On the contrary, wealthy Afrikaner farmers and professionals in the Cape province had long succored a more liberal and business-friendly brand of Afrikaner nationalism, in striking contrast with the more *verkramp* (narrow or conservative) version based in the Transvaal.

From within the Afrikaner community, there was a range of responses to the marginalized status of their fellows. Afrikaner nationalists in the Cape set up two financial institutions, Sanlam and Santam, that were to prove immensely powerful, not only in collecting and organizing the savings of thousands of Afrikaners, but also in nurturing what would become a significant force in financial markets. Santam and Sanlam were the product of the relatively liberal Cape Afrikaner bourgeoisie, but Callinicos argues that influence over them was increasingly exercised by the Broederbond, dominated by the Transvaal Afrikaner nationalists.[31]

---

[28] Ibid., 303–4.

[29] Marks and Trapido, "The Politics of Race, Class and Nationalism," 4.

[30] Clark, *Manufacturing Apartheid*, 39.

[31] Callinicos, *South Africa between Reform and Revolution*, 13. The Broederbond had been founded in 1918, initially as a predominantly cultural organization, "by a frustrated Afrikaner urban petit bourgeoisie with little chance for upward mobility in the English-speaking world of trade and business." It rapidly

Anxious to promote the manufacturing sector and thereby boost employment for Afrikaners, around the time of the First World War the state established two core parastatals, the Iron and Steel Corporation (Iscor) for the production of iron and steel, and the Electricity Supply Commission (Escom) for the provision of cheap and reliable electricity. Clark argues that H. J. van der Bijl, Escom's first chairman, was central in establishing the institutional ethos for the commission:[32]

Already on record as favoring private enterprise over state intervention..., van der Bijl announced his intention to operate the supply commission as if it were a private company... He argued that the company should not, like the railways, always look to Parliament to bail it out of financial difficulties. Such policies, he believed, would enable Escom to fulfill what he considered its primary function, the promotion of private enterprise throughout South Africa by a process of industrialization built on a foundation of cheap electricity.

Accordingly, Escom "was not to be state-controlled or state-financed, but it was to be state supervised."[33]

From the outset then, the struggle to build Afrikaner economic power never set out to create a business class that was dependent on the state. Instead, economic policy-making was marked by constant bargaining, interaction, and jostling for power, not only between the state and state-run corporations, but also between the state and the private sector as to what the role of the state in the broader economy should be.

This pattern of bargaining and mutual dependency was part of a broader tendency in the economy. By the end of the First World War, minerals were producing half of the country's national income.[34] If the state at this point had been weaker, the outcome might have been an economy entirely dependent on mining and any attempt by the state to industrialize and diversify the economy might well have failed, *a la* Michael Shafer's predictions.[35] If, for its part, the (English-speaking) mining industry had been weaker, the state's interventions in the economy might have been more successful and far-reaching,

became a highly influential secret society that dominated the ruling National Party and, for decades, shaped the direction of the state. Courtney Jung, *Then I Was Black: South African Political Identities in Transition* (New Haven, CT: Yale University Press, 2000), 113.

[32] Clark, *Manufacturing Apartheid*, 57.   [33] Ibid., 58.   [34] Ibid., 39.

[35] See discussion in the Conclusion. Shafer, *Winners and Losers.*

and South Africa might well have seen the development of a more dependent, and more explicitly ethnicized (Afrikanerized), business community. However, each of these parties constantly had to reckon with the power, influence, and interests of the other; neither could single-handedly dominate economic policy-making. Accordingly, "the creation of these two state corporations – Escom and Iscor – marked a compromise between state and capital in South Africa rather than a victory or defeat for one or the other."[36]

Voters effectively rejected the approach developed by Botha and Smuts when they voted that government out and voted in a new Pact government, which pledged to cleave less closely to the needs of imperial capital and instead to pay more attention to the plight of the Afrikaner working class and rural poor. The chief idea here was to secure employment for these constituencies through industrialization.[37] To further address the grievances of white labour, in 1924 the Pact government introduced the so-called "civilized labor" policies whereby the government substituted white workers for Africans in its employ. From the point of view of business, this represented a step away from its direct interests and an intensification of the role of ethnic partisanship in economic policy-making. Much of the business community including mining opposed the color bar because of the way in which it increased the cost of labor – but perhaps they did not do so vehemently enough, because the policy stayed on the statute books. After all, the state did not have a free hand in how it chose to tackle these problems:[38]

[The governments of the early twentieth century in South Africa] faced enormous constraints in responding to the concerns of the [Afrikaner, working-class] constituencies. Smuts created Escom to assuage disgruntled whites facing rural poverty and urban unemployment, yet he erected an institution that would have to fight for its markets against strong established producers. Hertzog's and Creswell's strident advocacy of "civilised labour" produced Iscor for much the same reasons as Escom had been established – to promote industrialization and provide jobs for whites outside the mining industry. But Hertzog and Creswell had to compromise with the mining giants, for the profitability of gold continued to determine government revenues.

---

[36] Clark, *Manufacturing Apartheid*, 68.
[37] Morris, "The Development of Capitalism in South Africa," 46–7.
[38] Clark, *Manufacturing Apartheid*, 69.

Of course, business was not a monolithic group and the respective influence of various fractions of business (such as mining, manufacturing, and services) was not the same with every government. Whereas Smuts had abjured protectionist measures in accord with the views of mining capital, the Pact government, by contrast, in 1925 enacted the Customs Tariff Act, a "more deliberate policy of protection," that was explicitly intended to facilitate industrialization and diversification of the economy.[39]

Business was divided over the issue of protection. Established chambers of commerce, dominated by the big import–export houses, tended to support the mining sector's free trade stance. Agriculture, on the other hand, tended to support industrial protectionist policies, as did local industry, organized into the South African Manufacturers' Association and, in later years, the South African Chamber of Industry.[40]

Under the Pact government then there was undoubtedly a shift toward a higher level of state involvement in the economy and a move away from laissez faire principles. Nonetheless, one should not overstate the extent – and character – of the state's involvement in the South African economy. Clark demonstrates convincingly that during the 1920s and 1930s, probably the formative years for the two key state corporations, Iscor and Escom "displayed considerable independence from official policies of the day." For its part, the state was "unwilling to press policies on them that would undermine their financial performance."[41]

It is important to note also what was not happening during this period: while the waves of independence in the 1960s resulted in widescale nationalization and Africanization of industry in much of the rest of the continent, as the Union won more and more autonomy from Great Britain, policies of comparable depth and reach were not adopted in South Africa. It was not considered economically or politically feasible to nationalize existing enterprises; business was too powerful and, besides, the South African government did not have the necessary capital to fund its existing state-owned enterprises (SOEs), let alone to acquire more. Instead, "the state looked to private capital to finance expansion,"[42] and thus had to reckon not only with the interests of local business, but with those of international capital too.

---

[39] Kaplan, "The Politics of Industrial Protection in South Africa, 1910–1939," 305.
[40] Ibid., 308. [41] Clark, *Manufacturing Apartheid*, 71. [42] Ibid., 72.

Moreover, existing state-run corporations had to operate within an economic context that included an important element of domestic competition and was dominated by an overall market-orientation. At their inception, for example, neither Escom nor Iscor could rely on a government-secured monopoly position or on government protection; instead they had to secure customers in an environment in which there were other, sometimes competing providers.[43] Given that van der Bijl was working to operate both corporations on business lines and without recourse to government subsidies, they were both run with a keen eye to profits and to winning customers through effective service provision. A similar pattern attended the 1939 establishment of the Industrial Development Corporation (IDC), intended "to fund the establishment of private, not state, corporations in partnership with private businessmen."[44]

For the most part, the grand strategy to industrialize the South African economy worked: the provision of iron and steel and of electricity was significantly expanded, and with this, the range of manufacturing and industrial firms that the economy could support. By the late 1930s, manufacturing had become a significant contributor to Gross Domestic Product (GDP).[45] Escom, literally, powered much of this expansion.

It was during and after the Second World War, however, that South African manufacturing expanded most impressively. Four factors contributed to this: the way in which the country was cut off from its traditional international supplies; a persistent and increasing local demand for goods;[46] the call from the Allies for South Africa to boost its production to meet also the Allied war needs; and ongoing, "massive" foreign investments.[47] After the war, for the first time in South Africa's history, manufacturing output topped that of both agriculture and mining.[48]

---

[43] Ibid.   [44] Ibid., 130.

[45] Martin J. Murray, "The Consolidation of Monopoly Capital, 1910–1948: The State Apparatus, the Class Struggle and Political Opposition," in *South African Capitalism and Black Political Opposition*, ed. Martin J. Murray (Cambridge, MA: Schenkman, 1982), 240.

[46] Clark, *Manufacturing Apartheid*, 45.

[47] Martin J. Murray, "Monopoly Capitalism in the Apartheid Era, 1948–80," in *South African Capitalism and Black Political Opposition*, ed. Martin J. Murray (Cambridge, MA: Schenkman, 1982), 397.

[48] Clark, *Manufacturing Apartheid*, 133.

Alongside this growth, the first Afrikaner conglomerate emerged: the Rembrandt group, led by Anton Rupert was entirely private sector-based. There was continued concern, however, about the domination of the economy by English-speakers. In 1939 then, along with the IDC, delegates at an Ekonomiese Volkskongres (an economic congress backed by Sanlam and the Broederbond) established the Reddings-daadbond (Savings Association) to boost savings and potential investment capital among the Afrikaans community.[49] South Africans had successfully diversified their economy – but had not significantly dented the ethnicized control of that economy. In the minds of many Afrikaner Nationalists, it was time to get serious about that second task.

Afrikaner state, English capital

In 1940, James Barry Hertzog, the founder of the original National Party, led his supporters back into a "purified" and reorganized (Herstigte) National Party (NP), infused with an economic national-ism motivated by the plight of rural and working-class Afrikaners.[50] The NP was a self-conscious attempt to unite all Afrikaners, regardless of their class origin, against "English capitalists."[51] Under Malan's leadership the party adopted a more focused brand of Afrikaner nationalism, less inclined to "cozy up" to the mines and their interests. Afrikaners had grown impatient. After all, in 1948 they controlled a mere 25% of manufacturing, 6% of industry and a scant 1% of mining.[52] The NP won the election in 1948, formed South Africa's "first purely Afrikaner government,"[53] and would govern uninter-rupted until 1994. Their electoral victory signaled a new division of power: whites would continue to run the country in every sense that

[49] The most thorough account is O'Meara's. Dan O'Meara, *Volkskapitalisme: Class, Capital and Ideology in the Development of Afrikaner Nationalism, 1934–1948* (Cambridge University Press, 1983), 107–16, 37–43.

[50] Dan O'Meara, *Forty Lost Years: The Apartheid State and the Politics of the National Party 1948–1994* (Athens, OH: Ohio University Press, 1996), 176–7.

[51] Jung, *Then I Was Black*, 114.

[52] Greenberg, *Race and State in Capitalist Development*, 178.

[53] T. R. H. Davenport and Christopher Saunders, *South Africa: A Modern History*, 5th edn (London: Macmillan, 2000), 378.

mattered, but within that community, while English-speakers dominated the economy, Afrikaners would attempt to chip away at that domination using the instruments of the state.

The NP was committed to fostering *volkskapitalisme* – the nation's capitalism.[54] Of course, the "nation" did not comprise all South Africans but was limited by race and ethnicity. Economic policy in Afrikaner nationalist circles at the time was ambivalent about capitalism, little wonder, given that capital was held mostly in English-speaking hands. From 1948, the Nationalists intensified the application of state policies designed to boost the economic status of poor whites and to build up the economic power of the Afrikaner community more broadly.[55] As elsewhere in Africa upon independence, under the NP the state established and consolidated a number of large, state-run concerns. We have already discussed Escom and Iscor. The regime used the IDC to establish a "new generation" of enterprises linked to the state.[56] These included Sasol (an initiative to manufacture and market fuel from coal), Safmarine (a shipping firm), Foskor (a phosphates company), and Alusaf (in aluminum production). And again, as elsewhere in the continent, parastatals played an important role in the ongoing process of industrialization.

Under the NP, state-run corporations moved further away from market principles in their operations. The operating styles of Escom and Iscor shifted as they increasingly secured monopoly control of their respective markets. The leadership of Escom set up a national electricity grid and a single integrated power generation and transmission effort for the entire country.

According to Sadie[57]

[o]f special interest to Afrikaners was the assumption of the entrepreneurial function by consecutive NP governments by way of the establishment, and the expansion of existing, parastatals [sic] ... Many of these became

---

[54] For the definitive work on the subject, see O'Meara, *Volkskapitalisme*.

[55] Nattrass and Terreblanche describe this as "the mobilisation of ethnic forces to foster Afrikaner accumulation." Cf. Sampie Terreblanche and Nicoli Nattrass, "A Periodization of the Political Economy from 1910," in *The Political Economy of South Africa*, ed. Nicoli Nattrass and Elisabeth Ardington (Oxford University Press, 1990), 12.

[56] Clark, *Manufacturing Apartheid*, 160.

[57] J. L. Sadie, "The Fall and Rise of the Afrikaner in the South African Economy" (Stellenbosch, South Africa: Unpublished mimeo, 2001), 76–7.

industrial or financial giants dominating their respective fields and served the role of prerequisites for the generation of economic growth ... They created opportunities for Afrikaners they would otherwise have lacked.

An additional tool employed by the Nationalist government to promote Afrikaner capital was the award of "lucrative" government contracts.[58] A frequently quoted example was the northern Afrikaans Press which received a large number of government contracts as a result of political connections. The Reserve Bank (the country's central bank) also provided bailouts to a number of commercial Afrikaner banks such as Trust Bank, Bankorp, and ABSA, an action much resented by English-owned banks who regarded this as unfair. In such actions might have lain the beginnings of what led elsewhere to the yoking of political and economic power – yet this outcome did not pertain in South Africa. This has much to do with the structural power of business which proved too formidable to be overrun or dominated by an ethnically mobilized or state-dependent set of Afrikaner economic interests.

We should take care not to dichotomize ethnic nationalist sentiment and business-mindedness. O'Meara writes convincingly about the numerous strands and tendencies within Afrikaner nationalism, and about the liberal and market-friendly nature, for example, of those (Cape) Nationalists who founded and directed the Afrikaner financial giant, Sanlam.[59] Nonetheless, it is evident that under the NP, there was a distinct and unmistakable shift toward higher levels of state intervention in the economy.

In response to government encouragement from the 1950s and higher levels of economic growth in the 1960s, the South African economy and white businesspeople flourished. More particularly, a

---

[58] Ibid., 66. Not all Afrikaner business developed or prospered because of its relationship to the Afrikaner state. While this is true of a large number of firms in the heyday of apartheid, it became less true as the economy developed in the 1960s and 1970s. In addition, there are examples such as the strikingly independent Afrikaner entrepreneur, Anton Rupert of Rembrandt. Despite the fact that his company may have benefited from its association with the NP, he was publicly opposed to the color bar. Other examples include Alton's Bill Venter and Pepkor's Christo Wiese, and serve as warning of the dangers of generalization. Nonetheless, much of what became Afrikaner capital grew out of a very particular conception of ethnic advancement and was fostered by the state.

[59] O'Meara, *Volkskapitalisme*.

stronger Afrikaner business class began to emerge. From the 1960s on, the transformation of the South African economy, away from an agricultural- and mining-based economy to an industrialized economy, was consolidated.

A number of Afrikaner firms managed to survive and thrive, and many of these were based in the new industrial and manufacturing sectors. However, this was also precisely the era when manufacturing began to chafe under the restrictions on the supply of skilled labor imposed by grand apartheid, and to realize the depressing effect of the system on black wages too, lowering the buying power of those in the domestic market for industry's goods. Manufacturers were not inclined to back the interests of the mining industry in a highly inter-ventionist state – or at least in a state that was intent on strict regulation of the labor market.[60]

While the NP came to power threatening to nationalize large swathes of industry, its actual policies were more moderate than might have been expected, as successive governments reached accommoda-tions with the existing business community.[61] In many ways, those governments had to. After all, South Africa had what many of its fellow African economies did not: a robust, preexisting, market-based busi-ness sector. Moreover, it was not only the state that had to reckon with the private sector; Afrikaner businesspeople did too. Despite its origins, Afrikaner capital ultimately had to learn to operate and survive in an environment that was predominantly market-based.

From the early 1960s on, the IDC increasingly reverted to the mode of operation at its original founding viz. "backing away from estab-lishing any further state enterprises and instead work[ing] as a conduit for government investment in private enterprise."[62]

Within the state, the Nationalists successfully consolidated Afrikaner domination of the parliament, of the bureaucracy, and of the para-statal sector.[63] According to Adam, writing in 1971, 71 percent of all white South African officials were Afrikaner-speaking (Afrikaners

---

[60] Greenberg, *Race and State in Capitalist Development*, 177.

[61] There are distinct parallels with perceptions, forty years later, about what the ANC's policies would be prior to its accession to power, and its actual policies while in power. See chapter 2.

[62] Clark, *Manufacturing Apartheid*, 166.

[63] Thompson, *A History of South Africa*, 187.

comprised only 58 percent of the total white population).[64] This process had required a significant increase in the economic reach of the state so that by 1970 "more than a fourth of all white workers ... were employed directly by the state and another 10 percent by the parastatals; half of all Afrikaner workers were employed in the public or semi-public sector."[65]

Afrikaner Nationalists used their political power to good effect beyond the state too, by harnessing the savings power of Afrikaners and making judicious use of the excess capital of the commercial farmers – and of state intervention: "The government ... directed official business to Afrikaners. Afrikaans businesspeople channeled Afrikaner capital into ethnic banks, investment houses, insurance companies, and publishing houses. By 1976, Afrikaner entrepreneurs had obtained a firm foothold in mining, manufacturing, commerce, and finance – all previously exclusive preserves of English speakers."[66]

The result was that Afrikaners' aggregate share of the economy, excluding agriculture, increased from under 10 percent in 1948 to 18 percent in 1963.[67] Furthermore, Afrikaners successfully entered that most English-speaking of economic preserves: mining. In 1963–4 the giant Anglo American Corporation (AAC) facilitated the purchase by an Afrikaner group (Federale Mynbou backed by Sanlam) of General Mining. It was the first significant Afrikaner purchase within the mining sub-sector and it was not uncontroversial.[68] Nonetheless, it incontestably signaled the success of the attempt to secure a share of economic power for Afrikaners. Broader figures bore out the scope of the victory: By 1971, 20 to 30 percent of the South African economy was controlled by Afrikaner capital.[69]

Ironically, this very success began to undercut the appeal of (a particular form of) Afrikaner nationalism:[70] "As Afrikaner business people became more ... successful, they became committed to the market economy, and consequently less dependent on political patronage and

---

[64] Adam, "The South African Power Elite," 75.
[65] Greenberg, *Race and State in Capitalist Development*, 402–3.
[66] Thompson, *A History of South Africa*, 187.
[67] Jung, *Then I Was Black*, 115.
[68] Some regarded the purchases as the ultimate betrayal of *volkskapitalisme* to the imperialist forces of big mining capital. See O'Meara, *Forty Lost Years*, 123–4.
[69] Adam, "The South African Power Elite," 97.
[70] Thompson, *A History of South Africa*, 223.

less tied to the rigid racial ideology of the past."[71] They began, in short, to develop a distinct sense of their interests as businesspeople, not as Afrikaners.

The policy interventions of Afrikaner businesspeople started to sound more and more like those of other (English-speaking) businesspeople, espousing classic free market and anti-state intervention sentiments. The most dramatic example is the polemic penned by Andreas Wassenaar, a member of the Broederbond, in the late 1970s.[72] In this tract, he rails against what is in his view the excessive involvement by the state and public sector in the running of the economy. For him the foe was not English-speaking capital but "the government, and the delegation by government to a bureaucracy of all its functions, including its power to control the economy."[73]

Historically, the Afrikaner community had been more closely associated with the political project of apartheid than their English-speaking counterparts. Adam's survey of businessmen found, on the issue of job reservation for whites for example, that opposition to this policy was higher among English-speaking industrialists than among Afrikaner industrialists.[74] Increasingly, however, all white businesspeople were becoming more impatient with those aspects of the apartheid system that restricted their capacity to do business.

More than 70 percent of businessmen surveyed in the early 1970s argued that their ethnic background was "irrelevant."[75] By 1972 the position of the Afrikaanse Handelsinstituut (AHI), which represented Afrikaner business, had become "indistinguishable" from its English-speaking counterparts.[76] Having once been a crucial political marker for economic mobilization, specifically Afrikaner identity had since become less important, trumped instead by the broader categories of race and class.[77]

This is not to argue that the historical enmity between Afrikaners and English-speakers vanished. In fact, as apartheid evolved, estrangement on political grounds between the more liberal-minded elements

---

[71] Leonard Thompson, quoted by Anthony Sampson, *Black and Gold: Tycoons, Revolutionaries and Apartheid* (London: Hodder and Stoughton, 1987), 231.
[72] A. D. Wassenaar, *Assault on Private Enterprise: The Freeway to Communism* (Cape Town, South Africa: Tafelberg, 1977).
[73] Ibid., 84–5.   [74] Adam, "The South African Power Elite," 86.   [75] Ibid., 98.
[76] Greenberg, *Race and State in Capitalist Development*, 190.
[77] Jung, *Then I Was Black*, 112.

of the (mainly English-speaking) business community and the more *verkrampte* elements of the Afrikaner political community may have worsened. In 1982, for example, Harry Oppenheimer (perhaps the single most important businessperson in the country at the time) could not obtain an audience with the then prime minister Vorster without going through Afrikaans intermediaries. Vorster's successor, President P. W. Botha, apparently refused even to be in the same room as Oppenheimer.

Some of this was doubtless posturing for public consumption. Nonetheless, the exigencies of maintaining white unity in the face of growing international isolation and determined levels of black resistance at home increasingly necessitated a strategic and ever more public alliance with English-speakers and with the business community.

The politics of business and government under apartheid[78]

From the late nineteenth century and through the first half of the twentieth century, business flourished in a political economy that had ensured a steady supply of cheap black labor. Increasingly, however, as the economy diversified away from agriculture and mining, the business community came to be dominated instead by manufacturing and industrial firms, which needed, on the one hand, skilled labor to produce their goods and, on the other hand, prosperous customers to buy those goods; these businesspeople began to pressure government to end its policy of job reservation. In 1950, for example, the Federated Chambers of Industry (FCI) issued a public policy statement that advocated the merits of building a stable, urban African workforce, in direct contradiction with the apartheid vision that tolerated Africans only as temporary sojourners in the "white" areas. The prime minister's response to FCI's call demonstrated the suspicion with which the ruling party regarded many in the business community; "the national desire for economic gain [on the part of business]," he blustered, "could not be allowed to take precedence over other more vital considerations."[79]

---

[78] Merle Lipton presents a masterful exposition of the relationship between business and the system of apartheid in *Capitalism and Apartheid: South Africa 1910–1986* (Aldershot, UK: Wildwood House, 1986).
[79] Greenberg, *Race and State in Capitalist Development*.

The 1950s and 1960s brought relatively rapid economic growth to the South African economy, and the economies of many developing countries the world over. In South Africa, however, this period also saw the implementation of "grand" apartheid in a wide range of social and economic spheres and, concomitantly, the growth of black resistance. The high rate of growth was rudely interrupted by political protests at Sharpeville and Langa in 1960. In Sharpeville, the more deadly of the two incidents, police opened fire on people who were protesting the pass laws, killing sixty-nine of them.[80] The impact on the economy was almost immediate. There was a sudden, swift outflow of investment as money "poured" out of the country (there was a similar investment response to political unrest in the 1970s, see figure 1.1);[81] the stock market fell sharply, as did retail sales.[82] In response, the Chamber of Mines joined with other business associations – specifically the Associated Chambers of Commerce (Assocom), FCI, the Steel and Engineering Industries Federation of South Africa (Seifsa), and the AHI – in "urging the government to smooth the areas of greatest 'friction'."[83]

Growing numbers within the business community began to turn against at least aspects of the apartheid system.[84] Historically, while the Chamber of Mines, FCI, and Assocom had opposed job reservation, the AHI had endorsed the government's labor policy. But by 1970, even the AHI "began to worry about the labor shortage in skilled areas, the restrictions on the prerogatives of management, and the need for freer utilization of labor."[85] The rise of manufacturing interests in the economy may explain this shift in sentiment. Relative to mining, as Greenberg argues, manufacturing and commercial subsectors were less concerned with labor costs and hence with a labor-repressive structure.[86] In terms of this logic, the AHI could not fail to be moved by the growing numbers of manufacturers and industrialists within its ranks.[87]

The other reason for the shift in business' policy preferences was the intrusion of politics on the smooth functioning of the economy. For

---

[80] Davenport and Saunders, *South Africa*, 413.

[81] Callinicos, *South Africa between Reform and Revolution*, 16.

[82] Greenberg, *Race and State in Capitalist Development*, 202.

[83] According to Greenberg these were "[t]he pass laws, influx controls, and to some extent, African trade unions" (the latter had not yet been legalized). Ibid., 172–3.

[84] Cf. Lipton, *Capitalism and Apartheid*, 227–254.

[85] Ibid., 185.   [86] Ibid.   [87] Thompson, *A History of South Africa*, 223.

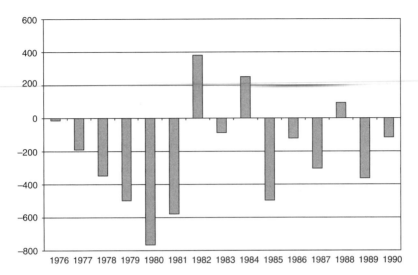

Figure 1.1 Foreign direct investment into South Africa, net (BoP, current US$ millions)
Source: World Development Indicators, World Bank Group

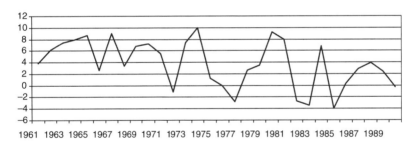

Figure 1.2 South African GDP growth (annual %)
Note: 1960 figures not available from this source
Source: World Development Indicators, World Bank Group

much of the twentieth century, while apartheid wrought devastation on the lives of black South Africans, white South African business had prospered. Increasingly, however, the repressive system began to impose a series of costs on business too. Growth, for example, slowed drastically in the immediate aftermath of the Sharpeville killings in 1960. It revived briefly but then slowed again after the Soweto uprising in 1976 (see Figure 1.2).

After that uprising the Transvaal Chamber of Industry and the AHI called again on the government to accept the permanence of an urban black population.[88] For its part, Anglo American pushed the mining industry to consider more seriously the challenges posed by ongoing labor unrest and by the mines' changing labor requirements. The Corporation declared, well ahead of any indication that government was prepared to consider this, that it was ready to grant recognition to "genuine" African trade unions.[89] None of this won business any friends in the NP government. In fact, business' relationship with Prime Minister Vorster was distant.

P. W. Botha took over from Vorster in 1978 and, initially at least, presented a business- and reform-friendly face to the world. In November 1979, for example, Botha hosted a conference of businessmen at the Carlton Hotel and presented the broad outlines of a reformist vision, arguing that apartheid was "a recipe for permanent conflict."[90] Sampson notes that "[m]any businessmen later looked back at the [Carlton] meeting with recriminations. 'What we rather naïve businessmen failed to realise was that we were, in fact, being "set up," ' said John Wilson of Shell seven years later: 'that those conferences were nothing more than a forum for the propagation of government policies.'"[91]

From the 1970s, ever larger numbers of black workers began to enter the "white" cities to provide labor. Alongside this, larger numbers of black South Africans became actively involved in the struggle against apartheid. It became evident that apartheid would not be sustainable, either politically or economically, and that ultimately business would be confronted with the need to become overtly politically engaged.[92] At first many businesspeople sided with the apartheid government, arguing that it was a safer bet than the forces of chaos and communism allegedly ranged on the side of the black opposition. They accepted Botha's argument that the country was under a "total onslaught" by communist forces from without and within and that it was necessary therefore to unite the entire white community, including

[88] Callinicos, *South Africa between Reform and Revolution*, 29.
[89] Greenberg, *Race and State in Capitalist Development*, 174.
[90] Davenport and Saunders, *South Africa*, 459.
[91] Sampson, *Black and Gold*, 134.
[92] The English-speaking business community traditionally regarded itself as "apolitical."

business, in a "total strategy" against that onslaught. This contributed to further narrowing the divide between Afrikaners and English-speakers.[93]

Botha was a Cape Nationalist, the inheritor of the *verlig* strain of politics, influenced by the values of that province's petty bourgeoisie. At the outset of his term of office, he introduced a relatively liberal monetarist policy and launched "an offensive against the welfare state for whites" that had been created by his predecessors. "Job reservation was abolished, fees were introduced in white state schools, [and] subsidies to white maize farmers were slashed."[94] In 1988, Botha announced his intentions to sell the state corporations.[95] In addition to these steps, "[b]usinessmen [were] drawn into cabinet committees as 'experts' on economic matters and their recommendations ... not infrequently found their way into state policy."[96] Initially, relations with business improved as a result of these initiatives. That first November conference with businesspeople was followed up in November 1981 with a conference in Cape Town. What this second conference demonstrated, however, was how little progress was actually being made on economic reform.

In a related development, Botha's political profile too began to shift, in this case rightward. Vehement opposition followed the introduction of a tricameral parliament that continued to exclude Africans from real political power, and the state responded with yet more repression. The government's declaration of a State of Emergency in 1985 seemed to smother any immediate prospects for genuine political reform. The first State of Emergency did not succeed in quelling the unrest – indeed, it may have fueled it – and additional States of Emergency were declared, granting ever widening powers of repression to the authorities.

The political crisis that developed over the course of the 1980s supplanted any ongoing economic reform or, indeed, any economic normality. The growth rate year to year fluctuated wildly but, overall, tended to lower. Government spending by contrast was moving in the opposite direction, driven higher by the costs of funding the bureaucratically complex apartheid system, and the security costs of defending

[93] Jung, *Then I Was Black*, 132.
[94] Callinicos, *South Africa between Reform and Revolution*, 153.
[95] Clark, *Manufacturing Apartheid*, 165.
[96] Marks and Trapido, "The Politics of Race, Class and Nationalism," 58.

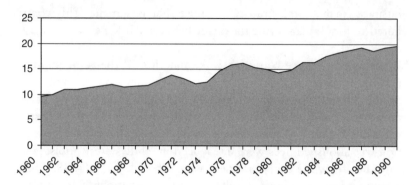

Figure 1.3 South Africa: general government final consumption expenditure (% of GDP)
Source: World Development Indicators, World Bank Group

that system (see Figure 1.3). The FCI condemned the resort to the States of Emergency and, in January 1986, called on the government to "create rapidly and urgently a climate for negotiation and a generally accepted framework within which negotiation can occur."[97] Botha responded testily, and, despite the concerns of the business community (both domestic and international), his government moved ever further right, thereby justifying Norman McRae's wry observation that South Africa "has evolved as 'probably the only country where the big business community is visibly to the left of the government'."[98]

In the spectrum of political views within South African business, industrialists tended to be more conservative than the bankers and hence more amenable to approaches from the NP. However, the mining group AAC was a notable exception. Perhaps the (literally) sunken nature of its assets, and its increasingly diversified ownership portfolio forced it to adopt a long-term approach, to recognize that economic development required a sustainable political solution to the country's problems. The corporation's chief executive officer, Harry Oppenheimer, subscribed to a point of view that came to be known as the "Oppenheimer thesis," namely that apartheid and economic growth were incompatible and that growth would "make apartheid

[97] Quoted in Callinicos, *South Africa between Reform and Revolution,* 159.
[98] Quoted in Adam, "The South African Power Elite," 76.

wither away as blacks were drawn into skilled jobs and middle class life."[99] The corollary of this view was that the development of a prosperous black middle class would ensure the political and economic stability of the country.

This view was adopted, at least in public, by forward-thinking elements of the business community. Ann Bernstein argues that the mid-1980s "represented a watershed in terms of the volume of business comment on political issues, the widespread and explicit rejection of apartheid [by business] and the greater clarity in enunciating principles and values on which a new order should be constructed."[100]

This response was probably a minority position within the business community. In the face of growing international isolation in the 1980s that was harming business prospects, the majority of the business community implicitly, perhaps even unconsciously, entered into an "unholy marriage" with the state.[101]

Nonetheless, the tendencies that Bernstein notes were important. Farsighted members of the business community realized that they would need to involve themselves in the country's political life. In January 1985, David Willers of the SA Foundation, a leading business organization,[102] met two representatives of the ANC in London. The following year, a group of businesspeople convened out of concern "that the South African economy and society would deteriorate and polarise irreversibly if something was not done."[103] Mandated by this grouping, the businessman Christo Nel began to meet with, first, the United Democratic Front (UDF)[104] and then ANC leadership. The group was formally constituted as the Consultative Business Movement (CBM) in 1988. The encounters changed both sides: "Mass

[99] Sampson, *Black and Gold*, 95.
[100] Ann Bernstein, "Business and Public Policy in South Africa," (Johannesburg, South Africa: The Urban Foundation, 1998), 3.
[101] Terreblanche and Nattrass, "A Periodization of the Political Economy from 1910," 17.
[102] Strictly speaking this is not the same organization as the one with the same name that figured prominently in the 1990s. The two organizations shared many members but did not overlap in time, and had different constitutions, boards, and missions.
[103] T. N. Chapman and M. B. Hofmeyr, "Business Statesman of the Year Award" (paper presented at the Harvard Business School Club of South Africa, 10 August 1994), paragraph two.
[104] The UDF was a wide-ranging association of civil society associations, closely aligned with the ANC (then banned and in exile) but not formally attached to it.

democratic movement representatives accepted that they needed to develop contact with a small minority of willing if unsure business leaders. And the business leaders realised that they had to take a leap of faith."[105]

Not all of the business initiatives of the 1980s were quiet or low level. One of the businesspeople who had met with the ANC was Chris Ball, the managing director of First National Bank, one of the largest banks in the country. A political storm erupted in 1987 when, after that meeting, Ball authorized funding for an advertisement that called for the unbanning of the ANC, precipitating a "spectacular row" with government.[106]

A number of business-minded think tanks were also established at this point, churning out policy recommendations concerning how best to reform the South African political economy. Chief among these was undoubtedly the liberal Urban Foundation, founded on the premise that black South Africans were – and should for policy purposes be regarded as – permanent and productive members of the South African economy. Government *did* heed the urgings of liberal business on at least one issue, the legalization of black trade unions. Whatever its failings, important fractions of business had, over time, demonstrated that they were able to articulate interests contrary to those of the ruling party and that they could and would act to secure a long-term future for capitalist development.

Black business, black politics

Needless to say, apartheid severely stunted the development of black entrepreneurship.[107] By the end of the 1980s, most black businesses were, at best, small (micro, even) or medium in size and restricted to petty trading and service provision.[108] An important exception was

---

[105] Chapman and Hofmeyr, "Business Statesman of the Year Award," paragraph two.

[106] Callinicos, *South Africa between Reform and Revolution*, 159.

[107] Scott Taylor, "The Challenge of Indigenization, Affirmative Action, and Black Empowerment in Zimbabwe and South Africa," in *Black Business and Economic Power*, ed. Alusine Jalloh and Toyin Falola (Rochester, NY: University of Rochester Press, 2002), 352.

[108] Okechukwu C. Iheduru, "Black Entrepreneurs in Post-Apartheid South Africa," in *African Entrepreneurship: Theory and Reality*, ed. Anita Spring and Barbara E. McDade (Gainesville, FL: University Press of Florida, 1998).

the development of the black taxi industry during the 1980s as restrictions on public transport were eased and/or ignored by the authorities.

From the very beginnings of capitalism in South Africa, a racialized hierarchy had crippled the capacity of Africans to pursue their economic livelihood. The 1913 Land Act for example restricted Africans' ability to occupy and own land and destroyed what Godsell describes as "the earliest recorded black entrepreneurs in South Africa," namely the commercial African farmers.[109] These restrictions were extended with the enshrinement of apartheid under the NP government after 1948. According to Iheduru, "more than 500 laws and more than 800 local ordinances and by-laws put all kinds of restrictions on black businesses."[110] At every level imaginable, from the training that they could have access to, to where they could trade, the kinds of businesses they could engage in, and how many businesses they could operate, black entrepreneurs experienced "external prejudice and discriminatory legislation that ... hampered their business enterprises."[111] Their white counterparts not only did not face these obstacles, but also benefited from a battery of direct and indirect subsidies.[112]

As grand apartheid was implemented, the elaborate fiction of "self-governing" homelands ironically created some limited room for African entrepreneurs, many of whom were "forced to move their operations to 'their' ethnic homelands or register their businesses in other people's names in order to circumvent laws restricting them to only one business operation in urban areas."[113] The catch was that those businesspeople then risked being associated with the corrupt and unpopular Bantustan governments.

[109] Gillian Godsell, "Entrepreneurs Embattled: Barriers to Entrepreneurship in South Africa," in *The Culture of Entrepreneurship*, ed. Brigitte Berger (San Francisco, CA: ICS Press, 1991), 93.

[110] Okechukwu Chris Iheduru, "The Development of Black Capitalism in South Africa and the United States," in *Black Business and Economic Power*, ed. Alusine Jalloh and Toyin Falola (Rochester, NY: University of Rochester Press, 2002), 580.

[111] Godsell, "Entrepreneurs Embattled," 85–6.

[112] Taylor, "The Challenge of Indigenization, Affirmative Action, and Black Empowerment in Zimbabwe and South Africa," 352.

[113] Iheduru, "The Development of Black Capitalism in South Africa and the United States," 580.

Within an increasingly polarized polity, the few black business-people who succeeded were often tainted by their association with the apartheid state and an exploitative capitalist system. The groundwork for these attitudes had long been laid. As Godsell points out, "[h]istorically, because of the limitations on trading in black townships, people who did manage to get licenses were regarded as being, if not corrupt in an economic sense, then certainly politically corrupt and in cahoots with the white administrative bureaucracy of the township."[114] The black townships became increasingly radicalized in the late 1970s and early 1980s and the environment within which black businesspeople had to operate grew ever more fraught. As township politics became more violent under the State of Emergency, businesspeople frequently found themselves labeled as collaborators and became the target of avarice, criminality, and political hostility.[115]

The legislative restrictions at least on black business began to ease under De Klerk's reform program of the 1990s as the country moved toward negotiations. However, this broader black hostility to busi-nesspeople in the 1980s was echoed in the ideological proclivities of the ANC. This had not always been the case.

Policy-making in the ANC

In January 1912, the South African Native National Congress was formed to represent the political concerns of black South Africans.[116] (A decade later it would change its name to the African National Congress.) At the outset, the politics of the Congress was determinedly moderate, centrist, and liberal. In 1945, the ANC's then president, Alfred Bitini Xuma, had argued that it was "of less importance to us [in the ANC] whether capitalism is smashed or not. It is of greater importance to us that while capitalism exists we must fight and struggle to get our full share and benefit from the system."[117] The Congress

---

[114] Godsell, "Entrepreneurs Embattled," 91–2.
[115] Ibid., 92–3. David Hirschmann, "Of Monsters and Devils, Analyses and Alternatives: Changing Black South African Perceptions of Capitalism and Socialism," *African Affairs* 89, no. 356 (1990).
[116] Saul Dubow, *The African National Congress* (Reading: Sutton Publishing, 2000), 1–2.
[117] From Xuma papers, ABX 45080/d, quoted in Robert Fine and Dennis Davis, *Beyond Apartheid: Labour and Liberation in South Africa* (London: Pluto Press, 1990), 52.

practised, in McKinley's words, the "politics of non-violence and incorporation," with a program of action dominated by letter writing and the dispatch of mannered delegations to government and to the Queen in London.[118] These tactics proved ineffective in blocking or overturning a battery of racist legislation.

Younger members of the Congress began to grow distinctly disillusioned with the "softly, softly" approach advocated by their elders. A younger generation of activists, most notably Nelson Mandela and Walter Sisulu, worked to reinvigorate the Congress' program, establishing the ANC Youth League in the early 1940s. Prodded by the Youth League, the Congress began to move away from its petty-bourgeois and elite origins and to connect more directly with the concerns of the mass of Africans now moving into the cities of South Africa.

The future partner of the ANC, the Communist Party of South Africa (CPSA), was founded in 1921. Like the Congress, the Party too would go through a name change as well as a serious reconsideration of its mobilizing ideology and organizing strategies. In an early indication that the two organizations might usefully coordinate their programs, the leaders of the Congress and the Party traveled together to Moscow in 1927,[119] and seven years later, the All Africa Conference "brought together for the first time Coloureds, Black Nationalists, communists and Trotskyists" and "put the ANC, for the first time, in at least indirect alliance with the CPSA."[120]

From the 1920s on, the two organizations shared many of their objectives and members although relations were neither uncomplicated nor always entirely harmonious. There was a strong Africanist tradition within the Youth League that was suspicious of, if not hostile to, the class-based ideological view of the Communists, as well as of their Indian and white adherents. Over time, however, as the South African Communist Party (SACP)[121] proved its courage in the struggle against apartheid, Party stalwarts became increasingly influential within the Congress. This process was reinforced by the formalization of Alliance politics in the 1950s, whereby the ANC consolidated its

---

[118] Dale T. McKinley, *The ANC and the Liberation Struggle: A Critical Political Biography* (London: Pluto Press, 1997), 6–7.
[119] Dubow, *The African National Congress*, 13.
[120] McKinley, *The ANC and the Liberation Struggle*, 10.
[121] The original CPSA disbanded and reformed itself with a different name.

relationship with a number of partner organizations including the
(white) Congress of Democrats, the Indian Congress, and the (colored)
African People's Organization.[122]

The non-racial character of the Congress movement was confirmed
in 1955 at the Congress of the People. At Kliptown, just outside
Johannesburg, a large crowd endorsed the provisions of the Freedom
Charter, including the foundational clause that "South Africa belongs
to all who live in it, black and white."[123]

To the extent that the Charter articulated an economic policy, it
was decidedly ambiguous. The Charter pledges to restore the national
wealth of the country to "the people" and seems to advocate nationalization of the country's mineral wealth, its banks, and monopoly
industry.[124] Over the years, this clause provoked heated debate about
whether it prescribed a socialist economy or not. It may have been
that the intention of the Charter framers was to leave the provision
deliberately vague.[125] At any rate, the apartheid state chose to believe
that the ANC was evincing distinctly communist tendencies. In the
second half of the 1950s, the state laid treason charges against 156
activists.[126]

After the Sharpeville massacre in 1960, both the Communist Party
and the ANC leadership went underground and into exile. Under
Mandela's leadership, the ANC formed *Umkhonto we Sizwe*, the
Spear of the Nation (or MK for short), to direct what would henceforth be an armed struggle against the apartheid state. According to
Dubow, MK played an important role "in helping to cement the
working relationship between the SACP and the ANC ... [as i]t was

---

[122] Dubow, *The African National Congress*, 37, and McKinley, *The ANC and the
Liberation Struggle*, 19.

[123] Unattributed, *The Freedom Charter* (website) (The African National
Congress, 1955 (accessed July 2007)) www.anc.org.za/ancdocs/history/
charter.html. There were also those who opposed the influence of the non-
Africans within the Congress. The Defiance campaign further radicalized
many of the ANC's members and in 1959 a number of the Africanists, under
the leadership of Robert Sobukwe, broke away to form the Pan Africanist
Congress.

[124] Ibid.

[125] See Dubow, *The African National Congress*, Tom Lodge, "Policy Processes
within the African National Congress and the Tripartite Alliance," *Politikon*
26, no. 1 (1999), McKinley, *The ANC and the Liberation Struggle*.

[126] Dubow, *The African National Congress*, 56.

largely through the Party's intimate links with Moscow that the ANC was provided with vital material and military resources."[127]

The ideologically polarized environment of the Cold War, and the fact that much military support for MK came from the Soviets, undoubtedly shaped the overall ideological direction of the ANC, inclining them, at the very least, to greater sympathy with the policy positions of the SACP. In addition, the tendency of Botha's government to label anyone who opposed it as communist boosted the appeal of communism for the average black South African.

The allegations about the ANC's "socialist" economic policy worried business greatly. On 13 September 1985, Gavin Relly (who had replaced Harry Oppenheimer as head of Anglo American) led a group of businessmen to the ANC headquarters in Lusaka, Zambia, to meet with Oliver Tambo and his team, and "naturally the issue about which Relly and company expressed most concern was the clause in the Freedom Charter providing for the nationalisation of 'monopoly industry.'"[128] This meeting came after Tambo's meeting in the early 1980s with the representatives of a number of important British and US banks and corporations.[129]

It was not just white, English-speaking business that understood the importance of the ANC's policy direction: leading black businessman and head of the National African Federated Chambers of Commerce (NAFCOC), Dr. Sam Motsuenyane, also traveled to Zambia's capital and reported on his return an "astonishing degree" of agreement between the ANC and his organization.[130]

Still, economic policy-making was not foremost on the minds of the ANC leadership. As evidenced in the 1988 Constitutional Guidelines, their thinking about the economy had not advanced very far beyond the general sentiments of the Freedom Charter, viz. a mixed economy and the imperative that the entire economy should serve the entire population.[131]

---

[127] Ibid., 76–7. This view is confirmed by McKinley, *The ANC and the Liberation Struggle*, 30.

[128] Callinicos, *South Africa between Reform and Revolution*, 134.

[129] McKinley, *The ANC and the Liberation Struggle*, 55.

[130] Callinicos, *South Africa between Reform and Revolution*, 135.

[131] See p. 355 of the Constitutional Guidelines. African National Congress, "Constitutional Guidelines for a Democratic South Africa" (South Africa: African National Congress, 1988). Quoted in McKinley, *The ANC and the Liberation Struggle*, 90.

The racial profile of the South African business community (white and predominantly English-speaking) and its political relationship with the country's government generated an extensive debate about the relationship between apartheid and economic growth in South Africa. At stake here were the political credentials of the business community: did businesspeople collude in, and profit from, the crime of apartheid (as many in the black community argued) or were they a liberal voice in favor of free markets and greater political freedoms (as many in the business community asserted)? Historically, the ANC and its allies had adopted the first view. As the ANC became more influential and moved into political power, this debate became vital for business and its role in economic policy-making in the 1990s. This story is told in chapter 2.

The South African political economy by the late 1980s

The 1980s saw South Africa in a state of profound crisis. Thompson describes an economy in "deep recession by the late 1980s, stifled by the impact of international sanctions and disinvestments, as well as by the distorting impact of apartheid itself on the economy."[132]

As growing numbers of businesspeople pressed the government to reform the way in which the state had structured both politics and the economy, the limits of what had been attempted over the previous sixty years became increasingly obvious. This was a state that attempted to use its power to boost the influence, stature, and prosperity of a small political elite, in this case white Afrikaners. And the state had, to a large measure, succeeded in this. However, both the attempt and the outcome differed from those which pertained in many other newly independent African states on a number of grounds: first, industrialization and the development of a large, established, and well-diversified capitalist economy in South Africa predated the emergence of a single, unified, and independent national government. Second, and not unrelated, when the state set out to reorder the economy, it had to contend with an already powerful and influential private sector. The result was that, regardless of its intentions, the state could not unilaterally restructure the economy. Third, in any event, many of those state interventions in the economy were not

---

[132] Thompson, *A History of South Africa*, 242–3.

intended to destroy the private sector, but rather to increase the ambit of that sector to include rather than exclude Afrikaners from its benefits.[133] This necessitated the state's paying some attention to what dominant fractions of the private sector required to consolidate their long term prosperity.

Historically, Afrikaner nationalism had been key to government's intervention in the economy, but the content and salience of that nationalism shifted over time.[134] That nationalism also could not secure (and arguably did not seek) wholesale capture of the business class by the state. On the contrary, the Afrikaner business class was itself "captured" by the preexisting English-speaking business class.

What would be crucial for South Africa henceforth was *African* nationalism and the views of its adherents regarding the appropriate role of business in South Africa. Similarly, business' view of the ANC in turn would shape relations with a new political elite. In January 1989, P. W. Botha suffered a stroke and effectively lost his leadership of both his party and the country. The *groot krokodil*[135] was replaced by F. W. de Klerk, and a new era opened in South Africa's history.

---

[133] Moreover, while there were a number of parastatals established, as I have outlined, they contribute only 7 percent to the economy. Reg Rumney, "Give Us Facts, Not Rhetoric," *Mail and Guardian*, 21 October 2002.

[134] Jung, *Then I Was Black*, 112.

[135] Botha was widely regarded as a dangerous political foe and dubbed the "large crocodile" in popular political discourse.

2 | The neo-liberal era in South Africa: negotiating capitalist development

I want to be a black Harry Oppenheimer.

(Tokyo Sexwale, former ANC guerrilla and premier of Gauteng Province, subsequently Director of Mvelaphande Holdings)[1]

In 1994, what had been "inconceivable" in South African economic policy-making came to pass.[2] At a gathering of the world's political and economic leaders in Davos, Switzerland, Nelson Mandela committed his country to wide-ranging economic reform that, far from moving in the direction of nationalization, pledged to advance privatization.[3]

This is a striking outcome in a country where the new black majority government, described as "quite far left of centre,"[4] had every reason to be hostile to a predominantly white business community. Business was tainted by its association with apartheid. In addition, the ANC was considered to be under pressure from the majority black population to end years of white economic privilege and increase state spending on welfare and poverty alleviation. Reinforcing these pressures was the ruling Congress' formal political alliance with the South African Communist Party (SACP) and the Congress of South African Trade Unions (COSATU), both of which explicitly advocated leftist economic policies. Yet, by the end of the 1990s, the ANC government

---

[1] Oppenheimer was one of South Africa's leading mining magnates. Antony Sguazzin, "Sexwale Takes Struggle into Oppenheimer's Sector," *Business Report, Sunday Times*, 24 April 2001, 2.

[2] In February 1990, Mandela had declared it "inconceivable" that the ANC would move away from a policy of nationalization. Cited in Nicoli Nattrass, "The ANC's Economic Policy: A Critical Perspective, " in *Wealth or Poverty: Critical Choices for South Africa*, ed. Robert Schrire (Oxford University Press, 1992), 64.

[3] Patti Waldmeir, *Anatomy of a Miracle: The End of Apartheid and the Birth of the New South Africa* (New York: W. W. Norton and Co., 1997), 256.

[4] Raymond Parsons, *The Mbeki Inheritance: South Africa's Economy 1990–2004* (Johannesburg, South Africa: Ravan Press, 1999), 105.

had consolidated a moderate – even conservative – set of economic policies.

To what extent did this shift reflect the efforts of business and what impact did business in South Africa have on economic policy-making? In the first half of the decade the business community sought a normalization of the political process and reassurance that large-scale redistribution was not in the offing. Here business had a very important impact on ANC policy-making, most obviously in its ability to withdraw capital and provide support for the national currency. Over the course of the decade, business split, most crucially along the lines of big versus small business, but also in terms of race and sub-sectors. Nonetheless, I conclude that business had a substantial impact on economic policy-making compared to our other cases, and consider how ongoing black economic empowerment (BEE) might impact business–government relations.

This chapter will begin by outlining the structure of the South African economy and the nature of the business community there. A brief discussion of policy-making within the ANC precedes a discussion of business' major policy demands in the 1990s.

The South African political economy

By the late 1980s, the South African economy was industrialized and well diversified with a sophisticated financial services structure. Manufacturing and industry contributed 44 percent of GDP, and services comprised 51 percent.[5] However this sub-sectoral diversity obscured some politically salient concentrations. The economy was (and still is) notoriously oligopolistic. Economic wealth was held almost entirely by a section of the white community. Not only had business long been dominated by English-speaking whites, but it was dominated also by a few large companies.[6] This boosted the political and economic influence of these firms.

---

[5] World Bank Group, "World Development Indicators 2000" (World Bank, 2000).

[6] In the mid-1990s, just five business groups controlled more than 70 percent of the assets listed on the Johannesburg Stock Exchange (JSE). McGregor BFA, *McGregor's Who Owns Whom in South Africa*, 24th edn (Florida Hills, South Africa: Carla Soares, Who Owns Whom, 2004).

By the late 1980s, the competitiveness of the South African private sector had also been damaged by the country's political situation. The private sector had been protected both by tariffs and by the international campaign to isolate the country in the last decades of apartheid. This isolation inevitably produced distortions and inefficiencies within the market. Nonetheless, for most of its existence the mainstream business sector had operated predominantly in terms of market-based incentives.

As a country with a long-standing private sector, South Africa had a large number of business organizations representing diverse sets of interests. These organizations were, for the most part, well resourced and well institutionalized, at least in comparison with those found in other African economies. A review of those most significant for economic policy-making follows.

Appropriately, the oldest business organization in the country was associated with mining, namely the Chamber of Mines, established in 1887[7] – but the other sub-sectors soon followed. The Association of Chambers of Commerce and Industry was established in 1892 and the Federated Chambers of Industry followed in 1917. They merged in 1990 to form the South African Chamber of Business (SACOB).[8] The firms represented by SACOB were predominantly small and medium-sized.

By contrast, the South Africa Foundation (SAF) membership comprised the fifty largest firms in South Africa and its board included some of the country's most powerful economic figures. Accordingly, the SAF was one of the heavy hitters in the policy terrain. It explicitly set out "to formulate and express a co-ordinated view on macroeconomic and other national issues and to promote the interests and further growth of South Africa's private sector."[9]

Business associations in the late 1980s were still organized on ethnic and racial lines. All of the associations outlined above, for example, were dominated by white English-speakers.[10] The Afrikaanse

---

[7] Chamber of Mines of South Africa, "News, Data and Policy Information on the South African Mining Industry" (accessed July 2007) www.bullion.org.za.

[8] Greenberg, *Race and State in Capitalist Development*, 176.

[9] South Africa Foundation, "Objectives of the Foundation" (Johannesburg, South Africa: South Africa Foundation, undated).

[10] In the latter half of the 1990s a number of these were pursuing "unity talks" with organizations such as the AHI, NAFCOC, and the Foundation for African

Handelsinstituut (AHI) was introduced in chapter 1 so I will not repeat that material here. The black business community was represented by a small number of organizations, most of these much more recent in origin than those in the white business community. The Foundation of African Business and Consumer Services (FABCOS), for example, was founded in 1988 to represent the informal business sector (historically dominated by the taxi industry).[11] The National African Federated Chambers of Commerce (NAFCOC) was somewhat longer-standing (founded in 1964) and represented a wide range of small and medium-sized enterprises and retailers. The Black Management Forum (BMF) represented the views of a range of professionals and businesspeople.

Two organizations aspired to be an encompassing voice for business in the 1990s. Business South Africa (BSA) probably represented the largest number of (mostly white) firms. It had a loose organizational structure and tended to be driven by consensus. The Black Business Council (BBC), its black counterpart, was a federation of eleven black business organizations.[12]

Economic policy-making in the ANC[13]

While it is one of Africa's oldest liberation movements, thinking about economic policy began late in the ANC's life. At the start of the 1990s, the ANC leadership had not had time to develop a systematic set of economic policy guidelines, but was generally ambivalent about globalization. They were aware that foreign investment was vital to supplement the country's low level of domestic saving, but for the most part activists sought to regulate and control that investment.

Business and Consumer Services (FABCOS). These resulted in the inclusive voluntary association, the Chamber of Commerce of South Africa (Chamsa) in 2003.

[11] Dumisani Hlophe, Malachia Mathoho, and Maxine Reitzes, *The Business of Blackness: The Foundation of African Business and Consumer Services, Democracy and Donor Funding,* Research Report no. 83 (Johannesburg, South Africa: Centre for Policy Studies, 2001), 8.

[12] In 2003, BSA and BBC merged to form Business Unity of South Africa (BUSA).

[13] This chapter focuses on policy-making within the ANC rather than the NP. Even before the ANC officially assumed power, economic policy was developed on the assumption that the NP could no longer make policy entirely on its own.

State ownership, they argued, should be extended and mining capital in particular should be more closely regulated.[14]

Before the ANC's accession to power, its locus of economic policy-making lay in the Economic Planning Desk established in 1990, then under the leadership of Max Sisulu.[15] The Desk came into its own when the young township activist from the Cape, Trevor Manuel, working closely with Tito Mboweni, replaced Sisulu the following year.[16] After 1994 when the ANC won the country's first nationwide elections, policy-making moved out of the party structures and into the heart of government.

Business' policy demands in the 1990s

At the outset of the 1990s, business, broadly speaking, wanted a "normalization" (read stabilization) of the political and economic climate. More specifically, business sought, first, a peaceful resolution of the ongoing political crisis and, second, some kind of reassurance that left-wing redistribution would be abjured in favor of more "moderate" macroeconomic policies. While black businesspeople favored a higher level of government intervention than their white colleagues, they too supported a peaceful political transition and the creation of a broadly free market environment.

Political normalization

Since the 1970s, but especially from the mid-1980s, it had become clear that government could not solve the country's economic woes without addressing the larger political problem of black disenfranchisement. Apartheid created an under-skilled but highly politicized and unionized workforce. The politicization of the labor market in the 1980s heightened the profile of organized labor. This environment profoundly affected business' ability to win influence with the political

---

[14] David Lazar, "Competing Economic Ideologies in South Africa's Economic Debate," *British Journal of Sociology* 47, no. 4 (1996): 614. Lodge, "Policy Processes within the African National Congress and the Tripartite Alliance."

[15] Moses Ngoasheng, "Policy Research inside the African National Congress," *Transformation* 18 (1992): 116.

[16] Lodge, "Policy Processes within the African National Congress and the Tripartite Alliance," 21.

powers to be, the ANC.[17] Moreover, as levels of "ungovernability" rose, so too did the cost of doing business. Beyond a labor force that had been deliberately under-educated, business had to contend with urban unrest and workplace disruptions. While not strictly an economic policy demand, a peaceful resolution of the political situation was, for business, the precondition for economic progress.

The Conference for a Democratic South Africa (CODESA) provided the opportunity for South Africans to negotiate just such a solution. It was not a smooth process but the parties did negotiate a more-or-less peaceful transition to democracy, preceded by a transitional power-sharing phase. Here, the ANC effectively ceded key economic ministries, such as Finance, and Mineral and Energy Affairs, to the National Party (NP), at least in the short term. This provided some reassurance to conservative elements of the business community, both at home and abroad, a guarantee of sorts that the ANC would not embark on a precipitate revolution in economic policy. While the transfer of political power was being negotiated in CODESA, it became apparent that there was a need for an equivalent forum in the economic sphere.

In 1992, COSATU pushed for the establishment of a National Economic Forum (NEF) as a meeting place for government, business, and labor. Derek Keys, formerly a high-profile businessman in the minerals industry, had been appointed finance minister by the NP. He was persuaded that government could no longer make economic policy on its own. Rather, it was only when there was cooperation and mutual confidence among these three sets of actors that the economy could flourish.[18] The NEF was succeeded, in February of 1994, by the National Economic Development and Labour Council (NEDLAC) which institutionalized the representation of organized business and government, along with organized labor and community-based organizations. NEDLAC's goal was "increased participation – by all major stakeholders, in economic decision-making."[19]

---

[17] By contrast, labor had a close relationship with the government to be. In 1990, the ANC, the SACP, and COSATU formally constituted themselves as a tripartite alliance. Ibid.: 7.

[18] The roots for this kind of tripartism had been laid down in the National Manpower Commission although that forum had been more limited in terms of the scope of issues it addressed.

[19] National Economic Development and Labour Council, "Founding Declaration of NEDLAC" (website) (NEDLAC, 1995 [accessed July 2007]) www.nedlac. org.za.

Business generally received these fora well. SACOB, for example, saw NEDLAC as a trust-building mechanism that provided an opportunity to make economic policy by means of discussion. Because it operated by consensus, however, it tended to produce "lowest common denominator" policy-making: outcomes tended to consist of options that were not necessarily any party's first choice, but that each of the parties could live with. In addition, NEDLAC privileged certain voices in the debate. Nattrass quotes a business representative arguing that NEDLAC was made up of "big business and big labour looking after Gauteng [the province that is the industrial and financial heart of the economy]."[20] There is some evidence for this view, as we shall see.

In September of 1993, South African negotiators concluded debt rescheduling with international financiers and some kind of normality began to return to South African financial and capital markets. With elections in 1994, the same might be said of the country's polity. The ANC won the country's first democratic elections by an overwhelming margin and, with Nelson Mandela in the presidency, formed a "government of national unity" with the NP. Business watched nervously.[21] The "normalization" of the business environment had begun but would not be complete until the business community more closely came to resemble the society's broader ethnic and racial profile.

The development of black business

In the previous chapter, I referred to the Oppenheimer thesis, namely the mining magnate's view that apartheid and political instability could be ended best by means of economic growth. Thabo Mbeki, then Mandela's deputy and Secretary General of the ANC, held a complementary view: that South Africa's long-term prosperity and stability could only be secured through a broad-based middle class, and, in particular, a flourishing black business community.[22] Given

---

[20] Nicoli Nattrass, "Collective Action Problems and the Role of South African Business in National and Regional Accords," *South African Journal of Business Management* 29, no. 3 (1997): 107.

[21] Of course, business did more than just watch. In addition to shouldering a share of the financial costs associated with the elections, sections of the business community were involved in ensuring that the elections actually happened.

[22] Jaspreet Kindra, "ANC Backtracks on Black Bourgeoisie," *Daily Mail and Guardian*, 2 June 2000.

that apartheid had denied black South Africans access to full participation in the economy, this would take some doing.

By the mid-1990s, only a small number of high-profile black capitalists were active in the private sector. Some had switched into business from a political background, like Cyril Ramaphosa, one of the founders of COSATU, a previous Secretary General of the ANC and the Congress' chief negotiator at CODESA. Others, such as Dr. Nthatho Motlana, had come from professional backgrounds. There was still a long way to go, however, in effecting a broader transformation of the face of business: In 1990, there were no black corporations listed on the Johannesburg Stock Exchange (JSE).[23]

Not surprisingly, black business was a key constituency agitating for greater opportunities for black businesspeople. As early as 1990, for example, NAFCOC published its "3-4-5-6 programme" which set targets for black participation in the economy by the year 2000.[24] The leadership of the ANC was sympathetic to such calls, but not entirely sure how to pursue them. The ANC's policy guidelines in 1992, for example, referred to the need to de-racialize the public and private sectors,[25] a sentiment that was reaffirmed in the Reconstruction and Development Programme (RDP),[26] but no concrete policy measures followed at this stage.

Instead, the first generation of initiatives to Africanize the business community, or Black Economic Empowerment (BEE) as it came to be called, took the form of highly leveraged purchases of equity capital by a tiny number of high-profile black entrepreneurs. The dominant

---

[23] McGregor BFA, *McGregor's Who Owns Whom in South Africa*, Charlene Smith, "Darkening the Corporate Pigment," *Mail and Guardian*, 28 November 1997.

[24] The targets were for 30% of directors, 40% of share ownership, 50% of suppliers, and 60% of management to be black. Neo Chabane *et al.*, "Ten Year Review: Industrial Structure and Competition Policy" (Johannesburg, South Africa: School of Economic and Business Sciences, University of the Witwatersrand, 2003), 22.

[25] African National Congress, "Ready to Govern: ANC Policy Guidelines for a Democratic South Africa Adopted at the National Conference" (website) (African National Congress, 1992 [accessed July 2007]); available from www. anc.org.za/ancdocs/history/readyto.html.

[26] Government of South Africa, "The Reconstruction and Development Programme: A Policy Framework" (Government of South Africa [accessed July 2007]); available from www.polity.org.za/govdocs/rdp/rdp.html. See section 4.4.6.3.

form for such transactions was the purchase through holding companies of (sections of) established white firms. Given the dearth of
moneyed black investors, most of these purchases required substantial
loans, the repayment of which, it was anticipated, would be facilitated
by the performance of the newly acquired company's share prices.[27]
New Africa Investments Limited (NAIL) was the paradigmatic example
of such a structure: "an investment holding company without a core
business."[28]

White business played a crucial role in these deals, as both financier
and seller. It was striking that an Afrikaner firm offered the first such
deal.[29] In fact, when Sanlam sold 10 percent of Metropolitan Life to
a BEE consortium in 1993, the black buyout was modeled closely on
the early Afrikaner *helpmekaar* model (see chapter 1).

Mining capital was not far behind. The giant Anglo American was
at the time readying itself for its London listing. As part of this process, the company unbundled a subdivision in May 1995 to create
three discrete units including Johannesburg Consolidated Investments
(JCI), which was then sold to a consortium of black investors.[30] The
close to 35 percent controlling stake bought by African Mining Group
"made history" as the first instance of black ownership of a mining
house in South Africa.[31] A slew of BEE buyouts and sales followed,
most structured in a very similar fashion.[32] The second half of the 1990s
became an era of deal making as selected black businesspeople were
presented with opportunities to acquire stakes in existing companies.

[27] Andrea Brown, *Black Economic Empowerment*, Global Equity Research, UBS
Warburg South Africa Research Team (Johannesburg, South Africa: UBS
Warburg, 2002), 15.

[28] Reg Rumney, Personal interview with author, 8 July 2004.

[29] What was probably the first black empowerment initiative actually occurred
under the old NP government, when National Sorghum Breweries was
consolidated and sold into black hands in 1990. Unattributed, "It's Not Enough
to Be Owned by Blacks," *Sunday Times*, 25 April 1999; Rumney, Interview.

[30] This move has been compared with AAC's decision to sell General Mining to
Afrikaner entrepreneurs thirty years earlier. Unattributed, "NAIL's Strange
Gambit in NEC-Johnnic Deal," *Financial Mail*, 1 November 1996,
Unattributed, "Black Empowerment Amid Echoes of History," *Financial Mail*,
6 September 1996.

[31] Chabane *et al.*, "Ten Year Review," 24. As Chabane *et al.* point out, while
AAC tried to present this as an "altruistic deal," in fact, the black investors
ended up paying an above-market price for their shares, due to a rival bid from
NAIL.

[32] Rumney, Interview.

These were heady days and seemed to promise a real transformation of South African capital: by the end of 1996, close to 10 percent of the JSE's capitalization was suddenly in black hands.[33]

These developments were facilitated by an important shift in the thinking of sections of the white business community: Having been initially hostile, a number of influential businesspeople came to understand that BEE could safeguard their own future:[34] "White business realized that this [BEE] would secure a capitalist economy; it would be looked on favorably and they would be allowed to influence government policy if they did this. They realized that there were many more capitalist-oriented businesses [in South Africa] than they had realized [and that it] would enhance their business interests if they cooperated."

Many of the early BEE deals involved borrowing large sums of money to buy into existing firms; this strategy worked relatively well so long as the South African share index was rising; the loans could be repaid as the prices of new acquisitions continued to rise. This changed abruptly when the South African bourse, along with those of other developing countries, was hit by the aftereffects of the Asian financial crisis, putting pressure on a number of these new companies.[35] For example, the shares of NAIL, the flag bearer of BEE, fell dramatically and company executives were forced to sell huge chunks of the company in an attempt to save it.

Certainly, BEE was not an unqualified success in the 1990s.[36] Its profile was damaged by the failure of a number of affirmative action initiatives, including Pepsi and African Bank in 1995, and by the later collapse in the value of share prices for the black-owned JCI.[37] New Age Breweries and National Sorghum Breweries had also floundered by 1998.[38] These failures served to underscore the critiques of this

---

[33] Robin McGregor, "How the Guard Has Changed since Rhodes Stormed the S.A. Economy," *Sunday Times*, 15 December 1996.

[34] Grietjie Verhoef, Personal interview with author, 5 July 2004.

[35] Brown, *Black Economic Empowerment*, 15.

[36] To be fair, the timing was not propitious. See Patrick Bond, *Elite Transition: From Apartheid to Neo-Liberalism in South Africa* (London: Pluto Press, 2000), 46.

[37] Okechukwu Chris Iheduru, "Social Concertation, Labour Unions and the Creation of a Black Bourgeoisie in South Africa," *Commonwealth and Comparative Politics* 40, no. 2 (2002): 77.

[38] Unattributed, "Honeymoon is over at NSB as Financial Misconduct Claims Fly," *Sunday Times*, 6 July 1997.

first generation of BEE deals, chiefly the argument that BEE was profiting only a very small minority, while the economic position of the vast majority of black South Africans remained unchanged or worsened.[39] Black entrepreneurs complained that BEE had opened up only limited opportunities in ownership, and ceded few openings for those wishing to be involved in hands-on management. From the white business community there was skepticism about the ability of black entrepreneurs, given their lack of business training, to "add value."

In 1993 the BMF adopted an affirmative action blueprint, with a set of targets for 2000 that differed from those proposed by NAFCOC.[40] This highlighted the diffusion of efforts and effect for the BEE campaign. Government grew impatient with the proliferation of bodies that purported to speak, with sometimes contradictory voices, on behalf of black businesspeople. Consequently, the Black Business Council (BBC) was formed to unify the various strands within that community and to evaluate the whole BEE process. To this end, the BMF established the Black Economic Empowerment Commission (BEEC), under the leadership of Ramaphosa, in November 1997, "to design concrete recommendations that could be accepted and implemented by government."[41] The timing was good. Having passed the Employment Equity Act in 1998,[42] government needed some direction on how to proceed on the BEE issue.

The Commission extended the definition of BEE beyond equity ownership to include issues of affirmative action and affirmative

---

[39] Iheduru, "The Development of Black Capitalism in South Africa and the United States," Georgina Murray, "Black Empowerment in South Africa: 'Patriotic Capitalism' or a Corporate Black Wash?" *Critical Sociology* 26, no. 3 (2000), Grietjie Verhoef, "'The Invisible Hand': The Roots of Black Economic Empowerment, Sankorp and Societal Change in South Africa, 1985–2000," *Journal for Contemporary History* 28, no. 1 (2003).

[40] The BMF's targets were that, by the year 2000, 30% of senior managers, 20% of executive directors and 30% of non-executive directors should be black. Brown, *Black Economic Empowerment*, 20.

[41] Black Economic Empowerment Commission, "Black Economic Empowerment Commission Presentation Prepared for the Portfolio Committee on Trade and Industry" (website) (2000 [accessed July 2007]) www.pmg.org.za/docs/2000/appendices/000913BEE.htm.

[42] This requires all firms above a certain size to publish their plans for achieving a representative workforce. Brown, *Black Economic Empowerment*.

procurement.[43] The BEEC Report was submitted to government in March 2001. It was followed by a document from the Department of Trade and Industry (DTI). BEE has since expanded into new areas: a series of "empowerment charters" for important sub-sectors of the economy,[44] increased funding from government for empowerment groups through the IDC,[45] and affirmative procurement on the part of both the public and private sectors.[46]

I began this section by inquiring into the normalization of the policy climate, an important component of which was addressing the racial composition of the South African business community. The chapter's key concern, however, remains the impact of business on economic policy. The agenda of BEE was both an objective of the black business community and a factor impacting on the capacity of white business to attain *its* economic policy goals. As a member of the Banking Council argued, "[e]verything that they [business] say about the need for growth, for tackling unemployment, that they cannot operate in an atmosphere of instability – all of this is what BEE can address. We cannot grow at 6 percent or tackle unemployment if we do not look at skills training, at establishing SMMEs, if half of all South Africans are in the informal sector."[47]

Racial issues aside, the political stability that followed 1994 contributed to a more routine business climate, one in which firms could begin to think about the specific kinds of policies they wanted. From the outset, their concern was with the broad outlines of macro-economic policy and, in particular, the specter of nationalization.

---

[43] Black Economic Empowerment Commission, "Black Economic Empowerment Commission Presentation", 1.

[44] Perhaps the most important charter was that developed for the mining sector. A charter for the petroleum and liquid fuels sector was published in November 2000, and was followed by discussions about financial sector and IT charter processes.

[45] Department of Trade and Industry, "South Africa's Economic Transformation: A Strategy for Broad-Based Economic Empowerment" (Pretoria, South Africa: Department of Trade and Industry, 2003) and Broad-Based Black Economic Empowerment Act No. 53.

[46] The Preferential Procurement Policy Framework Act No. 5 prioritizes the bids of companies with significant BEE credentials. Iheduru, "Social Concertation, Labour Unions and the Creation of a Black Bourgeoisie in South Africa," 60.

[47] Cas Coovadia, Personal interview with author, 27 July 2004. An SMME is a small, medium and/or micro enterprise.

A broadly liberal macro-economic framework

When Mandela in 1990, in line with existing ANC policy, had reaffirmed the ANC's historical commitment to nationalization, he provoked alarm in the business community. However, a considerable rethink commenced behind the scenes. The subtle beginnings of what would later become a policy shift were evident in a resolution on economic policy prepared for the 1991 ANC National Conference.[48] While the ANC still called for redistribution, a mixed economy with an extensive social security system, and a large role for the state, the wording of this resolution sounded a new emphasis on the importance of generating economic *growth*. Business gave the draft resolution a mixed response. The Chamber of Business welcomed the arguments about the need for fiscal and monetary discipline and competitive exports, but rejected the interventionist elements of the document and lambasted the ANC's "lack of understanding of the market."[49]

The concessions that the ANC made at CODESA provided further evidence of a shift.[50] Although principally concerned with a political resolution, CODESA committed a future government to a number of key economic regimes. Delegates resolved to guarantee the independence of the South African Reserve Bank (SARB) in the interim constitution and the Bank, in turn, prioritized conservative monetary objectives, chief among them, "[t]he curbing of inflation."[51] Finally, the Transitional Executive Committee signed a financing facility with the International Monetary Fund (IMF) for a modest sum which committed the new government to moderate macro-economic management.[52]

The closest to an economic policy think tank that the ANC had at the time was the Macro-Economic Research Group (MERG), which

---

[48] Lodge, "Policy Processes within the African National Congress and the Tripartite Alliance," 8.

[49] Matthew Kentridge, *Turning the Tanker: The Economic Debate in South Africa* (Johannesburg, South Africa: Centre for Policy Studies, 1993), 7.

[50] The business community was not formally represented at CODESA. However, many of the community's liberal economic interests were represented by the Democratic Party and (because it sought safeguards to restrain a potential ANC government) the National Party.

[51] South African Reserve Bank, "Annual Economic Report 1990" (Johannesburg, South Africa: South African Reserve Bank, 1990), 24, 37.

[52] Jonathan Michie and Vishnu Padayachee, eds., *The Political Economy of South Africa's Transition* (London UK: The Dryden Press, 1997), 32.

along with COSATU supported "closed economic Keynesian" policies.[53] But MERG and the unions were to lose the battle for ANC policy, outmaneuvered by the "defection" of several high-ranking ANC officials to liberal economics. If the Left in South Africa is to be believed, business was remarkably strategic in the way in which it plotted to win the support of the ANC.[54] Patrick Bond, for example, describes the "corruption of decades-old redistributive economic ambitions through a series of 'scenario planning' exercises" and "cosy seminars sponsored by business-oriented think-tanks."[55] The so-called Montfleur scenario planning exercise was particularly important because it drew in both Trevor Manuel and Tito Mboweni of the ANC's Department of Economic Planning. The exercise flagged a warning scenario of Icarus as the populist economy that flew too high, too early in an attempt to meet the expectations of the poor – and crashed and burned. Instead, ANC representatives endorsed an alternate vision, the conservative "Flamingo" scenario, because they felt that this would "help gradually to build local and international business confidence in the new government."[56] The various scenario exercises differed in the range of policy outcomes that they postulated. Significantly, however, all the scenarios emphasized the importance of negotiations and a social compact in charting South Africa's economic course.

In 1992 and 1993, key leadership figures in the ANC were invited to attend short courses and executive training at a range of international financial institutions, business schools, and economic policy think

---

[53] Stephen Gelb, Personal interview with author, 27 June 2001. See also Macro-Economic Research Group, *Making Democracy Work* (Cape Town, South Africa: Centre for Development Studies, 1993).

[54] The relationship was not one-sided. As the ANC began to make the transition from liberation movement to political party, it realized the need for ongoing fund-raising. And they had the perfect fund-raiser. The irresistible Mandela personally phoned the CEOs of twenty of South Africa's largest corporations to request no less than R1 million from each of them for the ANC's electoral campaign. Nineteen of them complied. Anthony Sampson, *Mandela: The Authorised Biography* (London: HarperCollins, 1999), 479.

[55] Bond, *Elite Transition*, 54–5.

[56] James Hamill, "The ANC Perspective: Meeting Expectations?," in *The New South Africa: Prospects for Domestic and International Security*, ed. F. H. Toase and E. J. Yorke (London: Macmillan, 1998), 66. The exercise was so named because it took place at the Montfleur Conference Centre in Stellenbosch.

tanks.[57] Exposure to an international neo-liberal policy environment further moderated the views of policymakers.

The ANC moves into government

The ANC inherited political power in a context that was hostile to assertively interventionist economic policy. Certainly, the wariness of investors and the dismal record of economic governance in the rest of the continent constrained the Congress' policy options. In addition, the ANC was muzzled by the perceived need to reassure the local business community; any unease on the part of that community was signaled directly to the government via jittery currency markets, sentiment on the JSE, and the Business Confidence Index.

Mandela's cabinet choices reflect this concern. In the vital post of Finance Minister, Mandela retained the services of Derek Keys, who had served De Klerk in the same post. When Keys later resigned, Mandela replaced him with another white businessman, Chris Lie-benberg of the financial group Nedcor.

The first comprehensive statement from the ANC about its economic policy came with the release of the RDP. The document was widely canvassed in various fora including the NEF (where business was represented). It was also presented to selected captains of industry including Harry Oppenheimer.

In spirit, the RDP drew on numerous sources but predominantly perhaps on the work of MERG.[58] It listed a large number of social and economic inequalities that needed to be addressed by the new government, but provided few suggestions as to how to prioritize these given a limited budget. On the ANC's accession to power, the document was bolstered by a White Paper. As drafts of the document progressed, however, they moved away from the MERG position, and became far less interventionist. As Mandela pointed out, the final White Paper contained "not a single reference to nationalisation ... not a single slogan that will connect us with any Marxist ideology."[59]

---

[57] Trevor Manuel, for example, who went on to become Finance Minister, attended an Executive Program at Stanford National University in Singapore.

[58] Lodge, "Policy Processes within the African National Congress and the Tripartite Alliance."

[59] Sampson, *Mandela*, 478.

When Mandela's term of office ended, he was succeeded by his deputy, Thabo Mbeki. In June 1999, Mbeki made his first presidential speech at the opening of parliament, to applause from organized business and the mainstream financial media. Big business regarded Mbeki as a sophisticated, cosmopolitan thinker,[60] and they remembered that he had been one of the first ANC members to meet face to face with South African businesspeople. The first Mbeki cabinet was, likewise, well received by business; in particular the private sector commended the retention of Manuel at Finance and Erwin at Trade and Industry respectively. Business seemed to be getting the second of its two concerns met.

Business makes its case – badly

The markets were surprised and pleased by the ANC in office. As early as 1995 exports had responded to the new environment[61] and business confidence surged to a ten-year high.[62] All was not entirely well, however, as evinced by the continued inability of the economy, even in recovery, to create jobs.[63] Then, in February 1996, volatility in international financial markets began to eat away at the value of the rand.[64] While the national leadership appeared committed to fiscal rectitude, investors remained nervous. A small group of private sector economists, led by Terence Moll of Old Mutual, began work on a document that would put business' case for more decisive economic policy reform.

Growth for All (*GFA*), as the document was called, was ultimately issued publicly by the South Africa Foundation. It began from the premise that the South African economy had not performed well for

---

[60] This view has since been obscured by Mbeki's puzzling stance on the relationship between HIV and AIDS, and his combative relationship with the opposition. However, he was highly regarded at the start of his term in office.

[61] Merchandise exports jumped 25 percent in 1995 despite the removal of incentives previously offered under its General Export Incentive Scheme (GEIS). South African Reserve Bank, "Annual Economic Report 1996" (Johannesburg, South Africa: South African Reserve Bank, 1996), 18.

[62] Business Confidence Index (data obtained from Bill Fine, South African Chamber of Commerce), also South African Chamber of Business, "The Voice of Business" (website) (SACOB, 2007 [accessed July 2007]) www.sacob.co.za/.

[63] South African Reserve Bank, "Annual Economic Report 1996," 11.

[64] It did not take much to trigger speculation. Rumors that Mandela was ill, provoked by the chance sighting of an ambulance in the vicinity of Mandela's Cape Town residence, led to a run on the currency.

decades and argued the need to attract substantial inflows of long-term FDI. This, in turn, necessitated bold, comprehensive measures to achieve sound macroeconomic policy, limited government spending, "market freedoms," and an outwardly oriented economy.[65] The document advocated five policy adjustments: dealing with crime and violence, streamlining government spending and revenues, privatization, a "flexible" labor market, and a vigorous export drive.

In June 1996, the government responded with the release of its own, long-awaited statement on macroeconomic policy, the program for Growth, Employment and Redistribution (GEAR). Led by Deputy Finance Minister Alec Erwin, GEAR originated in the work of a team mandated to think broadly about macroeconomic strategy in late 1995.[66] While the document began as a planning exercise linked to the RDP, it was subsequently shaped by the currency crisis that followed Manuel's appointment in 1996. GEAR was thus cognizant of the power of the markets. It argued the importance of such neo-liberal tenets as reduction of the deficit, rapid tariff reductions, exchange control liberalization, and privatization, and it even advocated reform of the labor market.

Most businesspeople welcomed the greater degree of policy predictability that GEAR offered, arguing that it "create[d] a more secure basis for investment and business decision-making." SACOB also welcomed the fact that GEAR resonated "with the broad thrust of economic policies found in successful market-driven economies visited by business people elsewhere."[67] Small and medium-sized business, however, regarded GEAR's employment goals as its "weakest link," arguing that job targets were too ambitious and that productivity had been given insufficient prominence.[68]

I will structure the remainder of this analysis around economic policy areas identified by *GFA* (such as the budget deficit, mix of private versus public ownership, and trade liberalization), considering the extent to which the expectations of business were met. The one area I will not examine in any depth is the first: crime. The demand for "something to be done" about crime was not explicitly an economic

[65] South Africa Foundation, "Growth for All: An Economic Strategy for South Africa" (Johannesburg, South Africa: South Africa Foundation, 1996), ii–iii.
[66] Lodge, "Policy Processes within the African National Congress and the Tripartite Alliance," 23.
[67] Raymond Parsons, *Business Day*, 11 June 1997.   [68] Ibid.

policy demand and neither, unlike political stability, was it a precondition for any kind of debate on more specific economic policy issues. In addition, I will consider a fifth policy area, conspicuously absent from business' list but prominent on the government's, namely competition policy.

The budget deficit

Contrary to what most expected, in its first years in office the ANC government managed to avoid any great jump in overall spending. This is remarkable given the country's stark and racialized inequalities, and the severe developmental backlog inherited by the new government. The markets took this as a reassuring sign of the government's fiscal rectitude. However, this apparent frugality may have been a reflection of administrative weakness rather than policy strength. Government departments, accustomed to serving much smaller (white) constituencies, and the newly created RDP ministry were simply unable to spend the budgets allocated to them.[69] The first few budget years ended with large sums of unspent "roll-over" expenditure, which stood at R6.4 billion by the end of fiscal 1995/6 – the equivalent of 5 percent of total government revenue in that year.[70]

Government dissaving had been one element that Finance Minister Keys highlighted in a presentation to the ANC leadership, just prior to their accession to government. They obviously took the lesson to heart. To address the income side of the equation, as part of an overall tax reform effort, a consolidated new South African Revenue Service was granted autonomy from the government in April 1996, and a program to "right-size" the civil service was introduced a month later.

It was soon evident that the ANC, led by Thabo Mbeki, was committed to market-driven policies.[71] From a high of 8 percent of GDP in 1994, the budget deficit dropped steadily to finish the decade

---

[69] South African Reserve Bank, "Annual Economic Report 1996," 50. The difficulties were such that the government shut the new RDP office in March 1996 and redirected RDP funds through existing line ministries. See Lodge, "Policy Processes within the African National Congress and the Tripartite Alliance," 14–15.

[70] South African Reserve Bank, "Annual Economic Report 1996," 50.

[71] At the South African Communist Party's tenth Congress in Soweto, Mbeki strongly defended GEAR as did Mandela in July 1998 at the SACP's annual congress in Johannesburg. Vuyo Mvoko, "Mandela Hits out as Allies Attack GEAR," *Business Day*, 2 July 1998.

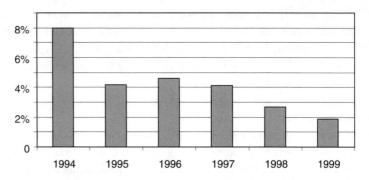

Figure 2.1 South African budget deficit (% of GDP)
Source: Economist Intelligence Unit

at under 2 percent[72] (see Figure 2.1). Organized business commended this trend and business sentiment in 1996 was evidenced in the largest increase in real fixed investment in a decade.[73]

Privatization

By contrast with other aspects of economic policy, business (and it is important to remember here that "business" was predominantly white) used words such as "sluggish" and "half-hearted" to discuss the privatization program. Part of the trouble may have been that the government's privatization program had a number of potentially contradictory goals, including providing services to previously under-served communities, and, where possible, selling to black-empowerment consortia. By the end of the 1990s, the ANC government had garnered R8.6 billion from privatization proceeds.[74] Movement was, in business' view, in the right direction but far from energetic.

Trade liberalization

In the early 1990s, a crucial set of international trade agreements were negotiated at the Uruguay round of the General Agreement on Tariffs and Trade (GATT). The South African negotiating position was

---

[72] Economist Intelligence Unit, "Country Data" (website) (EIU, undated, [accessed July 2007]) http://countrydata.bvdep.com.
[73] South African Reserve Bank, "Annual Economic Report 1996," 8.
[74] Economist Intelligence Unit, "Country Report: South Africa, First Quarter 2000" (EIU, 2002 [accessed 2002]) www.eiu.co.uk.

debated in the NEF where both COSATU and business ultimately endorsed South Africa's accession to GATT. Under the terms of the Marrakesh Agreement, signed in April 1994, South Africa further agreed to liberalize trade, introduce new tariff policies which would gradually lower duties over a five-year period, and begin to reform its General Export Incentive Scheme (GEIS), which was in violation of World Trade Organization (WTO) agreements.[75] Subsequently, Trade and Industry Minister Alec Erwin boasted that South Africa liberalized its tariffs at a rate faster than that required by the GATT and WTO.[76] More evidence of an overall shift in trade policy was evident by early 1995 when the new government made a start on exchange rate liberalization by abolishing the financial rand.

The South African economy began to respond to both the opening up of South Africa's international economic relations and to the changing domestic policy environment. The 1990s saw a broadening and diversification of the country's export base. For example, manufactured goods as a share of total exports rose from 40 percent in 1992 to 58 percent in 2000.[77] The economy began to grow more competitive in response to these new trading opportunities.

Labor framework

If there was one area in which the agenda of the organized trade union movement indisputably trumped that of business it was labor relations.[78] Four major Acts restructured the country's industrial relations: the 1995 Labour Relations Act, the 1997 Basic Conditions of Employment Act, the 1998 Employment Equity Act, and the 1998 Skills Development Act. Throughout, COSATU activists were formidably

---

[75] Ben Fine, "Industrial and Energy Policy," in *The Political Economy of South Africa's Transition*, ed. Jonathan Michie and Vishnu Padayachee (London: The Dryden Press, 1997), 135.

[76] Strictly speaking, this is true. However, the real rate of trade liberalization may have been lower than it at first appeared as exchange rate depreciation mitigated the impact of tariff cuts. Rashad Cassim, "The Political Economy of Trade Negotiations in Post-Apartheid South Africa" (paper presented at the ISP workshop, undated).

[77] Department of Trade and Industry, "Structure of South African Trade," in *South African Trade Statistics* (Government of South Africa, 2005 [accessed July 2007]) www.thedti.gov.za/econdb/raportt/rapstruc.html.

[78] Lodge, "Policy Processes within the African National Congress and the Tripartite Alliance," 18–20.

well organized: they had a clear policy agenda, they were well represented in the Department of Labour, and they were adept at operating
in NEDLAC institutions. While business was also well organized and
well represented, it lacked the conviction to engage in what would have
been a very fierce battle on this issue.

When the ANC first came into power, it had had every reason to be
more sympathetic to labor rather than to business. By the end of the
decade, however, relations between COSATU and the government were
cooling. This no doubt had something to do with the ANC's new status
as the employer of hundreds of thousands of civil servants. In July 1999,
the government resisted the salary increases that unions demanded in
favor of increases more closely in line with inflation. The government
finally broke off negotiations when the unions refused to negotiate down
to the government's level.[79] The government was playing hardball.

Business, on the other hand, was not. Private sector employers and
organized labor continued to devise ever more rigidly institutionalized
ways of regulating the labor market. In 1999 a group of leaders from
both labor and business visited the Netherlands and Ireland to
examine job creation and business–labor cooperation in these two
countries.[80] They came home inspired to set up the Millennium
Labour Council (MLC), a voluntary bipartisan forum for discussions
between business and labor on the development of a common economic vision for South Africa. It was yet another corporatist institution in the tradition of NEDLAC, and, like NEDLAC, it privileged
the interests of organized labor and business.

In the end, some analysts criticize the deal struck between big
business and big labor: "many small businesses ... feel left out of
corporatist deals as are the unemployed, the rural poor, traditional
communities and many weaker and less organized interests. In so far
as these outsiders are deliberately excluded from corporatist institutions, the vested interests of the big players are strengthened."[81]

SACOB, representing smaller and medium-sized white business,
expressed "serious concerns" about the labor legislation. The Chamber

---

[79] Parsons, *The Mbeki Inheritance*, 103.
[80] J. P. Landman, "Labour 1: Business 0" (website) (J. P. Landman, 2001
[accessed 2001]) www.jplandman.co.za.
[81] Heribert Adam, Frederick van Zyl Slabbert, and Kogila Moodley, *Comrades in
Business: Post-Liberation Politics in South Africa* (Cape Town, South Africa:
Tafelberg Publishers, 1997), 144.

argued that smaller businesses had special needs; in particular, they required a higher degree of flexibility on employment conditions.[82] High entry or exit barriers to employment reduced the demand for labor; selectively lowering such barriers, SACOB argued, would not necessarily compromise core labor rights. But it was not SACOB's position that won out.

By the late 1990s, the government had begun to consider ways to make the labor market less rigid and proposed new legislation that provoked significant opposition from organized labor. The proposed legislation was discussed in the MLC and agreement was finally reached on a compromise set of proposals that were less flexible than those that the government had proposed. What was significant here is that, in a policy area where one might have expected business to strongly support the government on labor market reform, the government instead found itself the odd one out in an agreement between organized business and organized labor. This is difficult to understand until one considers the nature of the business community in South Africa.

South African business associations tended, in the main, to be dominated by big business, which differed from small and medium-sized enterprise in its labor–capital factor ratios. In particular, labor costs formed a small share of the cost structure of big business; this was generally not the case for small and medium-sized enterprises. Wage hikes, therefore, had a lesser effect on the profitability of most big businesses. Big business, by contrast, would be substantially affected by the damage to the overall economic and political climate that wide-scale industrial action (in the form of wage-driven strikes, for example) would inflict. They were therefore inclined to cooperate with organized labor to raise wages for the existing, shrinking workforce. In addition, in an oligopolistic economy with a high entry barrier, even an inefficient company could enjoy high profits. The tendency then was for large rents to be shared between currently employed labor (in the form of relatively high wages) and shareholders (in the form of profits). Once again it was the unemployed, as well as consumers more broadly, who missed out.[83]

---

[82] Parsons, *The Mbeki Inheritance*, 68–9.
[83] I am grateful to Stephan Malherbe for this analysis.

Having reviewed four policy areas pursued by business, I wish to turn briefly to an area that government was keener on, viz. competition policy.

Competition policy

Given the oligopolistic nature of South African capitalism, it should come as no great surprise that competition policy was the one policy area where, even at the outset of the decade, the position of the ANC government was decidedly more "pro-market" than that of the private sector. A close analysis of the battle over this policy terrain then reveals much about the respective strengths of the protagonists and their characters.

In the late 1980s, the South African economy was uncompetitive in a number of important respects. As already discussed, the racialized nature of the South African economy had effectively excluded large numbers of potential domestic competitors. Structurally, the economy was characterized by high levels of industry concentration and "significant" price markups.[84] This may well be due to the dominance of a small number of large firms: in 1998, South Africa was ranked a poor nineteenth out of twenty-three African countries for its "monopolistic market dominance."[85] Four firms accounted for more than half of the output for almost half of the main product groups on sale.[86]

Levels of competition in the South African economy were thus compromised by interlocking, highly concentrated patterns of ownership. Historically, trade barriers had provided some protection from international competitors. A sharp decline in imports following the depreciation of the rand and capital flight in the politically turbulent 1980s were then compounded by the effects of trade sanctions and disinvestment.[87] The economy therefore was relatively uncompetitive

---

[84] Johannes Fedderke, Chandana Kularatne, and Martine Mariotti, "Mark-up Pricing in South African Industry" (Universities of Cape Town, British Columbia, and California at Los Angeles, 2004).

[85] Staff reporter, "SA Ranked Seventh in Africa Poll," *The Star*, 5 March 1998.

[86] Chabane *et al.*, "Ten Year Review," 5. See also Robin McGregor, "In Search of Competition," *Financial Mail*, 18 June 2004.

[87] Trevor Bell, "Should South Africa Further Liberalise its Foreign Trade?," in *State and Market in Post-Apartheid South Africa*, ed. Merle Lipton and Charles Simkins (Johannesburg, South Africa: Witwatersrand University Press, 1993).

in terms of both the structure of that economy and the behavior of many of its firms.[88]

As the net beneficiaries of this economy, few in big business were eager to see this structure dismantled. The government on the other hand was motivated to pursue a rigorous competition policy. In keeping with the ANC's leftist tradition, a particular kind of competition policy appealed to anti-conglomerate sentiment within the Congress.[89] The same sentiment was evident in the RDP White Paper.[90]

The ANC signaled early on that this was a priority area. In 1992, Mboweni convened a workshop involving local and international people working on competition policy; after 1994, as the Minister of Trade and Industry, Manuel periodically raised these issues in his speeches.[91] At this stage, the issue here was still one of redistribution; it was not yet being cast in terms of efficiency.[92] This would shift as the debate on economic policy deepened.

Big business, anticipating an attack on this front, responded somewhat testily to charges that it was uncompetitive; some countered that the important monopolies in the South African economy were not those in the private sector but those in the public sector (a reference to the parastatals). It was evident that discussions about competition policy raised the specter of a punitive (in business' mind) focus on breaking up the big conglomerates.

The government's first step to introduce competition began with trade liberalization.[93] As South Africa was reintegrated into a globalized

---

[88] Simon Roberts, Personal interview with author, 8 July 2004. Robin McGregor and Guy McGregor, "The Origins and Extent of the Lack of Competition in South Africa," in *McGregor's Economic Alternatives*, ed. Anne McGregor (Cape Town, South Africa: Juta and Co., 1990).

[89] The ANC's Laurence Harris, for example, described conglomerates as "represent[ing] huge concentrations of economic power which can severely weaken or even dominate the power of the democratic state over the direction of the economy." Laurence Harris, "The Economic Strategy and Policies of the African National Congress," in *McGregor's Economic Alternatives*, ed. Anne McGregor (Wynberg, South Africa: Juta and Co., 1990), 63.

[90] Government of South Africa, "The Reconstruction and Development Programme." See section 4.4.6.2.

[91] Reg Rumney, "We Need More Legal Muscle Says Manuel," *Mail and Guardian*, 9 December 1994.

[92] David Lewis, Personal interview with author, 27 July 2004.

[93] Trade liberalization arguably did lead to increased competition in some sectors, for example the entry of Hyundai into the motor vehicle sector. Brown, "Black Economic Empowerment," 38.

economy, international investors expressed concern about the country's conglomerate structure. This, together with the threat of action from the government, prompted preemptive action by business. A number of large firms commenced restructuring processes, preparing for foreign listings and unbundling the pyramidal structures that had characterized their cross-holdings.[94] Firms also consolidated and refocused their activities.

Over time, key thinkers within the ANC began to conceive of competition policy less as an anti-market measure (i.e. as a way to dismantle the conglomerates), and more as a tool to increase efficiency within the economy and attract higher inflows of foreign direct investment, in other words, as a pro-market measure.[95] There was a shift in emphasis, as Manuel and Mbeki came to realize the potential benefits of a rigorous competition policy for small and black business owners, and for consumers. In 1995, the DTI began three years of consultation on what a new competition policy might look like, including with the South Africa Foundation,[96] and released its proposed guidelines for competition policy in 1997.[97]

The formal negotiations, however, were conducted through NEDLAC, where BSA represented business. As with other policy areas, big business effectively dominated this debate. Given the private sector's free market rhetoric, it would have been extremely difficult for them to justify practices such as price-fixing and cartelization, although they did defend a certain degree of market concentration. Drawing on the experiences of the South Korean chaebols, for example, business cited the need for South Africa to foster "national champions" that could compete internationally. For the most part, however, business did not outright oppose the idea of competition policy; instead they contested the content of that policy.[98]

---

[94] For example, Gencor unbundled, South African Breweries divested, Edgars and OK Bazaars slimmed themselves down to focus more effectively on their core industries; even the giant AAC restructured itself, hiving off its non-mining and forestry assets.

[95] See, for example, Simon Barber, "Mbeki Attacks Industrial Conglomerates," *Business Day*, 11 September 1996.

[96] OECD, "Competition Law and Policy in South Africa" (Paris, France: Organisation for Economic Co-operation and Development, 2003), 16.

[97] Paul Richardson, "Pragmatism Rules as Delayed Talks on Competition Begin," *Sunday Independent*, 1996.

[98] Steven Friedman, Personal interview with author, 7 July 2004.

Business sought two things from a new competition regime. First, they wanted policy that focused on uncompetitive behavior, rather than on size *per se*. Second, business sought an independent decision-making body that would utilize a clear, predictable, and delimited set of rules. In particular, business negotiators sought to preserve the autonomy of the competition authority from more explicitly political objectives and to limit the discretionary power of the government.[99] The government's position was almost the reverse: it wanted, first, the inclusion of a broader set of issues associated with the "public interest," and, second, for the minister to have a high level of discretion in shaping decisions.

Steph Naudé of the AHI led the business negotiating team, which argued that "[a]ny deviation from internationally accepted 'norms' was ... damaging to the South African economy under the 'new' international global economic realities." In particular business cautioned that "structural remedies aimed at divestment would harm business confidence."[100] Small and medium-sized businesses potentially had the most to gain from a thoroughgoing competition policy. Curiously, however, they were not prominent in the debates.[101]

NEDLAC negotiations began early in 1998 and the Act was passed in October – a quick process and one described by a leading business magazine as "NEDLAC's most important success."[102] The old Competition Board was replaced by a new competition authority that secured funding from the levying of merger fees and hence could support a much larger number of staff than the old board.[103] Crucially, it was also to operate independently of the minister.

An OECD peer review of the authority praised the new competition regime. Strikingly, however, the report concluded that the new competition authority was strongest in the field of prospective mergers and left much of the existing market structure and practices

---

[99] Johan Coetzee, "Competition Bill Streamlined," *Finance Week*, 25 September 1998, Greta Steyn, "Business Concerned about Bill's Ability to Break up Conglomerates," *Business Day*, 19 May 1998.

[100] Chabane *et al.*, "Ten Year Review," 33.

[101] Small business was a little more prominent in the parliamentary debates on the subject and it was the latter process that gave rise to the public interest provisions.

[102] Coetzee, "Competition Bill Streamlined."

[103] OECD, "Competition Law and Policy in South Africa," 37.

undisturbed: "[t]o a surprising extent," it argued, "competition policy in South Africa is merger policy."[104]

Before assessing the broader "scoreboard" on policy issues, I will review the overall tenor of policy interactions between business and government in South Africa.

Business–government interactions

During the 1990s, business made two very public bids to engage with the government. The first of these was *GFA*, which was not a long document but which provided a powerful critique of the economy. In retrospect, it was prescient about the weaknesses of the South African economy and labor market in particular. Its public release, however, was greeted with fury and, from those sympathetic to business, bewilderment that the private sector could so clumsily present its case. The document had been relatively well received in a closed seminar with senior ANC leadership, and business was initially quite bemused by the heated response the document evoked. The hostility should have come as no surprise.

In a country where the emphasis had been on trust building in multiparty fora, treading softly in public and only negotiating hard behind the scenes, *GFA* broke all the rules. The language in the document was blunt and matter of fact. It came across as arrogant and heavy-handed, and it aroused historical suspicions of business as inherently exploitative and racist. In addition, by specifically targeting the labor market, *GFA* directly challenged a formidable opponent – organized labor – which was publicly allied with the government of the day. This made it very difficult for the ANC not to distance themselves from the document.

So, despite the fact that government and business agreed on many of the fundamentals, relations between the white business community and the ANC leadership (Mbeki in particular) continued to be difficult. Mbeki and his advisors appeared to distrust and dislike the private sector, reacting defensively and with charges of racism to any criticism of government from business. For their part, a good deal

---

[104] Admittedly, restrictive business practices such as price cartelization are much more difficult to tackle and require quite sophisticated investigative and analytical skills. Ibid.

of "Afro-pessimism" (poor expectations of the black ANC govern-ment) persisted within the white business community, despite the government's economic prudence. This was very much resented by the government.

The Truth and Reconciliation Commission (TRC) hearings turned a critical public eye on white business' past relationship with the apartheid regime.[105] For the most part, the private sector disputed the view that business was culpable in and had profited from apartheid; they argued on the contrary that apartheid was an economically unsustainable system, while some claimed that business had opposed apartheid (or at least elements of it). Not surprisingly, most of busi-ness stridently opposed any suggestion of a wealth tax to fund rep-arations for gross human rights violations. The TRC highlighted the white face of business and its role in an economy built on a racist foundation, and AngloGold's Bobby Godsell conceded that "the TRC damaged the relationship between government and business."[106]

It is not clear exactly what prompted the cooling – possibly a conjunction of the renewed emphasis on BEE (see above) and the TRC hearings – but by the late 1990s, Mbeki's relationship with white local business was worsening. As with previous generations of (NP) presi-dents, senior businesspeople found it almost impossible to get an audience with the political leadership, while international business continued to enjoy the ear of the government.[107]

The fact that business continued to be predominantly white undoubtedly had something to do with this. Mbeki was preoccupied with questions of race for much of his presidency. According to Friedman, "[for Mbeki,] foreign business at least had the virtue of

---

[105] Antjie Krog, *Country of My Skull* (Johannesburg, South Africa: Random House, 1998), 239–41, Nicoli Nattrass, "The Truth and Reconciliation Commission on Business and Apartheid: A Critical Evaluation," *African Affairs* 93, no. 392 (1999), Elizabeth Stanley, "Evaluating the Truth and Reconciliation Commission," *Journal of Modern African Studies* 39, no. 3 (2001).

[106] Bobby Godsell, Personal interview with author, 21 June 2001.

[107] In February 2000, Mbeki established a high-profile council of international businesspeople to advise his government on how best to attract international investment. Kenneth Creamer, "All the President's Business Men" (Martin Creamer's Engineering News Online, 2002 [accessed 19 August 2002]) www. engineeringnews.co.za/, Iheduru, "Social Concertation, Labour Unions and the Creation of a Black Bourgeoisie in South Africa," 57.

not being as involved with the old order as its white South African counterpart."[108]

In 1998 the new government's reformist resolve was tested by the international financial crisis that began in Asia but soon spread to other emerging markets. The crisis put further pressure on the rand, contributing to an outflow of capital, higher interest rates, and a slowdown in the economy. The rand fell further on news that Chris Stals, then still governor of the Reserve Bank, was to resign. The markets had admired his tough anti-inflation stance and feared that a successor might not sustain this. And the rand depreciated yet again when it was confirmed that Stals was being replaced by Tito Mboweni, the former Minister of Labour who had presided over significant extensions of rights for organized labor, and who was regarded by some as insufficiently qualified to head the Bank. Mboweni's impressive performance in the job subsequently silenced many of his early critics. However, the market's initial reaction stung the ANC leadership, who regarded it as nothing less than racist. What was particularly galling for the government was that Manuel's team had continued to record impressive achievements: the budget deficit fell faster than expected, inflation continued to drop, the economy recorded improvements in productivity, and some quarters saw an improvement in investment levels.[109]

In September 1998 organized business, led by big business, launched a second major initiative, the Business Trust, in which business consciously (and more adroitly than previously) set out to repair relations with the government. The Trust comprised a pledge by business to raise R1 billion for social investment in two areas: job creation (particularly in the tourist sector) and education development.[110] Business clearly felt the need to demonstrate its commitment to equitable development in South Africa in order to reopen channels of communication with the government.[111] In return for funding the Business Trust, business wanted access to the president. The Trust

---

[108] Steven Friedman, Personal interview with author, 8 May 2001.
[109] South African Reserve Bank, "Annual Economic Report 1998" (Johannesburg, South Africa: South African Reserve Bank, 1998), 1–3.
[110] Business Trust, "Business Trust: Together, We Will" (Johannesburg, South Africa: Business Trust, 2000), Mich Collins, ed., *The Business Trust: United We Stand* (Johannesburg, South Africa: Financial Mail, 2000).
[111] Renee Grawitsky, "Business's Jobs Plan Gets Off the Ground," *Business Day*, 16 September 1998.

delivered: Mbeki created a working group that would connect government – and the president – directly with big business.[112]

The policy outcomes

By the year 2000, the ANC had moved far from a reliance on slogans as a substitute for economic policy. The executive had developed a nuanced economic position that acknowledged the policy constraints attendant on developing countries in a highly globalized economy. On competition policy, the government's position was arguably more pro-market than that of business itself, although the ultimate outcome represented a compromise with business. The views of key government ministers had also moved beyond a blanket typecasting of South African business as exploitative to a more considered position of how best the public and private sectors could work together.

Undoubtedly, economic policy in South Africa had shifted and the economy began to respond to this shift. By the end of the 1990s, South Africa had emerged from an extended recession although growth rates were still lower than many had hoped. Inflation dropped along with the budget deficit. Exports expanded substantially but the liberalization process cost the economy thousands of jobs.

Of the four key reform areas proposed in *GFA*, which did business get? Most agree that the government delivered decisively and convincingly on its deficit targets, despite considerable strain on spending from provinces and increases in social spending. Progress was more equivocal on privatization.[113] The government had moved in a very considered way. There had been a number of smaller privatizations (for example, the telecommunications firm, TELKOM, had been restructured and commercialized) but the financial press were scathing about the absence of swift progress.

The third area, the labor framework, was probably the most important for business. Here there was, in the view of the broader business community, little positive progress. Indeed many small businesses

---

[112] He also created working groups for black business, commercial agriculture, and the trade unions respectively.

[113] James Jude Hentz, "The Two Faces of Privatisation: Political and Economic Logics in Transitional South Africa," *Journal of Modern African Studies* 38, no. 2 (2000).

complained that labor legislation became increasingly restrictive over the course of the 1990s.

The fourth area was the liberalization of trade and currency, which attracted a mixed verdict. Business argued for the most part that, while there had been some lifting of exchange controls, there was room for improvement. The government's achievements on trade liberalization were regarded as much more positive.

Two additional policy areas were important to business–government relations. BEE, initially raised by black business, was embraced with some diffidence by established big business. Competition policy legislation, again something that business was originally less than enthusiastic about, was negotiated and the policy which emerged was widely praised.[114]

Overall, business' hysteria at the start of the decade about a radically redistributionist ANC was largely assuaged and replaced with more mundane policy concerns. Business moved from being terrified about a possible socialist economic policy, to commending the performance of communists in the cabinet.[115] Interview after interview with businesspeople revealed similar sentiments,[116] namely surprise and relief that the new government had proved amenable to many of business' views on macroeconomic management.

Toward the end of the 1990s, concern mounted in two areas: first, over the disjuncture between policy and implementation, and, second, in specific policy areas such as education and labor. South Africa's debate on economic policy had shifted over the course of the decade, away from early crude distinctions between state- and market-led approaches, into fine-print questions of how to manage the economy, and these questions would divide business as much among itself as from government.

Why business won what it did

One way or another, organized business won much of what it sought by way of economic policy. Much of this was won indirectly, by the

[114] Chabane et al., "Ten Year Review," 33.
[115] SACOB's Raymond Parsons, for example, commented that "some of government's noted left-wingers have been among the most effective in implementing useful government programmes." Parsons, *The Mbeki Inheritance*, 124.
[116] Interviews conducted in Johannesburg, Durban, and Cape Town, 2001 and 2005.

strength and responsiveness of the market environment to policy signals from the government, exercised through instruments such as investor sentiment and currency fluctuations.

There is little doubt that the business community in South Africa was powerful, diversified, well institutionalized, and willing to engage with government. Business was not dependent on the government for its profitability and there was very little overlap between the country's political and economic elites. Shubane argues that business occupied an "autonomous [economic] sector, an area of political and economic significance which is beyond the reach of the state."[117] Similarly, Landman contrasted South Africa's situation with that of Zambia where[118]

business has to create space for itself. In South Africa, that space is open because of the nature of the economy. The currency markets, independent monetary policy, and the stock market all provide discipline for the state. This is much more important than having a united business organization. [Indeed,] the private sector becomes a place of refuge for the disaffected in the ANC but it is also a path to power for apolitical blacks.

While business won most of what it sought because of its autonomy and strength, it is ironic that what business lost (particularly the labor framework) it lost for the same reasons: namely the dominance of big business in its ranks (whence its strength) and its historic ethnic origins (whence much of its autonomy). Despite its structural strength, business was constrained by its ethnic profile and political past, specifically its association with the political and economic program of apartheid. The racially exclusive nature of the business community, historically at least, affected its broader political legitimacy and policy profile with the ANC government.

As for the state, the higher levels of openness and competition within the South African economy in the neo-liberal era constrained its capacity to unilaterally reorder incentives in that economy. The ANC government simply did not have the same range of policy options as the NP. The results have not been entirely unhappy:[119]

While business people grumble about the various administrative shortcomings of the new regime, from taxes that are too high to the quality of the

---

[117] Kehla Shubane, Personal interview with author, 8 May 2001.
[118] J. P. Landman, Personal interview with author, 25 May 2001.
[119] Adam, van Zyl Slabbert, and Moodley, *Comrades in Business*, 213–14.

civil service, a vast majority, particularly big business, feels comfortable and relieved … [O]rganized business is not only carefully listened to formally and informally, but also has the economic clout to make itself heard should the state contravene its vital interests. In fact, state and business interests coincide in the goal of a growing economy.

To argue that market-driven concerns and incentives pushed the ANC to adopt a centrist and moderate set of economic policies is not, however, to argue that business was unambiguously successful in shaping government policy. Far from it, as I have argued. The shift in ANC policy resulted predominantly from the influence of that "amorphous entity," the market.[120] The size and sophistication of the private sector meant that the economy was able to function largely without recourse to a vampiric relationship to the state. This was true despite the historical sponsorship by the state of Afrikaner business. The question remains how ongoing government efforts to foster BEE will shape that relationship.

South Africa in the 2000s: the waxing of neo-patrimonialism?

In the early 2000s, observers across the ideological spectrum began to express concern about political developments in South Africa. These focused on two areas in particular: first, critics alleged that the ruling ANC elite was increasingly unwilling to tolerate political opposition; second, observers pointed to new entanglements between the worlds of politics and business, often facilitated by BEE. I will briefly review these before concluding.

Developments in both of these areas were facilitated by the ANC's apparently "unassailable" hold on political power.[121] Even more so than the NP before it,[122] the ANC enjoyed a commanding electoral majority, winning 70 percent of the seats in the 2004 national election. The official parliamentary opposition was largely unsuccessful in

---

[120] In his early days as Minister of Finance, Trevor Manuel caused a quiver in the markets and a dip in the value of the rand when he described that market as an "amorphous entity" in a public forum. He swiftly learnt the value of a little circumspection in this regard.

[121] Tom Lodge, "The Future of South Africa's Party System," *Journal of Democracy* 17, no. 3 (2006): 163.

[122] It is worth remembering that the NP effectively dominated political power from 1948 to 1994, ruling for an incredible forty-six years!

extending its support base beyond the ranks of racial minorities and was regarded by many as little more than a poorly disguised attempt to protect white privilege.[123] This did not engender any complacency within the upper ranks of the ANC; they vigorously pursued power in those provinces and cities where they did not yet have it[124] and aggressively recruited opposition MPs to cross the floor to the ruling party. As the ANC consolidated its power in government, so too Mbeki built up the power of both his presidency of the state[125] and his leadership position within the party.[126] Internal challengers to Mbeki were excoriated in public and Mbeki engaged in heated exchanges with leftist critics of his economic strategy.[127]

Fears about Mbeki's aversion to opposition were inflamed by the conflict over Jacob Zuma's bid for leadership of the party in 2006. The struggle was played out in public when criminal charges of corruption and rape respectively were laid against Zuma. What was disturbing here was not so much the public evidence of dissent within the party or even the absence of agreed-upon mechanisms by which the party could choose new leadership. Most disturbing were hints that some were prepared to employ state institutions to selectively target their political rivals and reward their supporters.[128]

---

[123] Jeffrey Herbst, "Mbeki's South Africa," *Foreign Affairs* 84, no. 6 (2005).

[124] The Democratic Alliance's control of Cape Town, for example, was bitterly contested.

[125] Roger Southall, "The State of Party Politics: Struggles within the Tripartite Alliance and the Decline of Opposition," in *State of the Nation: South Africa 2003–2004*, ed. John Daniel, Adam Habib, and Roger Southall (Cape Town, South Africa: HSRC Press, 2003), 57.

[126] This argument is extensively documented in William Mervin Gumede, *Thabo Mbeki and the Battle for the Soul of the ANC* (Cape Town, South Africa: Zebra Press, 2005).

[127] SACP stalwart Jeremy Cronin was, for example, forced to issue a public apology in 2002 after he criticized the state of relations between the ANC and his party.

[128] Both Mbeki's supporters and his opponents appear to have abused the state's security-intelligence services. In 2001, an investigation was launched by the Ministry of Safety and Security into allegations that three prominent ANC officials and businessmen, Matthews Phosa, Cyril Ramaphosa, and Tokyo Sexwale, were plotting the assassination of Mbeki. No evidence was ever presented and the allegations were dropped. Nonetheless, all three men dropped out of contention for the leadership of the party. On the other side, four years later, the National Intelligence Agency mounted an unauthorized surveillance operation focused on Saki Macozoma, a member of the ANC's National Executive Committee, a prominent businessman and a key ally of

Sources of opposition within civil society remained vibrant and assertive, but their critiques were not always well received.[129] Similarly, in the relationship between business and government, the government did not look kindly on critical public remarks by prominent business-people.[130] On many issues then, organized business chose to cooperate with government and to express its concerns behind closed doors. This may have contributed to some degree of self-censorship. In 2007, for example, when First National Bank canceled a proposed public anti-crime campaign it emerged that the pressure to do so came, not from the government, but from within the business community itself.

It is difficult to know how to interpret these developments. On the one hand, there have always been those within business who preferred not to directly criticize the government (whether that was the apartheid gov-ernment or South Africa's new, democratically elected government), while other firms were more prepared to risk the government's dis-pleasure. On the other hand, if the government's reaction to criticism was experienced as unremittingly hostile, and if that hostility could be paired with powerful economic consequences through, say, the with-drawal of access to state contracts, over time this would undoubtedly damage business' willingness to constructively contest policy.

BEE explicitly favored the awarding of government contracts to companies that were majority black-owned. This principle was easily defended in an economy that continued to be disproportionately dominated by white business. What was unsettling, however, were indications that individuals within the state, the ANC, and business respectively were turning their political relationship to personal advantage.[131] As Friedman notes, "[o]nce business assumes that its

Mbeki. Vukani Mde and Karima Brown, "Power Behind the Throne, Pretender to it, or Just a Businessman?," *Business Day*, 24 October 2005.

[129] When Archbishop Desmond Tutu expressed his concern publicly about the tendency within the ANC to enforce a strict party line, the response was less than gracious.

[130] See, for example, Mbeki's response to perceived criticisms by the management of the petrochemical firm Sasol, and by Anglo American's Tony Trahar respectively. Thabo Mbeki, "Empowerment Good for the Economy and the Nation," *ANC Today* 3, no. 48 (2003), Thabo Mbeki, "Questions that Demand Answers," *ANC Today* 4, no. 36 (2004).

[131] One example of the latter was the 2002 sale of state forests in Komatiland to the BEE company Zama Resources, after the company's CEO allegedly paid the chief director of public enterprises R55,000 to facilitate the deal. Gumede, *Thabo Mbeki and the Battle for the Soul of the ANC*, 106.

future depends not on encouraging a society in which economic activity will flourish but on making friends in high political places, the line between co-operation and corruption becomes very thin."[132]

Individual instances of corruption are not necessarily proof of anything (except perhaps that the state's anti-corruption institutions are functioning), but more systematic violations are cause for alarm. In 2006, the Auditor General released a report which described extensive "business moonlighting" by a range of state officials from government employees to cabinet ministers. Within the party specifically, fears about political patronage were fueled by the often close connections between party and government officials, and BEE and other business deals. The financial relationship between the mining magnate Brett Kebble and the ANC Youth League is a case in point.[133] The trial of Durban-based businessman Schabir Shaik also uncovered shocking details about the extent to which the country's then Deputy President, Jacob Zuma, had literally indebted himself to Shaik.[134] The prosecutor argued, and the ruling judge appeared to concur, that Zuma had effectively been on a kind of retainer, the object of which was "to influence him to use his name and political influence for the benefit of Shaik's business enterprises or as an ongoing reward for having done so from time to time."[135]

Robinson and Brummer argue that "the murky relationship between money and politics has been at the heart of almost every major scandal faced by political parties and the government since 1994."[136] There are those in the ANC who are aware of these dangers and have warned against them. Indeed one of the most cogent assessments of the importance of BEE – and its challenges – was delivered by the

---

[132] Steven Friedman, "Corruption Thrives as Business Bankrolls SA's Elected Leaders," *Business Day*, 9 November 2005.

[133] Kebble was shot and killed in his car one evening in mysterious circumstances that have not yet been resolved. Rob Rose, "ANC Youth Leader on Tax Rap over Kebble Millions," *Business Day*, 29 June 2006.

[134] *The State* v. *1. Schabir Shaik, 2. Nkobi Holdings, 3. Nkobi Investments, 4. Kobigin, 5. Kobitech, 6. Proconsult, 7. Pro Con Africa, 8. Kobitech Transport Systems, 9. Clegton, 10. Floryn Investments, 11. Thint, 12. Chartley Investments*, Case No. CC27/04 (2005), Republic of South Africa.

[135] Ibid., 3–4. At the time of writing, Zuma's own trial on related charges was in legal limbo.

[136] Vicki Robinson and Stefaans Brummer, "SA Democracy Incorporated: Corporate Fronts and Political Party Funding," *ISS Paper* 129 (Pretoria, South Africa: Institute for Security Studies, 2006), 2.

organization's Secretary General, Kgalema Motlanthe, to a meeting of the Black Management Forum in 2004.[137]

It is early days yet but the question nonetheless bears asking: what kind of a business community is this process producing? It is, at least, fostering greater black ownership. The percentage of black capitalization of the JSE dropped from a high of almost 10 percent in 1998, to around the 5 percent mark at the end of the decade – still an improvement from levels of the early 1990s.[138] According to Iheduru,[139]

about 60 black-owned or black-controlled companies were listed on the JSE in 2000. Hundreds of other large, small and medium enterprise businesses have been established either separately or as "empowerment partnerships" with local and foreign (white) businesses and capital. The number of published "empowerment deals" grew from 52 with a combined value of about $1.6 billion in 1997 to some 130 investments worth about $3.8 billion in 1998.

So much for quantity; the quality or caliber of this emerging cadre is harder to assess. According to Friedman, the South African business community now comprises at least three categories of business-people:[140]

There is white business, and among black business there are straightforward businesspeople such as Don Ncube who was never a politico. And then there is "something else," an indeterminate category which starts with former struggle figures – people who have, or are assumed to have, political connections. Not everyone [in this latter category] is greedy and grubby ... There is not only one kind of elite; there are parasites and there are real entrepreneurs. We cannot unscramble it tidily.

We would do well to remember the precedent established by policies of Afrikaner empowerment under the NP which did not appear

---

[137] Kgalema Motlanthe, "Address to the Johannesburg Branch of the Black Management Forum" (African National Congress, 2004 [accessed March 2007]) www.anc.org.za/ancdocs/speeches/2004/sp0930.html.

[138] McGregor BFA, *McGregor's Who Owns Whom in South Africa*, 69.

[139] Iheduru, "Social Concertation, Labour Unions and the Creation of a Black Bourgeoisie in South Africa," 61. The same figures appear in Unattributed, "Paper Lions: South Africa – Black Economic Empowerment Not Working," *The Economist*, 17 April 1999, 65.

[140] Friedman, Interview, 2004.

to harm the economy. On the contrary, they may have strengthened it. Of course black South Africans constitute a larger share of the overall population than Afrikaners did and the effort required to empower this constituency is therefore likely to be greater, as are its costs. The key question is whether BEE's impact will be sufficiently powerful to shift the dominant mode of operating of business and government in a neo-patrimonial direction. At the time of writing, the answer was by no means clear.

Iheduru posits that the effort will in fact strengthen the development of an indigenous capitalism: "these 'comrade capitalists,'" he argues, "are helping to bring back legitimacy and community respect, especially among the working class, for black entrepreneurship."[141] The South African political economy could not be fairly described as neo-patrimonial. As Godsell argues, "yes, Afrikaner capital and BEE did organise on an organic basis but when they wade into the marketplace, the market trumps."[142] The signals are mixed but it seems clear that in South Africa, the state cannot have it all its own way. The private sector remains an important economic and political player and, in the marketplace of ideas, its preferences can exert powerful, albeit indirect, influences on policymakers.

Historically in South Africa ethnicity and race have, bizarrely, served to consolidate the structural power of the private sector and to secure for it some crucial political space. This has not been without value. The persistence of these historical inequalities, however – and their racialization – complicates ongoing relations between government and business. Should patterns of economic growth continue, systematically and disproportionately, to serve the interests of a minority only, this could threaten the country's hard-won political stability and ultimately its long-run economic development. The leading business newspaper expressed this thought as follows:[143]

The Zimbabwean model in which the black majority control politics, the white minority economics is, as we see now, untenable. Either we will have a growing black presence at the commanding heights of our economy in a

---

[141] Iheduru, "Social Concertation, Labour Unions and the Creation of a Black Bourgeoisie in South Africa," 73.

[142] Godsell, Interview.

[143] Unattributed, "There is Scope to Avoid a Business Nightmare," *Business Day*, 15 August 2002.

way which preserves prospects for growth, or in one which destroys it ...
That is why a Mauritius which builds its economic future on agreement
between business, labour and government grows, while countries which
faithfully obey the economic recipes but do not settle their conflicts stagnate.

The story of Mauritius follows.

3 | Business and government in Mauritius: public hostility, private pragmatism

[W]hen your members control 40 percent of exports you are listened to [by government].[1]

In the Mauritius of the 1990s there appeared to be few political incentives for the government to consult seriously with its business community. Not only was the private sector dominated by an ethnic minority, but it was dominated by the very ethnic minority that historically had oppressed the majority group which subsequently assumed political power. Common sense, and much politics literature, tells us that such a setup invites economic and political conflict.[2] Yet, despite a relatively high level of hostility between business and government, business was able to exert a moderate level of influence on economic policy in the 1990s and Mauritius has been described as "a case study in the successful management of an economy."[3]

This chapter investigates the contribution of the private sector in Mauritius to economic policy-making in the 1990s. While business' level of influence varied across the sub-sectors of the economy, the private sector overall had a high level of political capacity and received a surprisingly receptive hearing from government. Crucially, its challenge to government's leading role in the economy was ignored, but as this leading role has served business well, the outcome was still net positive.

Roland Lamusse, former economic advisor to the prime minister, argued that "if you want to talk about the relationship between the

---

[1] Leading Mauritian businessperson quoted in Barbara Wake Carroll and Terrance Carroll, "Civic Networks, Legitimacy and the Policy Process," *Governance* 12, no. 1 (1999): 11.

[2] For a recent example, see Amy Chua, *World on Fire: How Exporting Free Market Democracy Breeds Ethnic Hatred and Global Instability* (New York: Doubleday, 2003), 454–5.

[3] Tony Hawkins, "Investors Begin to Return," *Financial Times*, 18 December 2000.

business community and government in Mauritius, you have to start with sugar."[4] Accordingly, I begin this chapter by tracing the emergence of the island's business community from its origins in the sugar industry up until the end of the 1980s. I then proceed to lay out the nature of the Mauritian political economy at that point, and the country's economic and business associations. The bulk of the chapter thereafter considers the interactions between business and two successive governments on economic policy questions during the 1990s. Much of the chapter is spent discussing government initiatives, rather than those of business. This is no accident. In Mauritius, it was government that drove economic policy-making while business largely responded to government proposals.

Colonialism and the emergence of a local, sugar-based bourgeoisie

For much of human history, the islands of what would become Mauritius had no permanent human inhabitants. When they came to be occupied, Mauritius experienced "sequential colonialism,"[5] intermittently by the Dutch after the sixteenth century and sequentially by the French and British thereafter.

Mauritius had no indigenous people; this meant that none of Mauritius' subsequent human populations could claim "original" ownership of the land. It was also significant for the course of the island's economic development as it meant that there was no pre-capitalist or traditional peasant class that needed to be modernized. Rather, "the entire population has since the very beginning of colonialism been integrated into a capitalist system of production and consumption."[6] This facilitated the development of an autonomous, assertive, and structurally powerful capitalist class that was not shy to protect its interests and to pursue these with the state. Sandbrook points out that[7]

---

[4] Roland Lamusse, Personal interview with author, 24 July 2001.

[5] William F. S. Miles, "The Mauritius Enigma," *Journal of Democracy* 10, no. 2 (1999).

[6] Thomas Hylland Eriksen, *Common Denominators: Ethnicity, Nation-Building and Compromise in Mauritius* (Oxford: Berg, 1998), 19.

[7] Sandbrook, "Origins of the Democratic, Developmental State," 570.

[w]hereas other countries of the region comprised largely peasant societies that were inclined to clientelism and personal rule, Mauritius developed a powerful mercantile and agrarian bourgeoisie, a large class of small land-owners and merchants, and a rural and urban proletariat. This class structure facilitated the formation of a disciplined capitalist state.

Port Louis began as a free port and an anchorage for corsairs and privateers. The dearth of domestic capital in these early days meant that financing tended to be tied to the boom–bust cycle of what would become the island's major commodity, sugar.[8] The sweet stuff quickly came to comprise over 80 percent of the island's exports, and this figure would stay as high or higher for at least the next hundred years.[9]

After the French claimed the islands in 1715, a more stable capitalist class of planters and traders emerged, mostly from the community of French and European settlers who made the islands their permanent home.[10] Mauritius began as a monoculture colony, dominated by sugar, and the social and economic institutions associated with the sugar estates. Under the Dutch and French, tens of thousands of slaves were brought in from Madagascar, Senegambia, southern India, and Mozambique to work on the burgeoning sugar plantations.[11] Over time, Lamusse argues,[12]

[p]olitical and institutional factors … reinforced the predominance of the sugar industry. During the colonial era the plantocracy played a prominent role in the formulation and implementation of public policy through its

[8] Richard B. Allen, *Slaves, Freedmen, and Indentured Laborers in Colonial Mauritius* (Cambridge University Press, 1999), 6, 26.

[9] Ibid., 28.

[10] Suzanne Chazan-Gillig, "Ethnicity and Free Exchange in Mauritian Society," *Social Anthropology* 8, no. 1 (2000).

[11] Estimates of the numbers of slaves differ, but by 1910 there were some 61,000 slaves on the island. Allen, *Slaves, Freedmen, and Indentured Laborers in Colonial Mauritius*, 53. See also Eriksen, *Common Denominators*, Megan Vaughan, *Creating the Creole Island: Slavery in Eighteenth-Century Mauritius* (Durham, NC: Duke University Press, 2005).

[12] Roland Lamusse, "The Achievements and Prospects of the Mauritius Export Processing Zone," in *Economic Planning and Performance in Indian Ocean Island States*, ed. R. T. Appleyard and R. N. Ghosh (Canberra: National Centre for Development Studies, Australian National University, 1990), 34–5. Of course the state, and the British colonial state in particular, was crucial in providing much of the labor. Personal communication with Richard Sandbrook.

representatives on the Council of Government. Indeed, the sugar industry from its inception could be described as a political partnership: the estate owners (mainly of French descent) provided the capital and management and, when it became necessary, a source of labour and the imperial government provided (with some interruptions) a protected market.

French colonial rule was succeeded by that of the English in 1810. When slavery was abolished by the new colonial government in the 1830s, the sugar estates urgently required replacement labor. They lobbied the British to allow the importation of indentured Indian labor. Tens of thousands of Indians entered the country in the next couple of decades. By the 1860s, Indians had become the largest single racial group on the island[13] and by 1871 they made up more than two-thirds of the island's total population.[14] Their treatment on the sugar plantations was brutal, characterized by "severe exploitation" that was "denigrating in a fashion only too reminiscent of slavery."[15] Chinese immigration increased some decades after that although it never reached the same scale.

The structure of the sugar plantations and consequently of the Mauritian economy was such that, as in South Africa, ethnicity, race, and class coincided to a significant degree.[16] Nonetheless, some Indians did manage to accumulate the wherewithal to buy small plots of land or to open shops. Indeed, according to Vaughan, "the story of Indian indentured labour is in part a story of how a population of desperately poor and servile laborers carved out a central role for itself in the island's economy as independent landowners, traders and businessmen."[17]

By contrast, Creoles (mostly former slaves and their families) were less successful in holding onto their own small plots of land or building up the capital necessary to open a small business.[18] Rather they appeared to be displaced by the now much larger Indian population. As Vaughan puts it, "the game of multiculturalism had begun. And the Creole population, dispossessed by the twin processes of enslavement and emancipation, would lose."[19]

---

[13] Eriksen, *Common Denominators*, 10.
[14] Vaughan, *Creating the Creole Island*, 270.   [15] Ibid.
[16] Sandbrook, "Origins of the Democratic, Developmental State," 555–6.
[17] Vaughan, *Creating the Creole Island*, 271.
[18] Allen, *Slaves, Freedmen, and Indentured Laborers in Colonial Mauritius*, 181.
[19] Vaughan, *Creating the Creole Island*, 276.

Other than trying to nudge the sugar plantations away from their use of slave labor, the British chose to leave the economic hegemony of the French sugar barons largely undisturbed. Under English rule the (predominantly white) capitalist class consolidated itself by fits and starts, but mostly using financial resources from within the community.[20] This shaped the subsequent relationship between business and government, demarcating from the outset separate and relatively independent economic and political spheres.

Moreover, it was not just the elites of the society that were culturally demarcated. According to Miles, the colonized were also divided: "Educated Indo-Mauritians tended to be Anglophiles and upwardly mobile Afro-Mauritians to be Francophile." He continues:[21]

Sequential colonialism then, required Mauritians to differentiate, if not to choose, between two distinct metropolitan models ... Thus anticolonialism was not the clear-cut affair it was in monocolonial countries, for while the British represented political rule imposed from without, economic and cultural domination was wielded by Francophones ... For Hindus and Muslims, British governance constituted a check on the Franco-Mauritian and upper-class Creole aristocracies; whereas for these latter groups, the French language provided a medium of resistance to British colonial usurpation.

This history is significant for two reasons. First, ethnic groups tended to be associated with occupations and hence, to a large degree, with class. English-speaking Hindus followed the English into the political sphere and particularly into government and the civil service.[22] White Franco-Mauritians retained their dominance of the economy, joined by a small number of Sino-Mauritians, a few light-skinned Creoles and some Indians and Muslims.[23] Very early on in the island's history then, political and economic power were parceled out on largely ethnicized lines, what Srebrnik calls a "pronounced cultural division

---

[20] Allen, *Slaves, Freedmen, and Indentured Laborers in Colonial Mauritius,* 39–40, Chazan-Gillig, "Ethnicity and Free Exchange in Mauritian Society."
[21] Miles, "The Mauritius Enigma," 96.
[22] Sandbrook argues that the British explicitly sought to limit the influence of the Francophones by extending political rights to coloreds and to literate Indians. Sandbrook, "Origins of the Democratic, Developmental State," 573.
[23] Barbara Wake Carroll and Terrance Carroll, "Accommodating Ethnic Diversity in a Modernizing Democratic State: Theory and Practice in the Case of Mauritius," *Ethnic and Racial Studies* 23, no. 1 (2000): 135.

of labor."[24] Second, Mauritians developed the political capacity to constantly juggle and coordinate these two respective spheres of influence. As Miles remarks, "[d]ealing simultaneously with two sets of colonial influences develops unusually sophisticated political skills."[25] The two spheres of power were clearly demarcated but also co-dependent; Mauritius could not thrive without some kind of accommodation between the two.

The great depression of the early twentieth century hit Mauritius hard, impacting working-class Indians most harshly. The Hindu vote had begun to grow and in 1936 working-class Indians established the Labour Party (LP) to represent their interests. Real change arrived in 1948 when constitutional reform effectively enfranchised the islands' Indian populations; the sheer weight of numbers suddenly became the route to political power.[26] Hindus came to dominate the state as voters, and also as civil servants. Blocked from economic advancement in the hierarchy of the sugar industry, the now well-educated children of those small Hindu landowners looked for employment opportunities in the state and in the new movements agitating for independence: "Politics and the state provided the majority Hindus with a way of countering the economic power of the plantocracy."[27] The relatively long wait for independence (which came in 1968) provided a "gradual tutelary takeover" of the state by Hindus, avoiding the rushed Africanization processes that occurred elsewhere in Africa.[28] The result was a relatively well-organized bureaucratic state, with a demonstrably larger number of colonial officials and amount of state revenue per capita than most states on the continental mainland.[29]

Both elected offices and the civil service then have tended to be dominated by Hindus although, as Eriksen points out, this is often overstated in popular discourse in Mauritius;[30] while the government

---

[24] Henry Srebrnik, "Can an Ethnically-Based Civil Society Succeed? The Case of Mauritius," *Journal of Contemporary African Studies* 18, no. 1 (2000): 9.

[25] Miles, "The Mauritius Enigma," 96.

[26] Eriksen, *Common Denominators*, 104.

[27] Sandbrook, "Origins of the Democratic, Developmental State," 572.

[28] Arthur A. Goldsmith, "Africa's Overgrown State Reconsidered: Bureaucracy and Economic Growth," *World Politics* 51, no. 4 (1999): 538.

[29] Matthew Lange, "Embedding the Colonial State: A Comparative-Historical Analysis of State Building and Broad-Based Development in Mauritius," *Social Science History* 27, no. 3 (2003): especially 404.

[30] Eriksen, *Common Denominators*, 68.

did use the state to provide employment to Hindus – just as the National Party had done in South Africa for poor whites – this "was largely limited to the lowest levels of the public service."[31] Nonetheless it was true that, following independence in 1968, the public sector continued to be dominated by Hindus. Correspondingly, the private sector remained largely in the hands of non-Hindus. The stage would thus seem to have been set for serious conflict between these two sectors.

Reinforcing dissatisfaction with the ethnicized concentration of economic resources was popular resentment of the historical role of Franco-Mauritians. This made it risky for any mass-based party to identify or project itself as "the party of business." Until the early 1970s, business was closest to the largely Creole Parti Mauricien Social Démocrate (PMSD).[32] This is not as strange as it at first seems. While they occupied different ends of the economic status spectrum, they shared a common opposition to independence, rooted in the fear of what Hindu political domination would yield for their respective groups.[33]

And yet, despite occasional outbreaks of ethnic/communal violence, the Mauritian political economy from that moment was more often characterized by guarded cohabitation. Sandbrook argues that this is because those members of the bourgeoisie who stayed on in Mauritius after independence accepted an implicit division of power: "They yielded their political dominance and accepted some redistribution from growth in exchange for the legitimacy that a modest social democracy would generate – provided that social reform was limited to a tax-supported welfare state, and excluded asset redistribution."[34]

---

[31] Carroll and Carroll, "Accommodating Ethnic Diversity in a Modernizing Democratic State," 137.

[32] Ravi Gulhati and Raj Nallari, *Successful Stabilization and Recovery in Mauritius*, EDI Development Policy Case Series. Analytical Case Studies, No. 5 (Washington, DC: World Bank, 1990), 2.

[33] Perhaps for similar reasons, many Sino-Mauritians supported the PMSD at the time of independence. See Eriksen, *Common Denominators*, 94. Indeed, the PMSD's alliance with the Labour Party in the immediate post-independence period is regarded as an important part of the explanation for why the latter did not fulfill many of its more radical and left-wing platforms. In addition, the prominent Creole politician Gaëtan Duval was a great champion of the business community and almost single-handedly built a pro-business platform in the PMSD. Dani Rodrik, *The New Global Economy and Developing Countries* (Baltimore, MD: Johns Hopkins University Press, 1999), 207.

[34] Sandbrook, "Origins of the Democratic, Developmental State," 572. This trade-off closely resembles the deal that South African business sought – and

There was, moreover, real engagement between the sugar industry and the state. Mauritians are wont to refer to the "political price" of sugar, a reference to the fact that most Mauritian sugar was sold to the European Union (EU) at prices significantly above those in world markets,[35] generating some 3 to 7 percent of the country's GDP.[36] These prices were determined in a series of deals negotiated by both governments. In this sense then, the price received by the sugar industry was a political price, inflated above "market" levels.[37] Governments in Mauritius have always made sure to extract their own price in return for this favor, imposing high taxes on the sector to fund welfare and other projects and onerous labor provisions not applicable elsewhere in the economy.[38] In a real sense then, revenues accruing from the sugar industry funded development in Mauritius and fostered the island's political stability.

For all its economic benefits, however, the dominance by sugar of the Mauritian economy gave rise to three problems: first, a legacy of (frequently ethnicized and racialized) distrust between the economic and political elite; second, an economy rendered vulnerable by its extreme dependence on a single commodity; and, third, high levels of unemployment. Diversification into manufactured exports from the 1960s on promised partial remedy to all three of these.

Exporting unemployment, importing growth

In the mid-1960s the government of Mauritius adopted mildly interventionist, state-driven policies, similar to those being adopted elsewhere in the developing world. A small number of parastatals were

---

secured – during the 1990s after that country's transition to democracy. See chapter 2.

[35] Mauritius was almost certainly the biggest beneficiary of provisions for Africa, Caribbean, and Pacific (ACP) countries under the Lomé Convention and the agreements that replaced it.

[36] Deborah Brautigam, "Revenue, State Capacity and Governance," *IDS Bulletin* 33, no. 3 (2002): 16.

[37] It is, of course, difficult to argue that the international "market" level is a true reflection of any kind of market-driven price given the extent of state subsidization in the sub-sector.

[38] Generally, the sugar sub-sector paid the highest mandatory minimum wage on the island although big sugar estates and small planters had different obligations.

established, but overall levels of state ownership were low.[39] Government began to implement a variant of ISI, but given the small size of the Mauritian economy, the strategy had in-built limitations, not least the country's tiny internal market. Certainly it could not create the requisite number of jobs or create sufficient growth for a high unemployment, high-inflation economy.

The advent of political independence in the late 1960s provided an opportunity to switch economic direction. Professor Lim Fat of the University of Mauritius is widely credited with the idea that an aggressive export drive was the way for Mauritius to grow. It was an inspired choice. Not only was the policy switch perfectly timed to benefit from international receptiveness to increased trade but, crucially, the decision to favor a labor-intensive export route effectively solved the country's unemployment problem.[40]

Along with export orientation, Mauritians adopted a corporatist model of policy-making: the unions, government, and the sugar growers would meet on a yearly basis to negotiate production targets and wages that were, in turn, closely tied to the sugar quotas that Mauritius had been allocated.[41] This laid down a pattern of economic governance via negotiation.

Again, sugar was to prove the country's cash cow. Dani Rodrik describes "substantial" local investment in the new Export Processing Zone (EPZ) sector.[42] Between 1970 and 1983 Mauritian businesspeople provided almost half the total equity capital to the new sector – and 47 percent of that local equity capital came directly from investment by private sugar companies.[43] (This was a contrast to Ghana and Zambia where public investment dominated instead.)

As for international capital, much came from Hong Kong, and Mauritius' small Chinese population played an important role in

---

[39] Parastatals in Mauritius represent 1.9 percent of GDP; the African norm is around the 10 percent mark. Goldsmith, "Africa's Overgrown State Reconsidered," 536.
[40] The EPZs passed the sugar sub-sector as the largest employer in the economy in the late 1980s. Eriksen, *Common Denominators*, 19.
[41] Carroll and Carroll, "Civic Networks, Legitimacy and the Policy Process," 7.
[42] Rodrik, *The New Global Economy and Developing Countries*, 228.
[43] Roland Lamusse, "Adjustment to Structural Change in Manufacturing in a North–South Perspective" (World Employment Programme Research, 1989), 24.

attracting this.[44] It was fortuitous that the decision to adopt an EPZ strategy dovetailed with the interests of Hong Kong enterprises who, at that time, were looking for access to EU markets.[45] As with sugar, a "political price" of sorts was received for goods emanating from the EPZs: preferential access to lucrative developed country markets without quotas under the Lomé Convention markets was key to the subsector's success. The economy responded strongly to these incentives and grew at an annual average of 6.9 percent in the 1970s.[46] Within the space of a couple of decades, the export of knits and clothing displaced sugar as the chief source of employment and foreign exchange earnings in the country.

By the end of the 1970s, however, overall economic growth had begun to slow (see Figure 3.1). It became evident that there was a need for structural adjustment if the export sector was to regain its earlier momentum. A conventional set of stabilization measures commenced in 1979 with cuts in government spending.[47] Unlike in Ghana and Zambia, however, these measures were accompanied by consultations with business and other constituencies on, for example, the government's annual budget.[48]

In 1982, the leftist Mouvement Militant Mauricien (MMM) swept into power in a landslide victory.[49] The party firebrand, Paul Bérenger, was made the new Minister of Finance. To the surprise of many, he did not embark on any of the radical policies he had advocated for so long. Instead, in 1983, he launched a structural adjustment programme (SAP) and revived the flagging export program. Ultimately

---

[44] Arvind Subramanian and Devesh Roy, "Who Can Explain the Mauritian Miracle? Meade, Romer, Sachs or Rodrik?," in *In Search of Prosperity: Analytic Narratives on Economic Growth*, ed. Dani Rodrik (Princeton, NJ: Princeton University Press, 2003), 240.

[45] Lamusse, "Adjustment to Structural Change in Manufacturing in a North–South Perspective," 21.

[46] Sunil Kumar Bundoo and Beealasingh Dabee, "Gradual Liberalization of Key Markets: The Road to Sustainable Growth in Mauritius," *Journal of International Development* 11 (1999): 439.

[47] Ibid.: 440.

[48] These were not without precedent. The Industrial Relations Act of 1973 established tripartite wage negotiations involving government, labor, and business. Sandbrook, "Origins of the Democratic, Developmental State," 559.

[49] Deborah Brautigam, "The People's Budget? Politics, Participation and Pro-Poor Policy," *Development Policy Review* 22, no. 6 (2004): 662. Brautigam, "Revenue, State Capacity and Governance," 17.

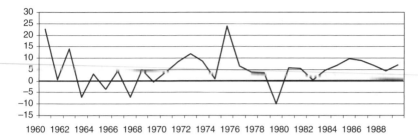

Figure 3.1 Mauritian GDP growth (annual %)
Source: World Development Indicators, World Bank Group

Bérenger lost his job as Finance Minister by making what were considered overly generous nods in the direction of the sugar barons without extracting any significant concessions from them in return. Nonetheless, the terms of economic policy under adjustment continued to be developed in consultation with important domestic constituencies including business.[50]

Bérenger's successor, Vishnu Lutchmeenaraidoo, continued his predecessor's pragmatic, centrist policies to restructure the economy. These measures paid off. The 1980s saw "intensive" economic growth, driven by the EPZs and the employment they had created (see Figure 3.1).[51] For much of Mauritius' history, class and ethnicity had overlapped, as had ethnicity and occupation. Ironically, ethnic politicking favored a diversification away from the much vilified sugar industry and toward export-led industrialization. The EPZs transformed the Mauritian economy.[52] Sugar remained an important foreign exchange earner, but in terms of providing employment as well as in overall contribution to GDP it had been superseded by manufacturing.

In the 1980s, Mauritians began to recognize the potential offered by the tourism industry. The pro-business Creole politician Gaëtan Duval was a crucial figure dynamizing the government's response in this regard. However, this was one of the few areas where the private sector in Mauritius played the lead role in developing a vision for its long-term

---

[50] Carroll and Carroll, "Civic Networks, Legitimacy and the Policy Process," 7. Brautigam, "The People's Budget?," 662.
[51] Rodrik, *The New Global Economy and Developing Countries*, 211.
[52] Eriksen, *Common Denominators*, 12.

development. (It was only as late as 1988 that the government established a specific Ministry for Tourism.)

The profits generated by both the EPZs and the tourism industry boosted the government's tax revenue, which in turn funded the expansion of education and other social services.[53] The Mauritian welfare state was born – but it depended crucially on profits coming from the private sector. The result was improved levels of social equity. Sandbrook points to the drop in Mauritius' Gini coefficient: from 0.5 in 1962 to 0.37 in the mid-1980s (where 1 is perfect inequality in income and 0 is perfect equality). "Nonetheless," Sandbrook continues, "wealth remains concentrated, with 1 percent of the population, mostly whites, owning just over half of the land under cane cultivation and about 65 percent of the stock of productive assets."[54]

The late 1980s then found Mauritius in much better economic shape than either Zambia or Ghana, with a large, increasingly diverse business sector that was distinct – in both its social and economic origins – from the state. In addition, despite their mutual antagonism, business and government had established a history of discreet cooperation. The 1990s brought a new set of challenges.

The Mauritian political economy by the late 1980s

By the 1990s, the population breakdown was as follows: Just over half of the population was Indo-Hindu, 27% were Creole, 16% were Indo-Muslim, and Chinese and European groups each comprised 2 to 3% of the population.[55] We should not assume homogeneity within these groups. The Hindu majority, for example, is internally divided along the lines of caste, place of origin in India, and language;[56] and Creoles are split between those who are better educated, French-speaking, and lighter skinned and the majority that speak only Kreol and are more poorly educated.[57] Nonetheless, the historical relationship

---

[53] Sandbrook, "Origins of the Democratic, Developmental State," 565.

[54] Ibid.: 557.

[55] Henry Srebrnik, "'Full of Sound and Fury': Three Decades of Parliamentary Politics in Mauritius," *Journal of Southern African Studies* 28, no. 2 (2002): 277.

[56] Ibid.

[57] Carroll and Carroll, "Accommodating Ethnic Diversity in a Modernizing Democratic State," 122. Rosabelle Laville, "In the Politics of the

that had been established between, on the one hand, these ethnicized groups and, on the other hand, distinct spheres of influence were, by the late 1980s, central to the Mauritian political economy.[58] Former Finance Minister Rama Sithanen argues that three spheres of influence existed in Mauritius: first, the economic sphere, historically dominated by white Mauritians (especially Franco-Mauritians), second, the print media sphere, dominated by Creoles, and, third, the political sphere, dominated by Hindus.[59]

As in South Africa, organized business associations have a long history in Mauritius: the first Chamber of Commerce was established in 1851 and the Chamber of Agriculture followed just two years later. Again as in South Africa, economic power in Mauritius was remarkably concentrated, both in terms of its racial profile and in terms of broader ownership structures, despite some diversification of the face of business away from being almost exclusively Franco-Mauritian.[60]

More so than in my other country cases, the politically salient divisions within the business community comprised the sub-sectors of the economy that various firms occupied. Business associations were clustered in three sub-sectors: sugar, the EPZs, and tourism.[61] This was reflected in both business associations and policy preferences. Many business associations were marked by the dominance of sugar. Not only was the processing and marketing of sugar a vital contributor to the Mauritian economy, but many businesses owed at least their origins to capital and to entrepreneurs based in the sugar industry. Sugar thus tended to straddle agriculture and industry.

Say the word "sugar" in Mauritius, and generally what is evoked by this are the large sugar estates controlled by the notorious "fourteen families" of Franco-Mauritians. However, there was also a significant

---

Rainbow: Creoles and the Civil Society in Mauritius," *Journal of Contemporary African Studies* 18, no. 2 (2000): 278, 281, 282.

[58] Thomas Meisenhelder, "The Developmental State in Mauritius," *Journal of Modern African Studies* 35, no. 2 (1997): 295.

[59] Ramakrishna Sithanen, Personal interview with author, 6 August 2001.

[60] In 2000, just four companies constituted half the market capitalization of the Stock Exchange of Mauritius, namely the State Bank, the Mauritius Commercial Bank, Sun Resorts, and New Mauritius Hotels. Hawkins, "Investors Begin to Return."

[61] Ganeshan Wignaraja and Sue O'Neil, *SME Exports and Public Policies in Mauritius* (London: Commonwealth Secretariat, 1999), xi.

Indian presence in the sector, comprising 35,000 small planters.[62] Moreover, the extent to which Francophone Mauritians monopolized the economic sphere had diminished considerably since colonial times with the emergence of significant Chinese and Indian entrepreneurs. Nonetheless, the perception of exclusive Francophone dominance persisted, rooted in their historical role as "sugar barons."

This sub-sector was represented principally through the Chamber of Agriculture, one of the oldest and most influential of the private sector institutions.[63] The Sugar Syndicate, the marketing organization in charge of exporting all Mauritian sugar, exercised its influence indirectly – through its participation, with government, in the negotiation of international agreements about sugar sales and prices. Its sister organization, the Mauritius Sugar Authority, was established in the mid-1980s to coordinate relations between the government, Ministry of Agriculture, and the various sugar industry institutions. These three institutions, the Chamber, the Syndicate and the Authority, worked closely together, and shared key membership and leadership figures.

Members of the sugar industry – the barons at least – traditionally have advocated deregulation and liberalization of the labor and tax structure. The small, Indian-owned estates barely featured in the formal business associations. Rather, this constituency exercised an indirect influence on the polity through its membership of the Hindu majority and the protection these numbers afforded.

Like sugar, manufacturing and tourism were represented by sub-sectoral associations. Perhaps the most important of these was the Mauritian Export Processing Zones Association (MEPZA). In terms of policy, MEPZA largely favored liberalization and devaluation of the national currency. Along with the sugar producers, they lobbied for a weak rupee to counter the depreciation of the euro.

Tourism was represented by the Association des Hôteliers et Restaurateurs de l'île Maurice (AHRIM), created in 1973. Its membership included both large and small hotels and restaurants as well as other

---

[62] The historical basis for this phenomenon lies in the late nineteenth century when the world price of sugar fell significantly. White estate owners began to sell off small sections of their estates to the handful of Indians who could afford to make such a purchase. Cf. John Addison and K. Hazareesingh, *A New History of Mauritius* (London: Macmillan, 1984), 53. Leslie Crawford, "Barons Braced for Rationalisation," *Financial Times*, 1994.

[63] Lange, "Embedding the Colonial State," 406.

enterprises engaged with tourism such as diving operations, tour companies, and car hire firms. The association was funded by member subscriptions. The tourism sub-sector has traditionally pressurized the government to allow greater tourist numbers.

The highest profile was enjoyed by the encompassing associations, the largest of which, the Mauritius Employers' Federation (MEF), was founded in 1962. According to its literature, MEF's mission is the "defense of the interests of its members and, by extension, the promotion of free enterprise in Mauritius";[64] generally, however, it limited itself to social and industrial relations-type issues. Members comprised both individual employers and firms, and ran the gamut from small enterprises to the largest. The MEF was entirely funded by members' subscriptions.

While not the largest, the Joint Economic Council (JEC), set up in 1970, was the apex of private sector organizations in Mauritius. Its officers met with government at the highest level, both in a set of regularized meetings and in a more ad hoc manner as important issues arose. The Council rested both literally and figuratively on the base laid by the sugar sub-sector.[65]

At a lower level, the Mauritius Chamber of Commerce and Industry (MCCI) represented a broad range of firms at Chamber level. Like the JEC, it tended to concern itself with broad macroeconomic issues.

While there had been a diversification of both membership and leadership, the major business associations continued to be dominated by Franco-Mauritians. Not surprisingly then, separate associations were established to represent businesspeople in other communities. The Chinese Business Chamber, for example, formed in 1998 to oppose the Consumer Protection Act. The Indian Traders' Association, active for some time, appeared to be moribund in the 1990s. However, these smaller groups were not seen as especially influential on policy questions.

In conclusion then, private sector associations in Mauritius had much in common with their counterparts in South Africa: they reflected the economic dominance of a minority ethnic group and the dominance,

---

[64] Mauritius Employers, Federation, "The Vital Voice of Mauritius Enterprise" (Mauritius Employers, Federation, undated).

[65] The JEC occupied the top floor of Plantation House, the building where the Sugar Syndicate and Chamber of Agriculture also had their offices.

within that group, of a small number of large, powerful firms. In addition, they displayed financial independence and significant organizational capacity including the ability to pursue an economy-wide set of policy proposals. By contrast with the South African private sector, however, they tended to follow the policy lead given by the government rather than proactively initiating policy change.

As for the state in Mauritius, it was widely regarded as effective and accountable and the civil service as relatively efficient and meritocratic. Perceptions that recruitment to the civil service was ethnicized persisted but were mitigated by an emphasis on merit in hiring and promotions.[66] In the late 1990s, the Mauritian state was twice ranked among the top three countries on the continent for having the lowest level of perceived corruption.[67] Indeed, observers argued that "Mauritius rank[ed] well above the average African country on all indices of institutional quality, political as well as economic, and also above the fast-growing economies on most indices."[68]

Economic policy-making in Mauritius

In Mauritius, parliament was the setting for lively, party-based contestations.[69] In the 1990s, there were three principal political parties. The predominant support base of the first of these, the LP, was solidly Hindu (traditionally supported by sugar workers). It remained vaguely left-wing, although in its policy-making it had never departed radically from the economic mainstream.

The MMM, the second, started out as a radical party, eschewing ethnicity for a class-based approach. This tendency did not survive as the party split often. The most significant offshoot of the MMM was the Mouvement Socialiste Militant (MSM) led by Sir Anerood Jugnauth.

Third, the Parti Mauricien Social Démocrate (PMSD), subsequently called the PMXD, traditionally drew support from the Creole

---

[66] Goldsmith, "Africa's Overgrown State Reconsidered," 539–41. For a contrary view, see Willy McCourt and Anita Ramgutty-Wong, "Limits to Strategic HRM: The Case of the Mauritian Civil Service," *International Journal of Human Resource Management* 14, no. 4 (2003).

[67] Goldsmith, "Africa's Overgrown State Reconsidered," 535.

[68] Subramanian and Roy, "Who Can Explain the Mauritian Miracle?," 231.

[69] For a guide to Mauritius' sometimes bewildering coalition politics, see Srebrnik, "Full of Sound and Fury."

community and adopted conservative economic policies that found favor with business.

Journalist Kiran Ramsahaye has pointed to the startling range of governing coalitions that Mauritius has seen, often allying parties on opposite sides of the political spectrum: "In Mauritius all political parties – no matter how far apart they may appear to be – are potential allies."[70] The frequently changing alliances are not economically disruptive; rather than evidence of political instability, the shifting coalitions "provide a safety valve, enabling politicians to let off political steam."[71] And despite the dizzying coalitional maneuvering, only four men have served as Prime Minister since independence in 1968.[72] Moreover, the actual distance between the various parties was often smaller than it at first glance appeared. While businesspeople grumbled, for example, that the LP was less amenable to their views than the other major parties, most felt that all the parties agreed on the broad parameters of economic policy.

To turn then to the period under review: what was the contribution of the Mauritian private sector to the development of that policy over the course of the 1990s?

The 1990s: a new set of challenges

The early 1990s promised a period of strong growth in Mauritius. The sugar and tourism sub-sectors were recovering from earlier doldrums and, after lagging initially, manufacturing too recovered, buoyed by increased consumer spending. However, there were signs of potential trouble ahead. In particular, three areas of the economy required attention.

In agriculture, there was an evident need to diversify out of sugar. While a number of entrepreneurs based in the sugar industry had moved into manufacturing, agriculture itself remained dominated almost entirely by sugar.

Moreover, the country's manufactured exports were not sufficiently diversified, in terms of either goods produced or markets sold into.

---

[70] "Leaders to the Fore; Ideology No More," *News on Sunday*, 1 March 1998, 7.
[71] Ibid.
[72] Rodrik, *The New Global Economy and Developing Countries*, 209.

The country's almost full employment status had pushed wages up, eroding the country's cost competitiveness. Historically founded on labor-intensive production, Mauritian industry now required a more skilled labor force and access to better technology if it was to retain its comparative advantage.

Of all three sub-sectors of the economy, tourism was the one in which the private sector had demonstrated the most independent initiative. However, by the early 1990s, hoteliers argued the need for better planning and coordination from government. In particular, a rash of construction projects had created an oversupply of accommodation.

In almost every sub-sector – bar tourism – business' policy preferences were, on the one hand, supportive of liberal macroeconomic policies but, on the other hand, also demanding some kind of government intervention in the sub-sector (most notably in manufacturing and sugar, the pressure was for government to continue to negotiate favorable access to international markets for those sub-sectors).

The section that follows will examine the private sector's capacity to shape policy-making in the 1990s, given these challenges. My analysis splits the decade in two, with an MMM/MSM government in the first half and various permutations of LP-led government for much of the second half. Throughout the decade, agriculture and the EPZ/manufacturing sub-sectors organized most assertively to defend their own interests, although hoteliers and traders occasionally weighed in. Against a politically turbulent backdrop, private sector institutions and their interactions with government were strengthened and good rates of national economic growth were maintained.

The "militant" governments

In the second half of 1990, a MMM/MSM coalition government took office with former radical Bérenger once again appointed Finance Minister. Despite his leftist credentials, Bérenger again implemented a remarkably liberal set of economic policies – as did his successor in the post, the economist Rama Sithanen. Between them, these two men galvanized the country's reform process and significantly improved the overall relationship between business and government. But Sithanen encroached where Bérenger before him had failed, and fallen: on the government's relationship with the sugar industry.

Sugar: a quiet transformation

Sithanen envisioned a different relationship between the sugar industry and the government. He hoped to "put an end to the straight-jacket [*sic*], narrow-minded and confrontational relationship that has beset the industry for centuries" and to "usher in a new dawn based on effective co-operation and partnership."[73] This was something that businesspeople based in the sub-sector had been seeking for some time.

Sithanen's most revolutionary step was to eliminate the export duty on sugar. This was politically dangerous because it could have been interpreted as pandering to the despised sugar barons. Indeed, in his budget speech, Sithanen could not quite bring himself to use the word "abolish"; at the tail end of a number of measures intended to mollify workers, he simply noted that the export duty on sugar would "no longer appear" as a revenue item for the government.[74] Instead, the money would be siphoned into, among other funds, the Sugar Investment Trust (SIT), which would give all planters and, crucially, all employees a share in the ownership of the milling companies. By linking the abolition of the tax with a new structure, funded in large measure by the barons, that would yoke the interests of workers and owners (large and small) in the sugar industry, Sithanen drew the political sting from his concession. In addition, the government secured an agreement from the EU that would entitle the country to an additional quota of 85,000 tonnes of sugar at the preferential price for six years. The barons had every reason to be pleased.

Manufacturing exports

As Finance Minister, Sithanen introduced a range of measures to improve the competitiveness of the economy. To the delight of business, many of these measures came directly from their suggestions. In the *White Paper on National Pay and Productivity Council*, for example, he adopted a proposal the MEF had made to link pay and productivity. I argued above that the manufacturing firms needed to upgrade their technology. In 1995, therefore, Sithanen announced a series of measures intended to boost investment in that sub-sector. He

---

[73] Hon. Ramakrishna Sithanen, Minister of Finance, "Budget Speech 1994–1995" (Port Louis, Mauritius, 20 June 1994), 25.
[74] Ibid., 27.

also proposed the establishment of a Business Licensing Authority as a one-stop clearing house for investors.

Tourism

The government and the private sector disagreed fundamentally over how the tourism sub-sector should be developed. The government wanted to preserve Mauritius as a top-quality destination for a limited number of big-spending tourists.[75] Hoteliers, restaurateurs, car hire agencies, and others associated with the tourist trade differed, arguing that the island could support a far larger number of visitors and calling upon the government, for example, to permit charter flights to the island. However, AHRIM, the sub-sectoral association, was barely functioning; it consisted largely of the smaller hotels and restaurants and made very little progress on this issue.

The private sector more broadly

The "militancy" suggested by the coalition parties' names was strikingly absent in its relationship with the private sector. The MMM government began to routinely include private sector representatives in its international and trade negotiations. For example, in 1991, the government asked the MCCI to receive all major delegations visiting the country, giving the Chamber the opportunity to engage with World Bank missions. This practice was extended to domestic policy consultation when Bérenger institutionalized private sector representation on a range of committees and processes dealing with national economic issues.[76] In 1992 then, the MCCI's annual report records monthly meetings with the Ministry of Industry and Industrial Technology to discuss issues relating to industrial development[77] and an Industrial Council was established to serve as "a permanent consultation mechanism" on industrial and technical issues.[78]

Sithanen institutionalized the structured public–private sector consultation that Bérenger had established. Prior to finalizing the budget, Sithanen invited proposals from the private sector, and incorporated

---

[75] In 1988, the government published a *White Paper on Tourism* which limited the number of tourists to a ratio of 1:3 with the local population.

[76] Mahmood Cheeroo, Personal interview with author, 21 August 2001.

[77] Mauritius Chamber of Commerce and Industry, "Annual Report 1992" (Port Louis, Mauritius: 1992), 4.

[78] Unattributed, *Industry Focus*, May 1993, 4.

suggestions from MCCI about eliminating anomalies in the tariff structure and reducing duty on imports for tourism and construction.[79] What is striking here is not just that the government met with and listened to private sector associations, but that these interactions were established by governmental initiative. As in their interactions, so too in policy-making: while much economic policy was favorable to the private sector, that policy emerged principally from the ideas and initiative of the government.

In a move intended to increase the role of market-driven incentives, Sithanen confirmed that the principal task of monetary policy (and by implication the Bank of Mauritius) was to reduce inflation and he introduced reforms intended to transform the Bank's role from "a market maker into that of a market player."[80] In addition, he set the stage for the listing of such state-owned companies as the State Bank, the State Investment Corporation, Mauritius Telecom, and Air Mauritius. The liberalization of exchange controls was finalized when Sithanen lifted the remaining 5 percent capital gains tax and paved the way for complete foreign exchange convertibility.[81]

Sithanen's tax reforms did not stop with sugar. In 1995, he began to reform the tax system and decrease the rate of income tax for both individuals and corporations over a five-year period. In pre-budget consultations, MCCI had requested a reduction in the rate of corporate tax applied to firms producing for the local market. This was granted, and personal income tax rates were restructured into three bands with the highest of these reduced by 5 percent.

The state of business midway through

The year 1995, an election year, provides a good opportunity to assess the coalition's record. In the decade to that point, the country had experienced average GDP growth of 6.5% p.a., inflation of 7.5%, unemployment had shrunk to a negligible 1.6% and the budget deficit averaged 2.2%.[82] "Business and government are working more closely

---

[79] Mauritius Chamber of Commerce and Industry, "Annual Report 1994" (Port Louis, Mauritius: 1994), 6, Unattributed, *Industry Focus*.

[80] Sithanen, "Budget Speech 1994–1995", 10.

[81] Bundoo and Dabee, "Gradual Liberalization of Key Markets."

[82] Tony Hawkins and Michael Holman, "Tiger in the Making," *Financial Times*, 27 September 1994.

than in the past, while in the political sphere there is a shared vision of the future," observed the *Financial Times*.[83]

Under the "militants" and especially under the stewardship of Sithanen, business had commended the general trend toward liberalization and deregulation of the economy, most particularly of the sugar industry. My interviews with businesspeople revealed a high level of satisfaction with the role that the government played to this point.[84] Despite this, Prime Minister Jugnauth's government was dismissed by the voters in favor of an alliance between the LP and the MMM. It was an unlikely coalition and collapsed by the end of 1997, leaving the LP to rule on its own. Business' interaction with this new government did not start off smoothly.

The Labour government

Within months of his appointment as the new Finance Minister, Rundheersing Bheenick had become extremely unpopular with the business sector, and relations between business and government slumped. He was ultimately dismissed as Finance Minister. Three issues contributed to this.

Top of the list of grievances for business was the 1996/7 budget. Perhaps the most positive thing that business could say about the budget was that it was an attempt to deal with the budget deficit. To the distress of the private sector, however, it did so by attending only to government revenue. Without any of the usual consultation, Bheenick announced the introduction of twenty-five new taxes, doubled sales tax, increased hotel and restaurant tax by 50 percent, and hit consumers with a 25 percent increase in the price of petrol. In addition he imposed a "windfall" levy of Rs300 million on the sugar industry – a result, the government argued, of "exceptional" income accruing to the sub-sector.[85]

The JEC fumed, denouncing the budget as a "big deception" and slamming the government's inability to cut its own expenditure.[86] MCCI raged that the budget was "not acceptable to the business

---

[83] Ibid.
[84] I interviewed a range of business people and business associations in Port Louis and Reduit in 2001.
[85] Needless to say, the sugar sub-sector hotly disputed any such windfall.
[86] Unattributed, "JEC Attacks the 'Big Deception,'" *Mauritius Times*, 2 June 1996, 5.

community."[87] Criticisms came from all sub-sectors of the economy including the MSPA and the newly revived AHRIM. The stock exchange reacted with a deluge of "sell" orders. It swiftly became evident that the budget was a political liability.

The government heard the dissatisfaction and responded with a series of changes to the budget.[88] Of vital interest to business, sales tax was somewhat reduced and a controversial withholding tax on interest withdrawn – but a second strike against the Finance Minister was not long in coming.

In Mauritius, it is rare for a businessman to be high profile in his political support for a particular personality or party.[89] Roland Maurel, a close friend and very public supporter of the new Prime Ministers, was the exception that proved the rule. It therefore raised a few eyebrows when Maurel, together with a Singapore-based firm, Amcol, developed a costly set of proposals for an entertainment complex and race course outside of the capital, Port Louis, shortly after his friend was made prime minister. The undertaking foundered when Amcol was declared bankrupt and withdrew from the deal. The general perception of what followed was that Maurel lobbied energetically to get himself bailed out by the government. No one seems sure of what Bheenick's precise involvement in the affair was (there was no concrete evidence that he acted improperly) but, in the minds of many, he did not act fast enough to distance his government from the affair. Business noted two strikes against the Finance Minister: the budget and Amcol.

The third strike followed the release by the Finance Ministry, in February 1996, of the annual "State of the Economy." The document was outrageously partisan and clearly intended to discredit the previous government. It alleged a massive shortfall in state finances and blamed former minister Sithanen for this, precipitating a rowdy debate on the economic policy record. At first, the fracas did not unduly

---

[87] Mauritius Chamber of Commerce and Industry, "Annual Report 1996" (Port Louis, Mauritius: 1996), 6.

[88] Indeed, according to one observer, "so many changes were introduced that even chartered accountants had trouble keeping track of measures." Unattributed, "Roasting Me Was a National Pastime," *News on Sunday*, 11 August 1996, 6–7.

[89] Businesspeople were usually more discreet on such issues and would often support a number of political parties financially at election time as a kind of insurance policy.

disturb the private sector, which saw it as an opportunity to reopen a policy dialogue with the new government.

In August, however, the government was confronted with evidence that Rs700 million had been transferred to the Bank of Mauritius under orders from Bheenick but without the authorization – or knowledge – of the prime minister. According to one newspaper, "[t]he transaction – described as being somewhat unusual – was apparently to make the budget deficit [inherited from the previous government] appear worse than it actually was."[90] This cynical manipulation of government accounting was the final straw and Bheenick was forced to resign.

Beyond their unhappiness with the new Finance Minister, by the mid-1990s the Mauritian business community was conscious of new threats to its profitability, emerging, first, from the government's management of the macroeconomy; second, from the ongoing stratification of the economy; and, third, from the labor market.

To start with the government's management of its own finances: revenue income had dropped as a result of reform in the tax system to introduce "Pay As You Earn" (PAYE) tax, and changes to the ratio of corporate tax; however, government spending continued to increase, much of this being recurrent expenditure.[91] There had been pressure on public spending in the first half of the decade as a result of cyclone damage and a steep hike in salaries in the civil service. MCCI also fretted about a "prevailing sluggishness" in Gross Domestic Fixed Capital Formation.[92] In response, the MCCI called on the government to reduce its consumption and increase its savings and investment.[93]

A second issue that recurred in private sector policy interventions was a concern with stratification within the economy. In the Chamber's view, this was the result of government policies that consciously sought to boost particular sub-sectors at the expense of others. The Chamber posited that the consequent lack of synergy between Mauritius' "stand alone" economic sub-sectors explained the failure to attract larger inflows of FDI. The MCCI explicitly called for an end

[90] Unattributed, "1996: A Year of Living Dangerously,"*News on Sunday*, 29 December 1996, 2–3.
[91] Ministry of Economic Planning and Development, "Mauritius Economic Review 1992–1995" (Port Louis, Mauritius: 1996), 35–7.
[92] Mauritius Chamber of Commerce and Industry, "Annual Report 1995" (Port Louis, Mauritius: 1995), 17.
[93] Mauritius Chamber of Commerce and Industry, "Annual Report 1994," 21.

to discrimination between the EPZ and those producing for local consumption.[94] This call was important because it challenged the economic role that the Mauritian government had carved out for itself; namely, that of a developmental state, intimately involved in prioritizing and privileging certain sub-sectors.

The Report went on to demand greater consultation with the LP government. MCCI argued that while the public and private sector cooperated very well at the international level to promote the national interest, the same was not evident at the domestic level: "to avoid a repetition of the unfortunate experience of the 1996/7 Budget, it is necessary that the collaboration between the Government and the private sector goes beyond sectoral and ad hoc issues. The time has come for a structured consultation on key macro-economic issues and national economic management."[95]

Prime Minister Ramgoolam temporarily took over the running of the portfolio, providing little reassurance to business. In an attempt to address a gloomy business climate, the prime minister, toward the end of the year, announced the launch of the Port Louis Fund, to facilitate investment in Mauritius' fledgling stock exchange; it was an explicit attempt to boost private sector confidence in the economy and "revitalise private and public co-operation."[96] As a next step, a medical doctor, Vasant Bunwaree, was appointed as Finance Minister in early December. This was a relief for the business community who welcomed not so much Bunwaree himself as the fact that someone – anyone – had been appointed to the vacant portfolio.

Shortly after his appointment, Bunwaree announced a "New Economic Agenda." It was not as grandiose as it sounded,[97] but it did set out the government's broad economic objectives for the following three years and succeeded somewhat in settling the nervous markets.

---

[94] For example, in its submission to the government on the 1998/9 budget, MCCI stressed the need for "a level playing field, not only between private and public operators, but also between the different sectors of the economy." Mauritius Chamber of Commerce and Industry, "Annual Report 1995," 6.

[95] Mauritius Chamber of Commerce and Industry, "Annual Report 1996," 26.

[96] The quote is from Junior Finance Minister Jacques Chasteau. Cf. Unattributed, "We're Your Friends," *News on Sunday*, 3 November 1996, 10–11.

[97] The announcement included nine measures aimed at boosting small enterprises and investment, and reducing the operating costs faced by business. Unattributed, "Drought Takes Toll on Sugar," *News on Sunday*, 3 November 1996, 4.

The new government also undertook a number of market-friendly policy measures, moving ahead with divestiture and privatization, and beginning to rethink certain taxes.[98] These developments were welcomed by the private sector.

Against this background then, what progress did business make on achieving its policy goals under the new regime? I will review developments in the sub-sectors, before considering the broader issues.

Sugar

To the delight of those in the sugar industry, in his first budget address, Bunwaree overturned Bheenick's "special windfall levy" on that industry (a review of the prices and exchange rate found no such windfall, just as the industry had claimed). Once again, however, payback was extracted from the industry for this concession. The government ordered the industry to offer interest-free loans for the purchase of SIT shares, to fund an Adult Literacy Programme and an additional five scholarships for each of the seventeen sugar estates, and to make a lump sum payment to the Mauritius Sugar Authority.

Manufacturing exports

Large firms with access to the best technology and design had been crucial in Mauritius' competitiveness in exports and this continued to be the case in the 1990s.[99] Large and small exporters alike (in both sugar and manufacturing), however, were uneasy about Bunwaree's announced intention to maintain a strong Mauritian rupee, part of a plan to force export enterprises to become more productive by making real quality improvements. Bunwaree later softened his stance, arguing that his intention had never been to inflate the value of the currency. Rather it would simply reflect the underlying strength of the economy.[100]

---

[98] Under the LP, privatization progressed at a very gentle pace. The government divested some of its shares in Air Mauritius, the Overseas Telecommunications Service, and the State Bank. A draft bill on BOT projects to involve the private sector in infrastructure development was proposed and a share of the National Pension Fund was to be opened up to private fund managers. In addition, Bunwaree announced the government's intention to adopt VAT.

[99] Ganeshan Wignaraja, "Firm Size, Technological Capabilities and Market-Oriented Policies in Mauritius," *Oxford Development Studies* 30, no. 1 (2002): 93.

[100] Supporters of the government argued that exports had profited from a depreciating rupee that had rendered further improvements in competitiveness unnecessary.

Tourism

A large number of new hotels had been built over the course of the decade without a corresponding increase in tourist numbers to fill them. Mauritius was affected by the global decrease in long-haul tourism in the wake of Gulf War-related fuel hikes – but the low number of tourists was also part of the government's tourism strategy, viz. to attract a small number of big-spending tourists, rather than the reverse.

I argued earlier that the Association had been moribund for many years after the larger hotels effectively abandoned it. AHRIM was revitalized in 1996 when the government had attempted to hike hotel and restaurant taxes, and the Association won some reduction in these. The tourism sub-sector had long demanded a relaxation of restrictions on the number of flights to the island but Air Mauritius energetically lobbied the government to maintain its monopoly on flights. In the end, Air Mauritius increased its number of flights and the government permitted greater numbers of visitors than it had originally planned for, but the government remained committed to its low-volume, high-spending tourism strategy.

The private sector broadly

There were indications that the government had learned some hard lessons about the importance of fruitful interaction with the private sector. Bunwaree began 1997 with a series of productive consultations with the JEC.[101] In pre-budget consultations, MCCI had pressed for a "low expenditure, low tax" budget. They argued once more for the need for a "level playing field" for all economic operators and for greater support for industries confronted with trade liberalization. The Chamber had reason to be satisfied that a number of these demands were incorporated into the budget.

The government paid close attention to business' borrowing costs. The 1997/8 budget recognized that lending rates were impeding new investment and the Bank of Mauritius was instructed to reduce (further) its cash reserve ratio with the expectation that this would lower bank lending rates.[102]

---

[101] These led to the amendment of the Landlord and Tenants Act, the setting up of the Board of Investment, proposals for Build, Operate and Transfer (BOT) projects, and low interest rates.

[102] In a rich but unintended irony, the budget speech then went on to argue that the policy of the government was to grant the Bank of Mauritius "the required

Exports remained the darling of government and EPZ firms enjoyed good access to government. Nonetheless both government and the private sector associations were able to accommodate the concerns of other sub-sectors. This was demonstrated when the government replaced General Sales Tax with VAT. Predictably, businesspeople complained about problems associated with the introduction of the new tax – but in reality it went rather smoothly (certainly by comparison with Ghana and Zambia). The strongest reaction was from retailers affected by the proposed Consumer Protection Act. In order to protect consumers from illegitimate price increases and preempt any potential inflationary impact, the government reintroduced price controls on a range of goods. Traders, as one might imagine, strenuously opposed this. In the end, the MCCI and JEC brokered a deal acceptable to both sides: traders would voluntarily restrain prices for four months and the government would soften the price controls on the twenty-six affected categories of goods. It was a good deal, and one that demonstrated the private sector's ability and willingness to regulate itself for the overall good of the economy. It considerably improved the overall relationship between business and the state.

The government's 1999/2000 budget was "generally well received" by the private sector[103] and endorsed by the MEF, JEC, and the Mauritian Export Processing Zones Association. Government proposals to streamline and simplify investment were welcomed as were the rationalization and reorganization of corporate taxes. Statements of a renewed commitment to cutting expenditure after two years of overshooting the budget deficit target were met with a little more skepticism. (As the business associations noted, there had been some macro-policy slippage under Labour from 1995: the government had not met its deficit targets and had not adjusted the prices charged for petrol and electricity quickly enough to ensure the profitability of the relevant parastatals.)[104]

autonomy" in the formulation of monetary policy. Vasant K. Bunwaree, "Budget Speech 1997–1998" (La Tour Koenig, Mauritius, 9 June 1997), 10.

[103] Economist Intelligence Unit, *Country Report: Mauritius* (London: Economist Intelligence Unit, 1999), 9.

[104] Government of Mauritius, *The Present State of the Economy* (Port Louis, Mauritius: Government of Mauritius, 2000), 14–16.

The analysis that MCCI had developed about a fractured private sector was incorporated into this budget. Bunwaree recognized the "dualistic pattern of technological capabilities" in the export zone and noted the existence of "a few large export-oriented firms with state-of-the-art technology and high quality management" while small and medium enterprises "lack[ed] technological skills, ma[d]e use of rudimentary design capabilities and suffer[ed] from poor quality management."[105] Significantly, however, he provided no systematic program to address this problem.

Bunwaree, in his second budget, confirmed the government's commitment to diversify its exports: henceforth, he argued, the emphasis would be on manufacturing, financial services and those based on information technology, high value-added textiles, and printing. Specifically, the government hoped to develop Mauritius as an offshore financial hub. Accordingly, a double tax treaty was signed with India and substantial capital flows between the two countries followed, bolstered no doubt by the prominent Indian diasporic community in Mauritius.[106]

From business' perspective, little progress was made on either improving the quality or reducing the costs of labor. To be fair, these were difficult and long-term problems. Politically, it was almost impossible for Labour to make labor cheaper. As for improving labor skills levels, the legislature did begin debating a series of education reforms but the outcome was inconclusive. The only reason this was not a greater problem was that Mauritius already had a relatively well-educated population.

Overall, the private sector was more supportive of Bunwaree's budgets than of his immediate predecessor's. In the Chamber's judgment, the 1997/8 budget "was prepared after better consultations with all stakeholders and its philosophy was nearer to the expectations of the private sector."[107] Despite the LP's leftist profile, Bunwaree's budget demonstrated that his government was open to input from business. His second budget, however, demonstrated also that the government had not abandoned its role as chief visionary for the economy.

---

[105] Bunwaree, "Budget Speech 1997–1998," 19.
[106] Subramanian and Roy, "Who Can Explain the Mauritian Miracle?," 240.
[107] Mauritius Chamber of Commerce and Industry, "Annual Report 1997" (Port Louis, Mauritius: 1997), 6.

The policy outcomes

Over the course of the 1990s, the Mauritian economy had continued to diversify despite less than ideal conditions in its tourist and export markets. In 1970, the EPZ had provided 2% of the country's exports; in the late 1990s, that had grown to 66%. The share of the sugar industry had shrunk from 88% in 1970 to 18%. Tourism had grown steadily from almost nothing to provide 20% of export earnings. Overall, growth was good (above 5% for most of the decade). Also, throughout the decade there was an ongoing reduction of import tariffs and protections, and continued promotion of exports,[108] and the budget deficit had been held within the 3% range from the late 1980s.[109]

Some important challenges persisted. Sugar continued to dominate agriculture (more than 90% of cultivated land was still under sugar). Good progress had been made on winning significant market share for profitable "special sugars" (such as demerara and muscovado) but medium-term planning assumed that the lucrative deal with the EU could be renewed indefinitely and that a depreciating rupee would secure the sub-sector's profitability vis-à-vis Europe.

Likewise, exports continued to be dominated by garments and woolens and, although there was some expansion into US markets, there was less diversification of export markets than had been hoped for. The Economist Intelligence Unit quipped that the "new economic structure of Mauritius [now] comprises not only a mono-agricultural sector but also a mono-industrial sector."[110]

Overall, the macroeconomy had been liberalized. Unlike liberalization in Zambia, however, the details of the program in Mauritius were negotiated with business and incorporated "concern for appropriate sequencing and sustainability."[111] In this environment then, how much of what business wanted did it get? Here we must distinguish between the specific policy demands of particular sub-sectors.

The sugar sub-sector experienced significant reform as a result of Sithanen's restructuring; taxes were liberalized although there was not

[108] Wignaraja, "Firm Size, Technological Capabilities and Market-Oriented Policies in Mauritius," 92.
[109] Bundoo and Dabee, "Gradual Liberalization of Key Markets."
[110] Economist Intelligence Unit, *Mauritius Country Profile 1998–99* (London: Economist Group, 1999), 10.
[111] Bundoo and Dabee, "Gradual Liberalization of Key Markets," 438.

a similar liberalization of the labor framework. Tourism did not consider itself a big winner, but flourished nonetheless. Manufacturing saw progress on most of what it wanted. What it did not win was an end to the government's distinction between those who manufactured for domestic sale, and those who did so for export. Both of these sub sectors reflect broader dynamics. While business won many of the liberal macro-policies that it sought, government did not even consider abandoning its broader role as manager of the economy. Government policy continued to champion particular sub-sectors. While the encompassing associations opposed this, firms situated in favored sub-sectors had every reason to support the government in this role – hardly surprising, given the concessions that they enjoyed both for sugar and for clothing and textiles.

Crucially, many of the most important "wins" for Mauritian business were items it barely had to ask for, in particular the continuation of these concessionary prices. Under Labour's first Finance Minister, Bheenick, business was reminded that it could not take the ear of government for granted. Business was reassured by subsequent developments under Bunwaree, and throughout the decade, much of what business got, it got by government initiative, strengthened and refined via consultation with the private sector.

Why business lost the big demand but still won overall

Mauritius enjoys both a relatively strong developmental state and a vibrant and autonomous business community. The country's particular policy outcomes can be explained in large measure by the quality of its state. Although not free of corruption or personalistic politics,[112] the Mauritian state is nonetheless much closer to the developmental state of Wade and Johnson[113] than to any archetypal neo-patrimonial state. Unlike the governments of Ghana and Zambia, the Mauritian state had the demonstrated capacity to prioritize particular sub-sectors, design programs to develop these, and carefully listen to firms within those sub-sectors.

---

[112] The scandal over illegal purchases by the police force under Commissioner Raj Dayal was one example of both personalism and corruption.

[113] Chalmers Johnson, *Japan, Who Governs? The Rise of the Developmental State* (New York: W. W. Norton and Co., 1995), Wade, *Governing the Market*.

But the quality of the private sector too in Mauritius has been high. Historically held at arm's length from the government, the business community was not able to rely on kickbacks from the government in order to survive. Rather, ethnicized hostility combined with the export orientation of the economy forced firms to look to their own competitiveness. Consequently, Mauritius developed a range of well-institutionalized business associations, capable of taking a long-range view of the economy. All of this accounted for the ability of business and government to have constructive policy discussions when out of the public eye.

As the Mauritian economy has diversified and the polity matured, there was some softening of the correlation between class and ethnicity, similar to what occurred in South Africa. In Mauritius this was driven, chiefly but by no means only, by upward economic mobility among the Hindus. Carroll and Carroll argue that "with the exception of the *ti-kreol* ..., all the Mauritian ethnic communities have been able to achieve success in some aspect of life, and this seems to have made it easier for the minority communities to accept forms of power-sharing that fall short of being proportionate to their numbers."[114] Many Creoles remain marginalized and this is an important source of potential conflict.[115] Nonetheless, for the most part, I would concur with Eriksen that while ethnic identities remain pervasive, "the ethnic groups of 1997 are culturally less distinctive than those of 1897 would have been."[116] For Eriksen this is the result of changes in the labor market: "Mauritians increasingly imagine themselves as competitors on the world market [and] individual merit is replacing kinship and ethnic membership as the most important principle for recruitment to the labour market."[117] Again as in South Africa, the predominant environment in which firms operate is not one marked primarily by neo-patrimonialism, but one which is dominated by the market, albeit in this case a governed market.

In addition, the parastatal sector was never as large, all encompassing, and inefficient as many of those found elsewhere in Africa. None of Mauritius' leftist parties ever followed through on their threats of nationalization. While Mauritius' politicians frequently took public

---

[114] Carroll and Carroll, "Accommodating Ethnic Diversity in a Modernizing Democratic State," 135.

[115] Ibid.: 138.   [116] Eriksen, *Common Denominators*, 14.   [117] Ibid., 164.

aim at their businesspeople, as their Ghanaian counterparts did, in Mauritius the business environment was more benign and the growth trajectory more robust.

Because of the government's stratified manufacturing and exports policy, the sub-sectoral divides within the Mauritian business community were stronger than elsewhere. Recognizing that these could weaken the economy-wide voice of business, private sector associations have challenged this – mostly unsuccessfully. After all, this would undermine the very foundations of the government's developmental approach.

A growing number of analysts regard the islands' ethnic diversity as an asset. In addition to having helped shape the relationship between government and business, the country's ethnicized history has impacted on its economic development in two important ways. The first of these was the economic role played by a population with close-knit diasporic ties to strategically important communities elsewhere in the global economy.[118] The role of Mauritius' Chinese community and its links to the Hong Kong capital that bolstered the EPZs is an important example, as is the role of the Hindu community and its links to the Indian capital that surged into Mauritius' newly created financial services sector. A less direct but absolutely vital second factor has been the accountability of the state. Subramanian and Roy argue that this too can be traced to the country's ethnic diversity as this "forced the need for participatory political institutions that were important in maintaining stability, law and order, rule of law and mediating conflict."[119]

Conclusion

While the Mauritian private sector was lambasted publicly by politicians, it retained a good, if guarded, working relationship with the government, regardless of which coalition of parties was in power at the time.[120] This included almost routine consultation with the government on major policy issues (most private sector organizations were

---

[118] Subramanian and Roy, "Who Can Explain the Mauritian Miracle?," 239.
[119] Ibid.
[120] This is not to argue that changes in government were inconsequential. In particular, the Labour Party was regarded as being more hostile to business.

consulted by the government prior to the preparation of the budget, for example).

Despite its idyllic aspect, ethnic conflict remains a feature of Mauritian society; Mauritians remain "communalist," acutely aware of ethnicized and racialized identifications. In addition, the Creoles have effectively been marginalized from many of the economic and political advances enjoyed by other groups on the island.[121] However, as Miles remarks, it is a "[w]illingness to compromise, not national unity [that is] the key to Mauritian political consciousness."[122] This was evident time and again in the 1990s, both in relations between business and government and in relations between sub-sectors within the private sector as they negotiated pragmatic compromises that were mutually advantageous and in the national interest.

There is recent evidence of the softening of rigid ethnic divisions within the private sector.[123] For example, the appointment of non-whites to represent the JEC, the MCCI, and the Chamber of Agriculture (all bastions of white business) would have been unthinkable in the 1980s and even in the early 1990s – but has since occurred. There is also the possibility of some softening of ethnic taboos in the political sphere; the head of the civil service in 2003 was a non-Hindu[124] and the 1990s saw the number of Creoles in the senior ranks of the civil service increase.[125] Most dramatically perhaps, in 2003 Paul Bérenger became the country's first white post-independence prime minister. (Until then, conventional wisdom was that the country would only ever tolerate or elect a Hindu – and more specifically a Vaish – premier.)

Ethnicity has profoundly shaped both the positive and the negative aspects of the private sector's interaction with government. It accounts for the government's public posturing (especially vis-à-vis sugar) and may also have hindered the development of all-pervasive neo-patrimonial ties between the public and private sectors. Because of their divergent ethnic compositions and historical origins, political and economic elites simply do not overlap to any great extent. In Mauritius, the island's

[121] See Sandbrook, "Origins of the Democratic, Developmental State," 560.
[122] Miles, "The Mauritius Enigma," 101.
[123] For a less rosy picture, see Laville, "In the Politics of the Rainbow." Given the social unrest of early 1999, this caution would seem warranted.
[124] McCourt and Ramgutty-Wong, "Limits to Strategic HRM," 612.
[125] Carroll and Carroll, "Accommodating Ethnic Diversity in a Modernizing Democratic State," 139.

ethnic mosaic and the pervasiveness of intricate sub-ethnic divisions resulted in a pattern of unstable and constantly shifting coalition governments. All of these factors created a situation in which, despite public hostility and bickering between the economic and political elites, business and government were able to interact fruitfully on policy issues.

PART TWO

Business and the neo-patrimonial state

4 | The emergence of neo-patrimonial business in Ghana, 1850–1989

[In Ghana] a class of African businessmen, supplied with African capital ...
did not exist. [Instead,] there had arisen the large petty bourgeois stratum ...
which was able to step into the power vacuum caused by the absence of
a true African capitalist class.[1]

In contrast with South Africa and Mauritius, Ghana's economic history has been marked by an unhealthily close relationship between the fraternal worlds of money and power. In what later became south and central Ghana, an ongoing entanglement of political and economic elites was epitomized in the institutions of the pre-colonial Asante empire and colonialism did not necessarily disarticulate these linkages. Following independence, Kwame Nkrumah and the ruling Congress People's Party (CPP) institutionalized the dominance of the political sphere over the economic, consolidating a neo-patrimonial fusion of economic and political elites.

This was not inevitable. Given certain similarities, it is not unthinkable that Ghana's development might have more closely resembled South Africa's: like South Africa, Ghana had a leading sector (cocoa in Ghana's case)[2] which might have provided the basis for the development of an assertive, indigenous economic class. Ultimately, however, successive Ghanaian governments over-exploited that sector before it was yet strong enough to defend its interests. Instead of growing out of a profitable and market-driven cocoa sub-sector, much of Ghana's business class would emerge instead from a profoundly state-driven economy. And given that the state in question rapidly became neo-patrimonial, this pattern of development severely compromised the nature of the local capitalist class.

---

[1] Bob Fitch and Mary Oppenheimer, *Ghana: End of an Illusion* (New York: Monthly Review Press, 1966), 47.
[2] Ghana's gold mines were not as lucrative as South Africa's.

139

Two threads run through this story. The first is cocoa, which in Ghana is "king."[3] However, this potential source of capital and entrepreneurialism was bled dry; instead it was the state and, to a lesser extent, foreign firms that directed the development of the economy. The result was the growth of a state-based economic class. Much more so than in South Africa, the state constricted the development of a distinct entrepreneurial class. This, I will argue, was largely because the Ghanaian private sector was nascent at a point when the state had already acquired real muscle; later attempts in Ghana to foster indigenous business came too late, and only served to reinforce neo-patrimonial ties between business and the state. Neo-patrimonialism then, trumped any productive business–state engagement.

The second, and lesser, thread in this story is the impact of ethnic identifications on business–government relations, and the way in which these interacted with other political fissures. There is an important and recurrent overlap between three constituencies in Ghana: first, the people of the Asante region (ethnic identification), second, the cocoa-based entrepreneurial class (class identification), and, third, the liberal political tradition that emerges from that region and class (partisan political identification). For much of Ghana's post-independence history, the liberal, cocoa-based Asante elite did not dominate political power, but instead found themselves in some form of political opposition.[4] (The one exception was the government of Kofi Busia, 1969–72.) However, the role of ethnicity was rapidly overshadowed by changes in the country's resources base and the constitution of its economic elites. As state decisions became the major allocative mechanism, neo-patrimonialism became the dominant dynamic. As in South Africa, the degree to which the political economy was ethnicized varied over time but, overall, ethnicity and race featured at a substantially lower level in Ghana. Ethnicity did, at points, influence who was "in" and who was not, but the central determinant of power in Ghana was connections to the ruling party.

---

[3] Deborah Pellow and Naomi Chazan, *Ghana: Coping with Uncertainty* (Boulder, CO: Westview Press, 1986), 137.

[4] Again, this suggests the possibility of "the South Africa option." In South Africa, much of the business class identified with both political and ethnicized opposition to the state. See chapters 1 and 2.

The region that comprises modern-day Ghana is ethnically complex, the result of large-scale migrations and ongoing trade.[5] There are about a hundred distinct ethnic groups in Ghana[6] and some 44 percent of the population are from the large Akan group (including Asante, Fante, Nzima, and others).[7] The number of expatriates in Ghana is tiny – around 2 percent. While expatriates (for a time) disproportionately dominated some important sectors of the economy, they never dominated the economy's most important sector, cocoa. Nonetheless, their prominence obstructed the expansion of the local labor force and hindered local industrial development.[8]

I will argue that the dominant influence on Ghana's business class was not ethnicized politics but its own weakness and its relationship with a particular kind of state. This chapter will begin by considering how the yoking of political and economic power under the Asante state laid the basis for a neo-patrimonial political economy. The colonial government established diverse controls over the economy. These were consolidated after independence by policies that promoted the role of the state in fostering industrialization. However, rather than promoting competitive and independent entrepreneurs, many of these measures favored foreign firms and a class of state-dependent actors. The chapter concludes by considering the profound shift in government policy that commenced with the adoption of neo-liberal reforms in the mid-1980s.

The pre-colonial origins of Ghana's entrepreneurial class

As in Zambia, the business community in Ghana grew out of a historical relationship with the state. Unlike Zambia, however, Ghana possessed more fertile soil for an indigenous business community. In colonial Ghana (then known as the Gold Coast), an indigenous economic stratum was associated with the remnants of the Asante kingdom, its gold and its cocoa farmers.

The territory which became Ghana has a long, lively trading tradition.[9] The Asante empire of the eighteenth century was built on a prosperous

---

[5] Pellow and Chazan, *Ghana*, 96.   [6] Ibid., 100.   [7] Ibid., 3.   [8] Ibid., 148.

[9] Polly Hill, *Studies in Rural Capitalism in West Africa* (Cambridge University Press, 1970), 7. Douglas Rimmer, *Staying Poor: Ghana's Political Economy 1950–1990* (Oxford: Pergamon Press, 1992), 18.

trade in gold, ivory, and slaves. Locals exported other commodities too such as palm oil and timber,[10] but ultimately those would all be overshadowed by cocoa. The growing prominence of the British in the region, their abolition of the slave trade, and their later annexation of the southern states began to change some of these economic patterns.[11] Asante accumulation patterns in the eighteenth and nineteenth centuries also began to be reorganized around participation in the Asante state as "membership in the state became the only certain avenue to the possibility of acquiring great wealth."[12]

Colonialism and the Ghanaian political economy

Asante society was divided into three classes: chiefs, ordinary citizens, and slaves.[13] Prior to the emergence of chiefdoms, economically successful individuals in the region were recognized simply with the title of "big men." However, in the eighteenth and nineteenth centuries, the increasingly institutionalized Asante state "politicised, structured and formalised this crucial appellation."[14] War and trade respectively presented the two most common means of economic accumulation.[15] This was not asocial capitalist accumulation by atomized profit-seekers. It was profoundly political and closely connected with the Asante state. It was also profoundly social in two senses: first, it relied on social networks and, second, the possession of wealth imposed on the wealthy a social obligation to use their resources to bolster the collective fortunes of the Asante state.

Political and economic power in Asante was embodied in the Golden Stool (or Sika Dwa), "the highest level at which political power was exercised," and the Golden Elephant Tail (or Sika Mena), "the highest level at which wealth was appropriated." As Wilks describes it, these two institutions epitomized the link between money and advancement:[16] Access to one (say, political power) provided

---

[10] Adu Boahen, *Ghana: Evolution and Change in the Nineteenth and Twentieth Centuries* (London: Longman, 1975), 89.

[11] Ibid. See also Rimmer, *Staying Poor*, 19.

[12] T. C. McCaskie, *State and Society in Pre-Colonial Asante* (Cambridge University Press, 1995), 38.

[13] Boahen, *Ghana*, 102.

[14] McCaskie, *State and Society in Pre-Colonial Asante*, 42.   [15] Ibid., 52.

[16] Ivor Wilks, *Forests of Gold: Essays on the Akan and the Kingdom of Asante* (Athens, OH: Ohio University Press, 1993), 144.

access to the other (economic power) and vice versa, generating a tradition "of using political authority to accumulate, display and enjoy wealth."[17] This is far from the liberal ideal of a public sphere of government that is structurally and politically separate from the private sphere of commerce.

In any state, taxes are perhaps the most obvious connection between private wealth and the political power of the state. The Asante state employed a range of "taxes" including tolls, fines, and death duties. On the death of a wealthy man, all of his stores of gold dust would accrue to the king.[18] This transfer was not always without conflict; there were a number of independent-minded businessmen who resisted taxation. McCaskie describes how, in the late 1870s, Asante reacted against the new king and, in particular, against the death duties: "Taking as their model the individuals' rights of disposition over wealth in English law, and the low level of taxation apparent in *laissez-faire* capitalism as practiced in the Gold Coast Colony, they totally repudiated the fiscal and political authority of the Asante state."[19] The economic elite were learning the benefits of systems of economic exchange that provided a higher degree of autonomy – and a lower level of taxation – for their class. Ultimately, however, that elite did not decisively win their battle. This is important because "[m]any of the ways of looking at money, commerce, land, office, investment, and consumption described ... for nineteenth century Asante are still important determinates of behaviour in late twentieth century Ghana, and constitute a set of constraints upon the emergence of a capitalist order."[20]

The pre-colonial Asante kingdom had facilitated trade and production in a number of ways, including the enforcement of a single currency zone and the securing of trade routes.[21] The humiliating sack of Asante's capital, Kumasi, in 1874 by the British dramatically reduced the political underpinnings of much of this authority, not least through the abolition of the slave trade, which forced Asante traders to redirect their attention to gold, rubber, kola nuts, and,

[17] Rimmer, *Staying Poor*, 46–7.   [18] Wilks, *Forests of Gold*, 147.

[19] McCaskie, *State and Society in Pre-Colonial Asante*, 71.

[20] Wilks, *Forests of Gold*, 159.

[21] Gareth Austin, *Labour, Land and Capital in Ghana: From Slavery to Free Labour in Asante, 1807–1956* (Rochester, NY: University of Rochester Press, 2005), 40–1.

ultimately and perhaps most profitably, cocoa.[22] Because it damaged
the political authority of the Asante state, this moment presented an
opportunity for the flourishing of an organized "middle class" that
defined its interests separately from the polity.[23]

The emerging cocoa industry was "an exclusively Ghanaian enterprise achieved by Ghanaians themselves since all the cocoa was produced on farms of varying sizes owned and operated by Ghanaians."[24]
Commercial cocoa production for export purposes really began in the
late nineteenth century when Tete Quashie planted cocoa in Akuapem
and made his first export of cocoa six years later.[25] The region
presented ideal growing conditions for the cocoa plant, cultivation
spread quickly, and cocoa rapidly became Ghana's biggest and most
important export.

The development of this sub-sector thus presented an opportunity
for the emergence of an indigenous capitalist class. The cocoa sub-
sector was developed with very little help from the colonial government[26] or from the large commercial (mostly foreign-owned) banks
who did very little lending to Ghanaians. Instead, those who needed
money to expand their businesses or invest in their farms had to rely on
their personal connections.[27] Nonetheless, the sub-sector flourished.[28]

By the end of the colonial period, half of the adult male population
of Asante was profitably engaged in cocoa production.[29] This represented "a massive process of indigenous capital accumulation."[30] Had
this process of capital accumulation been fostered, institutionalized,
and diversified, the Ghanaian political economy might have developed
in a very different direction. Instead of powering the growth of a full-
blown capitalist class, however, cocoa "became a fount of public
employment and instrument of political patronage,"[31] as the colonial
state sought to regulate the sub-sector. By establishing a mono-
psonistic marketing board, the state effectively "taxed" cocoa farmers,
paying them a lower price than they would have received on an

---

[22] Ibid., 47–8.
[23] As the state weakened, the logic goes, so would the connections linking the
political and economic class, allowing for the emergence of a less politically
dependent economic class. Wilks, *Forests of Gold*, 158.
[24] Boahen, *Ghana*, 92.   [25] Pellow and Chazan, *Ghana*, 23. Boahen, *Ghana*, 92.
[26] Rimmer, *Staying Poor*.   [27] Ibid., 39–40.
[28] Pellow and Chazan, *Ghana*, 23.
[29] Austin, *Labour, Land and Capital in Ghana*, 51.   [30] Ibid., 68.
[31] Rimmer, *Staying Poor*, 202.

open international market and pouring the difference into the state's coffers.[32] This effectively reduced the impact of market-related incentives on the sub-sector, substituting instead the regulatory power of the state.

There was another lucrative natural resource that might have succored the development of a local capitalist class: gold. The region had long been famed for its gold wealth, and the Asante mined the precious mineral using labor-intensive methods up to the late twentieth century. Despite its home-grown origins, however, gold mining quickly came to be dominated by European investors and firms who began to acquire concessions in gold-rich areas during the 1870s. Three Fante businessmen, Messrs Biney, Brown, and Ellis, were the first owners of a lucrative Obuasi mine that would ultimately form the core of the giant mining corporation, Ashanti Goldfields.[33] The three entrepreneurs commenced mining operations in 1890, employing 200 men.[34] Before the end of the decade, however, unable to access the credit that they needed to further develop the mine, they sold their concession to an Englishman who would found the Goldfields Corporation.

This story mirrored broader trends: indigenous miners were confounded by their lack of credit to purchase new technologies, thus facilitating expatriate buyouts of lucrative concessions, not only for gold but also for other minerals such as manganese, diamonds, and bauxite. These transactions were not always and only disadvantageous to locals (some local tribal authorities benefited from mining concessions).[35] Nonetheless, the end result was domination of the gold sub-sector by expatriates.[36] The same trend prevailed in the timber industry: because of the capital requirements there, timber too came to be dominated by expatriates.

There were important individual exceptions: Austin points to Bibiani Logging and Lumber, owned by B. N. Kufuor, as well as the firms of P. A. Yeboah and W. K. Enmin.[37] In addition, there was some

[32] P. T. Bauer, *West African Trade* (New York: Augustus M. Kelley, 1967), Rimmer, *Staying Poor*, Fitch and Oppenheimer, *Ghana*, 44–52.

[33] T. E. Anin, *Essays on the Political Economy of Ghana* (Ilford, Essex: Selwyn Publishers, 1991), 39. For more on Ashanti Goldfields, see chapter 5.

[34] Boahen, *Ghana*, 94.   [35] Pellow and Chazan, *Ghana*, 22–3.

[36] Boahen, *Ghana*, 96, Austin, *Labour, Land and Capital in Ghana*, 53.

[37] Austin, *Labour, Land and Capital in Ghana*, 54.

indigenous activity in the service sub-sector, notably transport. Extremely competitive commercial lorry fleets were Asante-owned and run in the early twentieth century – but these were exceptions.[38] The origins of Ghanaian manufacturing, for example, lay with the missionaries. Peil argues that the first modern industry in Ghana may have been the Presbyterian Press, set up in 1859 in Accra. Over the next six decades, other enterprises followed, including saw milling, furniture manufacture, oil crushing, and car assembly. The Accra Brewery which opened in 1931 was, she argues, the first firm to use large-scale production methods.[39] But all of these ventures were dominated by foreigners.

There was some attempt to "Africanize" the managerial structure of British companies in West Africa. This was not easy as many of the country's "best and brightest" preferred careers in the public sector, rather than the private. Milburn cites the following communication by Holts Company in West Africa in January 1949: "Some District Agents have told us, from time to time, that they are having difficulty in obtaining learners and cadets with suitable educational qualifications and of the right type; and that the best products of Yaba, Achimota and King's College Lagos, are going into Government Service."[40] As independence approached, firms became increasingly conscious of the need to promote Africans within their ranks, but they did not appear to make great progress.[41]

There is some debate about whether the colonial government promoted or limited the operation of market forces.[42] In its earliest incarnations, the relationship between business and the colonial government was relatively hands-off. Pellow and Chazan describe British indirect rule up till 1927 as "*laissez-faire*," "intended to back up the native authority in the colony states and no more."[43] After the 1930s, however, the colonial government adopted a more interventionist role, epitomized by the purchase and marketing of cocoa.

In the late 1930s, cocoa planters organized a series of cocoa boycotts.[44] These "hold-ups," intended to challenge the effective tax on

[38] Ibid., 68.
[39] Margaret Peil, *The Ghanaian Factory Worker: Industrial Man in Africa* (Cambridge University Press, 1972), 14.
[40] Josephine Milburn, *British Business and Ghanaian Independence* (London: C. Hurst and Company, 1977), 74.
[41] Ibid., 95–6.   [42] See Austin, *Labour, Land and Capital in Ghana*, 27.
[43] Pellow and Chazan, *Ghana*, 19.   [44] Ibid., 26.

the cocoa farmers, had also been intended to loosen the stranglehold of expatriate firms on the purchase and marketing of cocoa. Rather than being abolished, however, the marketing board was refashioned in 1939 to fall under the direct control of the colonial government. With this quiet, incremental step, the institutional foundation of a new form of state-based accumulation was reinforced.

With the benefit of hindsight, this might have been the single most consequential act for business–government relations; it would privilege the state over any nascent capitalist class as the leading economic actor in Ghana, transforming the relationship between the state and a core economic commodity. According to Austin, "[t]his institutional innovation began a trend in the political economy of Ghana, for the substitution of administrative and political mechanisms, including patronage, for the market as the major channels through which resources were allocated and fortunes pursued."[45]

World war further bolstered the role of government and further restricted the opportunities available to Ghana's entrepreneurs. Until the 1920s, Ghanaians had been active not only in the production of cocoa but also in its purchase, buying from farmers and selling into international markets.[46] However, strict wartime quotas favored European firms and eroded the position of Ghanaian importers.[47] Many of the smaller Ghanaian enterprises suffered from shortages of supplies and trained personnel,[48] and European traders, formerly confined to the coast, began to expand into the interior. Syrian and Lebanese firms had also become more active from the late nineteenth century on. By the end of the 1930s, few Ghanaian firms survived.[49]

In the late 1940s the colonial government established the Industrial Development Corporation (IDC), which initially operated mostly "as a loans board."[50] Later, Peil argues, it became more entrepreneurial, establishing a number of firms of its own.[51] In contrast with the relatively efficient and market-related activities of the South African IDC, however, many of these enterprises failed because of "inadequate planning, poor demand for the products and/or poor management."[52] By 1962, when the surviving IDC-funded industries

---

[45] Austin, *Labour, Land and Capital in Ghana*, 39–40.
[46] Boahen, *Ghana*, 97. [47] Ibid., 157.
[48] Peil, *The Ghanaian Factory Worker*, 14. [49] Boahen, *Ghana*, 97.
[50] Ibid., 156. [51] Peil, *The Ghanaian Factory Worker*, 17. [52] Ibid.

were transferred to the Ministry of Industries, the IDC had fallen "prey to political manipulation, being used to provide employment for party supporters, to purchase privately owned businesses at inflated prices, and to make unsecured loans to political clients."[53]

British rule constructed in Ghana a paradigmatic colonial economy, dominated by the production for export of unprocessed natural resources (cocoa and, to a lesser extent, gold and timber). The racial hierarchy of political power was reproduced within the ranks of the emerging business community: Garlick describes a pyramidal structure with a small number of larger, interterritorial European firms forming the apex, large and medium-sized Indian and Levantine firms below that, smaller Indian, Levantine and African firms below that, and the base of the pyramid comprised by thousands of petty African traders.[54] As Ghana moved toward political independence, the level of involvement of European firms dropped and the state began to assume even greater prominence.

The movement toward political independence

As the basic institutions of a future Ghanaian economy were being established, so too were those of the country's political future. The United Gold Coast Convention (UGCC), a liberal political party, was founded in the 1940s. The party's support base lay in Ashanti and with coastal Akan groups[55] and was profoundly middle class: business people, cocoa farmers, and professionals. Crucially, UGCC represented a broad liberal strain in Ghanaian politics. Known as the Busia-Danquah school, it tended to regard business as "the principal engine of Ghana's economic development and to view the role of government as being to facilitate the activities of the business sector."[56]

Hoping to boost their popular appeal, the party leadership invited Kwame Nkrumah to become the organization's Secretary General.

[53] Rimmer, *Staying Poor*, 64.
[54] Peter C. Garlick, *African Traders and Economic Development in Ghana* (Oxford University Press, 1971), 7.
[55] William Easterly and Ross Levine, "Africa's Growth Tragedy: Policies and Ethnic Divisions," *Quarterly Journal of Economics* 112, no. 4 (1997): 1218.
[56] Joseph Ayee, Michael Lofchie, and Caroline Wieland, *Government–Business Relations in Ghana: The Experience with Consultative Mechanisms* (Washington, DC: Private Sector Development Department, The World Bank, 1999), 3.

Nkrumah was perhaps the most prominent Ghanaian nationalist leader at the time and the UGCC were delighted when he accepted their invitation. However, Nkrumah was schooled in radical politics and deeply suspicious of businesspeople and before too long he chafed at the UGCC's policies. Over time, tensions between liberal and radical factions split the movement, creating a political fissure that continues to characterize present day Ghanaian politics. Nkrumah quit the UGCC and established instead the rival Congress People's Party (CPP).

In contrast with that of the UGCC, Nkrumah's support base was the urban working class, war veterans, some poor farmers, and the unemployed. While far from communist, the CPP was distinctly anti-capitalist in its outlook. It saw the business sector as inherently exploitative and corrupt,[57] implicated in the structures of colonialism. Rejecting the liberal model, the Nkrumahist tradition instead supported a state-centered model of development.

Nkrumah's CPP decisively won the 1951 election and Nkrumah was released from jail to become the Leader of Government Business. The colonial government that Nkrumah was made the leader of was relatively small and undeveloped, employing under 90,000 people[58] – but if the Ghanaian public sector was relatively undeveloped, its private sector was even less so. There were very few large private firms and almost all of those were foreign- or expatriate-owned.[59] The CPP won the 1954 election too, preparing the way for independence under the rule of the CPP.

Chazan and Pellow argue that Nkrumah's top priorities included, first, securing his political support base and position, and, second, consolidating the state's control over the lucrative cocoa sector. These goals were linked: as Nkrumah moved loyal CPP activists into key government positions, he was better able to reward his urban supporters.[60] Cocoa profits were especially important for this. In 1952 then, the CPP government created the Cocoa Purchasing Company as an agency of the Cocoa Marketing Board (CMB) – and, in effect, of the CPP too: "all of the directors of the Company were leading figures in the CPP and most of its loans were given (on very lenient terms) to farmers who joined the farmers' Council and those whose support was

---

[57] Jerry John Rawlings echoed these same themes later.
[58] Rimmer, *Staying Poor*, 41.   [59] Ibid., 43.   [60] Pellow and Chazan, *Ghana*, 31.

needed by the party."[61] Two years later, despite having promised farmers that he would raise the cocoa price, Nkrumah supported a bill that would freeze it. The cocoa sector was effectively being stripped of its ability to organically "seed" a new capitalist class.

Nkrumah's first decade in government did not present a complete break with the policies of the colonial government; indeed, many of his policies extended trends begun under colonialism. The civil service, for example, was the same service that had administered the colony. Historically, that bureaucracy had been relatively well regarded and the new Ghanaian recruits to the civil service were of high caliber. This reputation was compromised, however, by the "enormous growth" in hiring that commenced just before independence:[62] In 1949 there were 17 Ghanaians in senior civil service positions; by 1957 there were 3,000.[63] Furthermore, the civil service itself increasingly was over-shadowed by the rise of a "parallel bureaucracy" in the CPP as the party assumed prominence in day-to-day decision making.

The CPP used two strategies to entrench its position, namely the deliberate channeling of economic resources from the state to the party, and the systematic hobbling of opposition parties[64] – both of which pushed Ghana's political system further in a neo-patrimonial direction. Boahen noted "disturbing elements of hero-worship and blind adulation of the party leader coupled with regrettable evidence of dictatorship and intolerance of criticism within the ruling party."[65] The pluralism of the broader political system was compromised by the repression of the opposition National Liberation Movement (NLM) and by growing disdain for other political parties.

The government sought to co-opt or repress a wide range of voices in the society. Since at least the 1940s, the relationship between the unions and government had been "close," reinforced, Rimmer argues, "by the circumstances that government was itself the predominant pro-vider of regular jobs."[66] Over time, however, the Trades Union Congress was subordinated to the ruling party, "so that it became an agent for promoting government policy rather than workers' demands."[67]

---

[61] Rimmer, *Staying Poor*, 47. Victor T. Le Vine, *Political Corruption: The Ghana Case* (Stanford, CA: Hoover Institution Press, 1975), xix.
[62] Le Vine, *Political Corruption*, 92.   [63] Boahen, *Ghana*, 178.
[64] Pellow and Chazan, *Ghana*, 38–9.   [65] Boahen, *Ghana*, 179.
[66] Rimmer, *Staying Poor*, 37.   [67] Peil, *The Ghanaian Factory Worker*, 227.

Likewise, suppressing the indigenous private sector was an important part of consolidating the state's political power. Here again, Ghana differs from South Africa. While in South Africa the Afrikaner government tried to downplay the power of mining capital by promoting manufacturing, the Nkrumah government had no interest in displacing cocoa entrepreneurs with any other potentially uppity businesspeople. A close confidant of Nkrumah, Dr. Ayeh Kumi, argues that Nkrumah was motivated by the fear that "if he permitted African business to grow, it will grow to the extent of becoming a rival power to his and the party's prestige[sic]" Kumi continues: "It was not possible to enact a law against private Ghanaian businessmen; what was done was to place a squeeze on them and their operations. The banks were not allowed to offer them credit and if they had to, it should be up to a certain limit only. They were not to be issued with enough licenses for importation, they should buy through large firms or government agencies."[68] The initial impulse of the new Ghanaian state was not to foster an indigenous business community, but to quash it.

The second strategy of the CPP, namely the appropriation of state resources, went well beyond the flow of funds from state to party. In the post-independence era, there was "a great increase in corruption in public life."[69] The expanded role of the state in the wider economy and the growth of state corporations and marketing boards in particular provided many opportunities for growing corruption.[70] The linkages between economic and political elites that had been a legitimate and explicit feature of Asante reemerged under the CPP:[71]

the politicians showed great enterprise in maximising the new income opportunities to which their positions gave them access. A good many were small businessmen and contractors before they went into politics in the mid [19]50s; these men simply continued and expanded their business activities while in public office. In addition, many who came to government from the civil service and professional ranks started businesses while they were in office.

A neo-patrimonial system then that extended well beyond the public sector to thoroughly encompass the private sector was consolidated with the advent of formal political independence.

---

[68] Cited in Anin, *Essays on the Political Economy of Ghana*, 59–60.
[69] Boahen, *Ghana*, 179.   [70] Le Vine, *Political Corruption*, 17–18.
[71] Ibid., 63–4.

Independence and the flowering of neo-patrimonialism

Nkrumah

On 6 March 1957 Ghana won its independence from colonial rule. It was by no means a rich country, but its overall fiscal situation looked relatively healthy. Ghanaians enjoyed the highest per capita income in the region[72] and the ratio of the country's debt to the value of its exports, for example, was less than 0.5 percent, a very favorable ratio.[73] The country had accumulated significant foreign reserves that were ten times the level of the country's relatively insignificant foreign debt.[74]

The source of both the country's wealth and its vulnerability was cocoa. Ghana produced more than one-third of the world's total supply of cocoa and, in turn, the trade provided more than two-thirds of the country's export earnings and employed one-fifth of its labor force.[75] By contrast, manufacturing was almost nonexistent: in 1960, a mere 9 percent of the employed worked in that sub-sector.[76] Although Ghana's dependence on cocoa was not as severe as, say, Zambia's dependence on copper, it nonetheless complicated any attempts at economic diversification.[77] And there were signs of trouble ahead: while world consumption of cocoa was rising, production was rising faster and would cause a long-term drop in price.[78]

While cocoa production was dominated by locals, the formal business sector in Ghana was not: 90 percent of the import trade was controlled by foreign firms, 96 percent of timber concessions were owned by foreign firms, all of the country's gold mines and half of its diamond concessions were foreign-owned, and banking and insurance were overwhelmingly dominated by foreign firms and ownership.[79]

Nkrumah was deeply motivated to secure Ghana's total economic independence from both the British and the capitalist world system of which they were a part. This goal, Pellow and Chazan argue, "could be achieved either by state control or by the establishment of an

---

[72] Pellow and Chazan, *Ghana*, 140.   [73] Rimmer, *Staying Poor*, 40.
[74] Baffour Agyeman-Duah, "Ghana, 1982–6: The Politics of the PNDC," *Journal of Modern African Studies* 25, no. 4 (1987): 615.
[75] Pellow and Chazan, *Ghana*, 138.
[76] Peil, *The Ghanaian Factory Worker*, 1.
[77] Pellow and Chazan, *Ghana*, 139.
[78] Ibid., 137.   [79] Boahen, *Ghana*, 196.

indigenous entrepreneurial class."[80] Such a class could have been fostered from among the ranks of the prosperous Akan and their educated professional offspring, from the Asante cocoa growers, and from the ranks of the chiefs – but many here opposed Nkrumah politically and were aligned instead with the UGCC and NLM. Not surprisingly then, Nkrumah chose state control, and the state that he built was increasingly buttressed by neo-patrimonialism.

Given the importance of cocoa both politically and economically, Nkrumah sought to bring more of the sector under state control. In the mid-1960s, Nkrumah subordinated the large cocoa farmers into the United Ghana Farmers' Council (UGFC) as part of a broader attempt to weaken those constituencies that had supported his political opposition.[81] He also took more explicit steps to suppress dissent. In 1957, for example, his government passed the Avoidance of Discrimination Act, and a year later the Preventive Detention Act. Both of these measures were actively used against those perceived as hostile to the ruling CPP.

The growing prominence of the state in the economic sphere began to blur any distinctions that might have existed between the public and private sectors. Garlick outlines the cases of two prominent Ghanaian citizens who epitomized the fusion of political and economic power (they were both successful businessmen and high-profile politicians). The first of these, C. C. K. Baah, owned an important building construction firm and served as a back-bencher of the CPP government; in 1964 "almost all" of his business came from government contracts. However, after speaking out publicly against the government's tax policy and fearing for his safety, he hurriedly left the country. The second case, that of A. W. Wiafe, is similar. He was the owner of Youngsters Stores Ltd. and a ministerial secretary who had benefited from a "substantial" allocation of the limited number of import licenses. After publicly criticizing the government's economic policies, he was detained under the Preventive Detention Act.[82] The state could grant access to economic goodies to its favored sons, but it could also withdraw it – and did so in response to the slightest dissent.

---

[80] Pellow and Chazan, *Ghana*, 148–9.   [81] Ibid., 45.
[82] Garlick, *African Traders and Economic Development in Ghana*, 120–1.

Ostensibly, economic policy-making in Nkrumah's Ghana was guided by a succession of developmental and seven-year plans. However, the private sector remained firmly "outside the plan"[83] – or at least, the Ghanaian private sector did. Instead, Nkrumah's government developed a series of policies that, to the extent that they boosted private business at all, favored international and foreign-owned business. Initially Nkrumah's government was not unduly concerned about the role of expatriate firms in the Ghanaian economy. Syrian and Lebanese retailers flourished in the late 1960s[84] and "the government went out of its way to give grants and interest-free loans to expatriate mining companies that were not making much profit, thus enabling them to continue in operation."[85]

The Ghanaian state focused on expanding its own role in the economy and in the key agricultural sector. In 1957, the government established the Ghana Farmers' Marketing Co-operative and the Ghana Co-operative Marketing Association (the latter competed with the expatriate firms and ultimately forced their withdrawal from the field). In the financial sector, the Ghana Commercial Bank was established in 1952 and, within eight years, controlled almost half of all deposits and credits by commercial banks.[86]

For its part, the state itself was also increasingly "Ghanaianized"[87] – and, in the process, its character was systematically molded in a neo-patrimonial direction. The relative independence of the civil service, for example, was undermined in 1961 when Nkrumah personally assumed control of public service appointments.[88] Having once been a genuinely popular party, the CPP's support base became narrower over time and the party lost much of its coherence; increasingly, its program centered on Nkrumah and on the maintenance of his political power as he became "a cult figure, a deity, and the sole decision maker in Ghana."[89]

Constitutional developments reinforced these processes. In 1960 Ghana became a republic, granting an indefinite term of office to President Nkrumah. In a referendum four years later, an "implausible" 99.9 percent of voters[90] supported the transformation of the republic into a one-party state. These two acts, Frimpong-Ansah argues,

---

[83] Rimmer, *Staying Poor*, 87.   [84] Boahen, *Ghana*, 197.   [85] Ibid.
[86] Ibid., 198.   [87] Pellow and Chazan, *Ghana*, 44.
[88] Le Vine, *Political Corruption*, 92.   [89] Pellow and Chazan, *Ghana*, 41.
[90] Le Vine, *Political Corruption*, xx.

constructed "a highly state-centric system with power concentrated in the President," which led to the further "reduction of competition within and outside the party."[91] In addition to expanding the overall number of government departments, the 1960 constitution facilitated the process by which "[t]he party machine began to encroach on the process of administrative decision-making."[92]

From 1960 on there was a dramatic intensification of these policies as governmental decision making turned in a more determinedly "Nkrumahist" direction. Government spending grew in the late 1950s in preparation for the "big push" of the 1960s.[93] According to Rimmer, Nkrumahism advocated "a larger public sector, growth in the bureaucratic regulation of economic life, and the discouragement of large-scale private enterprise, more especially if it was African."[94] The "Plans" and "Programs" that followed[95] would increasingly sideline the private sector. Indeed, Nkrumah explicitly warned that Ghanaians "would be hampering [their] advance to socialism if [they] were to encourage the growth of Ghanaian private capitalism in [their] midst."[96] Instead, the state (and party) bureaucracy should be bolstered, and SOEs would drive industrialization.

In 1961, the government established the Ghana National Trading Corporation (GNTC)[97] and, a year later, the State Farm Corporation.[98] In addition, the UGFC replaced the Cocoa Purchasing Company; henceforth, instead of competing with expatriate firms, the state-run Council would serve as the only licensed buyer of cocoa and, increasingly, also as a "repository of patronage."[99] State-owned industries proliferated in the 1960s[100] but failed to advance a sustainable process of industrialization. Those that were profitable "owed their profitability to monopoly power, protection against imports, preferment in the allocation of import licenses and implicit subsidization through input prices."[101] Most of these enterprises, however, simply became a drain on the treasury. More insidiously,

[91] Jonathan H. Frimpong-Ansah, *The Vampire State in Africa: The Political Economy of Decline in Ghana* (London: James Currey, 1991), 97.
[92] Ibid. [93] Rimmer, *Staying Poor*, 79. [94] Ibid., 85.
[95] Ibid., 87. Pellow and Chazan, *Ghana*, 43.
[96] Garlick, *African Traders and Economic Development in Ghana*, 122–3.
[97] Ibid., 122. [98] Pellow and Chazan, *Ghana*, 149.
[99] Rimmer, *Staying Poor*, 78. [100] Peil, *The Ghanaian Factory Worker*, 17.
[101] Rimmer, *Staying Poor*, 91.

they impacted the broader patterns of accumulation: instead of fostering a competitive economy, state enterprises "became avenues for private accumulation for fractions of the national bourgeoisie which were either located in the CPP bureaucracy or in a position ... to manipulate the party and state bureaucracies."[102]

In 1961 open general trading licenses in Ghana were revoked. Henceforth, the GNTC would be the country's principal importer and marketer of foreign goods. In the same year, the State Mining Corporation was granted control of six mines. Similarly, the Accra State Diamond Mining Corporation assumed control of all diamond mining in Ghana. The State Construction Corporation was established in 1962 and, within just a couple of years, had secured three-quarters of all state construction work.[103]

In the industrial sub-sector, the number of state-owned enterprises grew from thirteen to twenty-two by 1965, when twenty more such industries were also being built.[104] In a single year the number of state-owned firms in manufacturing jumped from thirty-eight to forty-six.[105] By 1965[106]

[t]here were thirty-one ministries, the functions and responsibilities of which had been periodically reshuffled. [There were fifty-three s]tate enterprises ... and there were also a dozen joint state/private enterprises and two dozen public boards, but it is not certain that anyone knew at the time how many of these bodies there were (certainly no-one was keeping count of the debts they contracted).

These institutions were established and maintained because they were integral to the support base of the ruling party.[107] This bolstering of the bureaucracy and SOEs began to shape the country's class structure and "established a new social stratum directly dependent on the state."[108]

Over time, neo-patrimonial modes of behavior became an attractive and even necessary part of operations not only for those working in the state, but for private businesses too. The allocation of import

---

[102] Kwame A. Ninsin, "State, Capital and Labour Relations, 1961–1987," in *The State, Development and Politics in Ghana*, ed. Emmanuel Hansen and Kwame A. Ninsen (London: CODESRIA Book Series, 1989), 20.
[103] All from Boahen, *Ghana*, 213.   [104] Ibid., 214.
[105] Peil, *The Ghanaian Factory Worker*, 17.   [106] Rimmer, *Staying Poor*, 91.
[107] Pellow and Chazan, *Ghana*, 149.   [108] Ibid., 45.

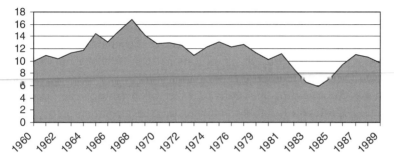

Figure 4.1 Government consumption of expenditure, Ghana (% of GDP)
Source: World Development Indicators, World Bank Group

licenses was a key example and "decent importers were compelled to accept improper methods of obtaining licenses as the only means to survive."[109]

I have argued that Nkrumah's initial economic policies (implicitly at least) favored foreign capital and the state, suppressing prospects for the emergence of a distinct, prosperous, and structurally powerful indigenous private sector. Even as the Ghanaian government began to shift its strategy and to foster a home-grown set of private enterprises, state and foreign interests had already been accorded decisive dominance of the economic terrain. Crucially too, this new effort "took the form of discriminating against foreigners,"[110] rather than creating a market-friendly environment.

To nurture the development of local firms and operations, the government adopted exchange control and import licensing measures. Consequently, Ghana's imports increased steadily alongside government expenditure. These bills were not matched, however, by growing receipts from the country's exports;[111] and ever rising government spending posed the danger that government expenditure soon would exceed the revenue it could collect (see Figure 4.1).[112] The danger did not take long to materialize: by 1962, the government had effectively

---

[109] Quoted in Rimmer, *Staying Poor*, 94. Originally from Government of Ghana, 1967, *White Paper on the Report of the Commission of Enquiry into Alleged Irregularities and Malpractices in Connection with the Grant of Import Licenses*, Accra: Ministry of Information W.P.4/67
[110] Rimmer, *Staying Poor*, 105.   [111] Pellow and Chazan, *Ghana*, 44.
[112] Rimmer, *Staying Poor*, 79–80.

exhausted once substantial CMB surpluses; henceforth, increased government spending would be funded by borrowing.[113] However, those in government remained convinced that cocoa would save them. Cocoa production was on the rise, motivated by strong international prices. It hit its highest ever level in 1964/5 – a whopping 572,000 tons – consolidating its status as "the milch cow of the Ghanaian state."[114] Much of that revenue was plowed into attempts to industrialize the Ghanaian economy.

Nkrumah succeeded to a remarkable extent in transforming the Ghanaian economy. From a largely agricultural economy, it grew in the 1970s into one in which the industrial sector contributed almost 20 percent of GDP – but these advances came at a cost. Like many other newly independent states, the Ghanaian state did not have the capacity to play a dominant role in directing the economy. The result was both appalling inefficiency and corruption.

By 1965, less than 10 percent of state-owned factories were generating a profit. State farms had mostly "failed completely"[115] and corruption pervaded governmental instruments, including exchange controls and import licensing:[116]

Local elites ... lived or died on the basis of access to foreign currency ... [I]mport licenses were given out to government institutions, government corporations and companies that government, or government officials, had special interests in. Those who did not have privileged access through the government had to pay bribes of between 5 and 10 percent of the contract.

By all accounts, the state's involvement in the economy gave rise to extraordinarily high levels of corruption.[117] According to Le Vine:[118]

[an] important set of linkages was inherent in the relationship, both formal and informal, between Nkrumah and his principal economic and financial advisers, between various government units and the Ghanaian business

---

[113] Ibid., 80.   [114] Ibid., 113.   [115] Boahen, *Ghana*, 216.

[116] Jeffrey Herbst, *States and Power in Africa* (Princeton, NJ: Princeton University Press, 2000), 218.

[117] In Zambia, the high regard with which Kenneth Kaunda was held as well as his own levels of personal integrity are generally credited with having kept corruption there at acceptable levels. In Ghana, Nkrumah's demise and the chaotic array of inept leaders that replaced him provided no equivalent check. Cf. Le Vine, *Political Corruption*.

[118] Ibid., 74.

community, and between all these interests and the several secretariats that controlled such entities as the state corporations and in turn were controlled (after 1964) by the president. This large and somewhat ponderous aggregation contributed many of the most important components in a system of intermeshing networks of corruption.

In a dynamic reminiscent of the workings of the Asante empire, political and economic power fused in post-independence Ghana: "Political power," Rimmer argues, "was regularly sought as a means of accumulating personal wealth, which was desired not only for its own sake but for the prestige it conferred in dealing with dependants and clients. No less significantly, political support was given in the firm expectation of material recompense."[119]

One might imagine that these trends would alienate at least some fractions of business, and to some extent they did. However, the relationship between business and government was not one of simple opposition. As in Zambia, entrepreneurs based in the state exploited their political access to acquire wealth; these individuals moved with facility between the "public" and "private" sectors, further blurring the identities and functioning of the two spheres.

Ultimately, the result of all of these efforts to bolster the power of the state was to undermine its developmental effectiveness. Under Nkrumah's rule, Ghana's foreign reserves were almost completely depleted and the country's external debt grew 2,000 percent.[120] By 1964, Nkrumah and the CPP had "reduced the role of the state to that of a dispenser of patronage."[121] The organizational coherence of both the civil service and the ruling party was in decline. Power lay no longer with the CPP, but instead with particular individuals.[122] Worse, the person at the centre of that system, Nkrumah himself, seemed to be falling apart; according to Boahen, "Nkrumah became obsessed with his own power and ambition; he also became the subject of a most nauseating personality cult, and most surprisingly of all, he became superstitious, corrupt and immoral."[123] On 24 February 1966, while on a trip abroad, Nkrumah was displaced by a coup which established a military government led by the National Liberation Council (NLC).

[119] Rimmer, *Staying Poor*, 97.   [120] Figures from Boahen, *Ghana*, 216.
[121] Pellow and Chazan, *Ghana*, 45.   [122] Rimmer, *Staying Poor*, 70.
[123] Boahen, *Ghana*, 209.

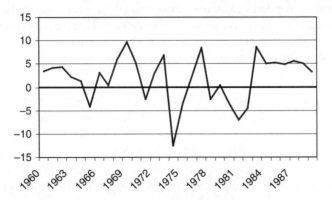

Figure 4.2 Ghanaian GDP growth (annual %), 1960–1989
Source: World Development Indicators, World Bank Group

The remainder of this chapter will review developments between the fall of Nkrumah and the end of the 1980s. Sadly, the economic and political decline that had commenced toward the end of Nkrumah's rule intensified after his removal from office (see Figure 4.2). The successive coups and ongoing malgovernance that followed brought abrupt changes of policy and mixed fortunes for the business sector, but never provided a sustained period in which the growth of that sector was possible.

Post-Nkrumah – a liberal interlude?

Led by Lt. General Ankrah and with the assistance of the World Bank and IMF, the new NLC government undertook some stabilization and liberalization measures. Economic policy moved rightwards as the NLC divested some SOEs and state farms, and provided more support for private business, temporarily boosting business confidence.[124]

Initially it seemed that both the NLC and Busia governments were more partial to the concerns of business than the CPP had been. In practice, however, what this meant was that these governments were more inclined to take a number of anti-market measures to boost the position of Ghanaian businessmen: "So far as the NLC and Busia

---

[124] Garlick, *African Traders and Economic Development in Ghana*, 129.

government did encourage private enterprise," Rimmer concludes, "it was in an illiberal way."[125]

There was some consultation with British firms about economic policy[126] and spotty evidence that the government was hearing some of the concerns of local businesspeople too. Chief among these concerns was the prominence of Pakistani, Indian, Syrian, and Lebanese traders. In response to lobbying by Ghanaian businesspeople for protection against this and other international competition, the government enacted the 1968 Ghanaian Enterprises Decree[127] according to which all small firms would be restricted to Ghanaian ownership.

Declining economic conditions in Ghana fueled resentment of the economic activities of expatriate businesspeople[128] (and even of non-Ghanaian Africans such as the small but not negligible number of Nigerians). The 1969 Aliens Compliance Order expelled 150,000 foreigners (mostly other Africans) who lacked the proper documentation to legally live and work in Ghana.[129] The Ghanaian Business (Promotion) Act of 1970 raised the capital limit on wholesale and retail firms with sales of less than NC500,000; it further restricted petty trading, commercial transport, printing, baking, and the manufacture of cement blocks to Ghanaians.[130] As Garlick remarks, with these steps the government effectively eliminated competing foreign firms.[131] Far from being pro-business, these measures damaged the Ghanaian economy, "dissolving crucial trade networks, making certain commodities altogether unavailable, and depriving the country of the expertise necessary in running such business."[132]

In the management of the public sector too, there was an ideological shift, but no sustained measures to improve institutions' quality or effectiveness. Rather, the bureaucracy was further politicized by a purge of the civil service in which it seemed that only the positions of those who were Akan were secure, inflaming suspicions of ethnicized partiality on the part of the government.[133] The SOEs were transferred to the Industrial Holding Corporation and, in keeping with the

---

[125] Rimmer, *Staying Poor*, 126.
[126] Milburn, *British Business and Ghanaian Independence*, 112–13.
[127] Pellow and Chazan, *Ghana*, 53.   [128] Ibid., 43.
[129] Rimmer, *Staying Poor*, 126.
[130] Peil, *The Ghanaian Factory Worker*, 16–17.
[131] Garlick, *African Traders and Economic Development in Ghana*, 131.
[132] Pellow and Chazan, *Ghana*, 148.   [133] Ibid., 55. Rimmer, *Staying Poor*, 107.

more liberal stance of the new government, some of the worst per-
formers were privatized or closed.[134] Despite the government's
apparent liberal turn, Rimmer notes that "forty-three of the fifty-three
public enterprises and boards in being at the end of 1965 were still
operating in 1971 and five such bodies were newly created."[135] That
was the extent of the "reform" of this sector.

To be fair, the reform program of the Busia government was fore-
shortened: following the government's devaluation of the currency in
1971, it was displaced by another military coup. The new government, the Supreme Military Council (SMC) of Colonel Acheampong,
immediately revalued the currency[136] and made a sharp turn back to
the left. Acheampong's government moved against the foreign owners
of capital: in 1973 the state acquired controlling shares in four
timber firms and, two years later, in the mining company Ashanti
Goldfields.[137] The government declared that henceforth it would own
a specified percentage of all firms producing necessities such as soap
or petroleum products. It further extended the requirements for
Ghanaian ownership by firm size and in banking and insurance.[138]

Deprived of much-needed imported inputs and investment capital,
the capacity of industry and manufacturing shrank – and, along with
it, the overall economy. Rimmer outlines the "plunge into the abyss of
national poverty" that followed.[139] Since 1970, he argues

income per head had fallen by three-tenths, real wages by four-fifths, import
volume by two-thirds and real export earnings by half; the rate of exports to
GDP had been reduced from 21 to 4 percent, the domestic savings rate from
12 to 3 percent and the investment rate from 14 to 2 percent; and the
government's debt had risen from 0.4 to 14.6 percent of GDP and now
constituted 65 percent of its total spending.

This significantly shaped the emerging economic elite – and its economic base:[140]

Ghanaians report that the country's rent-seeking officialdom benefited even
amidst this decline. By the 1970s it had [become] painfully obvious that
Ghana had become polarised into two fundamentally opposed classes. The

---

[134] Peil, *The Ghanaian Factory Worker*, 17.   [135] Rimmer, *Staying Poor*, 125–6.
[136] Easterly and Levine, "Africa's Growth Tragedy," 1218.
[137] Rimmer, *Staying Poor*, 164.   [138] Ibid., 164–5.   [139] Ibid., 133.
[140] Le Vine, *Political Corruption*, 14.

division was not one of socio-economic class, as between capitalists and workers, but between political groupings. The operative socio-economic divide was between governmental officials who had access to rent-seeking opportunities and Ghanaians who did not.

The result was not only a bifurcated Ghana but also a bifurcated business community: one stratum was state-based[141] and sympathetic to the state-led model of development; the other was generally associated with the opposition, and concentrated in the professional and trading classes.

The retreat into subsistence

Acheampong governed for six years before being replaced from within the military by Lt. General Fred Akuffo, heralding a period of even greater political and economic disruption. In the decade from 1972 to 1982, there were five changes of government in Ghana, and only one of those occurred by constitutional means (compare this figure with Mauritius' record of exceptional stability where a single government was in office during the same decade, returned to power in each instance by constitutional means).[142] The condition of the state became so degraded that one analyst coined the term "the vampire state" to describe its relationship with the economy and broader society.[143]

The state-based sector continued to expand, even as the "real" economy deteriorated. The result was constantly shrinking output and the increasing "informalization" of the Ghanaian economy. The term used in Ghana to describe this black market economy was *kalabule*, defined by Agyeman-Duah as "the system of economic graft that created almost instant cedi millionaires through fraud and manipulation in the poorly regulated business sector."[144] The black market currency exchange premium, for example, reached its "historical peak" in 1982: the exchange rate as traded in the back alleys of Accra was twenty-two times what you would get from official sources![145]

---

[141] In the sense that even if the individual businessperson in question was not formally employed by the state, the conduct of business and opportunities for profit were reliant on state-based activities.

[142] Rimmer, *Staying Poor*, 142. See chapter 3 for Mauritius.

[143] Frimpong-Ansah, *The Vampire State in Africa*, 111.

[144] Agyeman-Duah, "Ghana, 1982–6," 627.

[145] Easterly and Levine, "Africa's Growth Tragedy," 1218.

The economy had become one that was dominated by the incentives emerging from state-driven behavior: "everyone's advantage was served if he or she could buy or borrow in the official economy and sell or lend in the parallel economy." Consequently, "realization of the subsidies implicit in official prices became the leading purpose of commercial activity and a major use of labor resources" – hardly productive economic activity.[146]

As the neo-patrimonial state was consolidated, the citizenry's attitudes toward that state further exacerbated the cycle of corruption: "To Ghanaians, government means power located on a 'no-man terrain,' somewhere in Accra. It is considered a tribute to one's smartness to be able to steal huge sums of money from that land, without being detected."[147]

While the Ghanaian economy shrank in the 1970s,[148] government spending continued to increase.[149] The output of gold dropped to half the level of the early 1960s.[150] Those expatriate businesspeople and foreign investors who had not already been excluded by legislative measures, now withdrew from an economy in which it was extremely difficult to continue to operate.[151]

By the late 1970s the economy was in a state of "unprecedented" chaos.[152] Official cocoa exports fell to a miserly 177,000 tons,[153] decimated by cross-border smuggling and the lack of incentives for farmers to invest in new trees. In addition, the price of coca had collapsed from £3,000 per ton in the late 1970s to £800 in 1982.[154] The result was a further drop in government revenue[155] and, on the part of farmers, a further retreat into subsistence. In the decade after 1973, the economy shrank at an annual average rate of 1.3 percent.[156] Manufacturing and industry plunged as a share of the economy.

---

[146] Rimmer, *Staying Poor*, 168.
[147] J. Mawuse Dake, "Reflections on Party Politics and Impact on Democratic Development in Ghana," in *Civil Society in Ghana*, ed. F. K. Drah and M. Oquaye (Accra, Ghana: Friedrich Ebert Foundation, 1996), 93.
[148] Rimmer, *Staying Poor*, 133.   [149] Pellow and Chazan, *Ghana*, 154–5.
[150] Ibid., 142.   [151] Ibid., 148.   [152] Ibid., 58.
[153] Rimmer, *Staying Poor*, 145.   [154] Agyeman-Duah, "Ghana, 1982–6," 629.
[155] Rimmer, *Staying Poor*, 157.
[156] Economist Intelligence Unit, *Ghana Country Profile 1990–91* (London: Economist Group, 1990), 13.

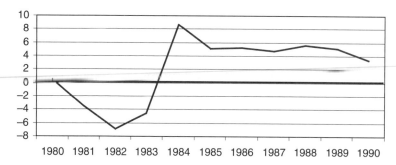

Figure 4.3 Ghanaian GDP growth (annual %), 1980–1990
Source: World Development Indicators, World Bank Group

By the early 1980s, over 80 percent of those formally employed in all industries were employees of the public sector.[157] While those associated with the state-based political elite had been the most obvious beneficiaries of the system, ultimately the whole system was undermined from within. As the economy approached collapse, the capacity of both the private and the state-based sectors to continue to support the ever expanding networks of patronage and rent-seeking decreased, inciting a series of political crises.

Enter Jerry Rawlings

The apparently miraculous way in which the government of Jerry John Rawlings ("JJ") engineered the recovery of the Ghanaian economy after 1983 (see Figure 4.3) led some of his more enthusiastic supporters to dub him "Junior Jesus." The tale of his first and second coming has been told often and only a brief account will be offered here. Twice (first in 1979 and then again in 1981) Rawlings the populist revolutionary came to power by military means on an avowedly anti-elite mission. In both instances, he almost immediately attacked the wealthy and influential, blaming them for the country's woes.[158] More modest citizens such as street traders and market

---

[157] Figures from Ghana's Statistical Services, *Quarterly Digest of Statistics*, Accra, Ghana. Quoted in ibid., 16.

[158] *Ghanaian Times*, 7 July 1979, cited in Jeffrey Herbst, *The Politics of Reform in Ghana, 1982–1991* (Berkeley, CA: University of California Press, 1993), 26.

women were also targeted. Several marketplaces in major cities were razed, including, most famously, Makola market in Accra.

The result was not cheaper or more easily available goods but "enhanced deprivation"[159] as the range of goods for sale shrank and their black market price rose. Individual traders and businesspeople were interrogated about their income. Their stocks were confiscated and some individuals were publicly flogged.[160] An embittered business community did not soon forget these humiliations.

Under the governance of the Armed Forces Revolutionary Council (AFRC) there was an abrupt intensification of class antagonism, along with heightened ethnicized tensions.[161] People's Defence Committees and Workers' Defence Committees were created to police the measures put in place by the government, such as price controls.[162] These devolved forms of political authority and the profoundly anti-elitist views of the AFRC produced some "excesses": "People with private cars were ridiculed as 'exploiters', and many Ghanaians of high social or business standing were removed from their posts without any evidence of malpractice."[163] Rawlings developed a reputation for being "anti-business" and "anti-profit."

The two military Rawlings governments were separated by an all-too-brief period of democratically elected government (1979–81) under the leadership of Hilla Limann. Conditions were hardly ideal for the consolidation of that democracy, however. When Limann's government floundered, Rawlings moved again in 1981 to assume power by force, this time under the Provisional National Defence Council (PNDC), by which time "the center of Ghana had virtually collapsed."[164]

Policy-making in the PNDC

Economic policy under Rawlings in this first phase resembled the populist and protectionist model of policy under Acheampong. The PNDC government took a decision, for example, to freeze private

---

[159] Joseph Abbey, Personal interview with author, 7 March 2001.
[160] Rimmer, *Staying Poor*, 169.   [161] Pellow and Chazan, *Ghana*, 50.
[162] See Agyeman-Duah, "Ghana, 1982–6," 618–20.   [163] Ibid.: 620.
[164] Pellow and Chazan, *Ghana*, 75.

bank accounts.[165] Rawlings himself regarded businesspeople and traders as exploitative profiteers:[166]

They say there is a lot of money in the country, but we know that this is in the hands of only a few very rich people. Therefore, if you sell your goods at high prices, what you are saying is that only the rich should be able to buy. The poor people cannot buy. If they cannot buy, they will be forced to steal in order to be able to buy, it is therefore in the interest of all to ensure that prices are within manageable limits … If this appeal is not heeded to, we shall be left with no alternative but to use our own method to ensure that citizens are assured decent living.

The PNDC "method" proved ineffective and only served to further alienate "[t]he declared enemies of the [Rawlings] revolution," the entrepreneurial classes.[167] Okudzeto quotes from the statement issued in response to the murder of three High Court judges in June 1982: "There has been a systematic campaign of 'hate' setting the so-called 'rich' against the so-called 'poor.' Achievement has become a national crime."[168] Inflation rose to its highest rate ever – over 100 percent[169] – and there were repeated attempts to overthrow the government in its first few years in office.

In 1983, the Ghanaian economy was hit by two more traumatic events: first, a severe drought, and, second, the forced and sudden repatriation of, by some counts, more than a million Ghanaians from Nigeria.[170] The returnees went from being a source of remittances for their families, to yet another mouth to feed in an already desperate economic situation. Now, "[e]ven the members of what had once been prosperous classes were visibly malnourished."[171] As the informal economy grew, the state's control and resources shrank accordingly.

---

[165] Agyeman-Duah, "Ghana, 1982–6," 635.

[166] Jerry John Rawlings, *A Revolutionary Journey: Selected Speeches of Flt. Lt. J. J. Rawlings, Chairman of the Provisional National Defence Council, December 31 1981 – December 31 1982*, vol. 1 (Tema, Ghana: Information Services Department, Ghana Publishing Corporation, undated), 9.

[167] Frimpong-Ansah, *The Vampire State in Africa*, 112.

[168] Sam Okudzeto, "The Role of the Association of Recognised Professional Bodies in the Political Struggles of Ghana," in *Civil Society in Ghana*, ed. F. K. Drah and M. Oquaye (Accra, Ghana: Friedrich Ebert Foundation, 1996), 117.

[169] Frimpong-Ansah, *The Vampire State in Africa*, 112.

[170] Rimmer, *Staying Poor*, 178.   [171] Ibid., 179.

These events intensified a raging policy debate within the PNDC between the "scientific socialists" who equated profit with exploitation,[172] and the "moderates" who argued that, given the bankruptcy of the state, there was no option but to move in a neo-liberal direction.[173]

As a rule, the charismatic and energetic Jerry Rawlings was central to PNDC decision making. However, Rawlings was less interested in the details of economic policy-making and so here he delegated authority to his Finance Minister, Dr. Kwesi Botchwey.[174] The National Economic Review Committee (ERC), established to "take stock" of the economy, revealed the completely desperate state of the government's finances, and underlined the urgent need to seek donor support.[175] Botchwey had previously been a relatively orthodox Marxist. Confronted with the full dimensions of the crisis, however, he resolved on a pragmatic set of policy options. The policy document that was to form the basis of Ghana's negotiations with the IFIs was dramatically revised, from an earlier "left-of-center" version to a more circumspect statement.[176]

The policy battle within the PNDC was effectively settled when the country's international socialist allies refused its requests for assistance, referring the Ghanaians to the IMF and the World Bank. The year 1983 brought, not so much a change of heart as a change of key personalities as the ultra-leftists departed and the moderates launched a distinctly neo-liberal Economic Recovery Programme (ERP).[177]

This second phase represented a profound shift, not only for the Rawlings regime, but indeed in the broader management of the country's economy. It was characterized by relatively rigorous adherence to the broad elements of the Washington consensus. Between 1983 and 1986, the ERP, designed and directed by the small but influential ERC, undertook most of the steps generally considered necessary to stabilize an economy in crisis.[178] Structural reform, intended to alter fundamentally the nature of the Ghanaian economy

---

[172] Frank Damali, Personal interview with author, 27 March 2001.
[173] Agyeman-Duah, "Ghana, 1982–6," 630–1.
[174] Atu Ahwoi, Personal interview with author, 5 April 2001.
[175] Abbey, Interview.   [176] Ibid.
[177] P. V. Obeng, Personal interview with author, 11 April 2001, Kwesi Jr. Pratt, Personal interview with author, 30 October 2000, and Alban Bagbin, Personal interview with author, 20 March 2001.
[178] Obeng, Interview.

(exports in particular) and to advance price and currency reform, began in 1987.

Agyeman-Duah describes "four pillars" of the economic recovery program: liberalized trade and exchange policies; assistance to the agricultural sector (and cocoa in particular) including higher prices for agricultural produce; the rehabilitation of the country's transport infrastructure; and the expansion of the country's energy supply.[179] The Investment Code, released in 1985, epitomized this new approach that was, in theory at least, more hospitable to business and the private sector.[180]

Little by little, the country's reform program won the confidence of the IFIs. Ghana's business and middle classes, however, did not warm to the PNDC.[181] Years of hostile relationships with a succession of governments, as well as the specific history of Rawlings and his followers, had rendered Ghanaian businesspeople cautious.[182] This was exacerbated by the PNDC's "excessively technocratic and bureaucratic" approach to policy-making, which did not institutionalize potentially reassuring consultations.[183] In addition, sections of the business community did not like the new scrutiny that they were subjected to as the government tried to tighten up accounting standards and ensure greater tax compliance.[184]

The Ghanaian political economy by the late 1980s

By the mid-1980s, there was evidence that the ERP was having some effect. Government revenue recovered[185] and economic growth

---

[179] Agyeman-Duah, "Ghana, 1982–6," 631–2.

[180] Government of Ghana, "Investment Code" (Accra, Ghana: Government of Ghana, 1985).

[181] E. Gyimah-Boadi, "The Search for Economic Development and Democracy in Ghana," in *Ghana under PNDC Rule*, ed. E. Gyimah-Boadi (London: CODESRIA, 1993), 8.

[182] Ernest Aryeetey, Personal interview with author, 2 March 2001. For an extended discussion of relations between the PNDC and the Ghanaian business community, see Roger Tangri, "The Politics of Government–Business Relations in Ghana," *Journal of Modern African Studies* 30, no. 1 (1992).

[183] Kwasi Anyemadu, "The Economic Policies of the PNDC," in *Ghana under PNDC Rule*, ed. E. Gyimah-Boadi (London: CODESRIA, 1993), 42.

[184] Professor E. Gyimah-Boadi, Personal interview with author, 13 March 2001.

[185] Jonathan H. Frimpong-Ansah, "Flexibility and Responsiveness in the Ghana Economy: Reflections on Post-Decline Atrophy Syndrome" (Accra, Ghana: Ghana Academy of Arts and Sciences, 1996), 50.

recovered decisively from the negative rates of the early 1980s (see Figure 4.3). Government spending moved into surplus and its arrears decreased steadily over the late 1980s.[186] By the end of the decade, the program was widely regarded by the IFIs as a success.[187]

Nonetheless, the reform process was far from complete. Crucially, by the end of the 1980s, the reforms had not achieved the long-anticipated recovery of the private sector. The reforms were also deeply unpopular with a range of important political constituencies, including sections of the middle class. It need not have been this way. The business community was a potential ally in the reform process. For instance, Anyemadu describes the agreement between the government and the Association of Ghanaian Industries, for example, on the need for a moderated program of trade liberalization.[188] Yet, almost a decade of structural adjustment had done little to repair the business–government relationship.[189]

Conclusion

Nugent observes of Ghanaian history that "if wealth could not always capture power, it was generally the case that political power opened up fertile lines of accumulation for those who enjoyed access to it. The leadership of the CPP was most adept at making the conversion … [but t]he overthrow of Nkrumah did not bring this pattern of politics to a definitive end."[190]

In this chapter, I have argued that Ghana's history produced a weak business community, characterized by its dependency on the state rather than by its efficiency as a productive sector. Nonetheless, the economic reforms instituted by Rawlings' PNDC government in the 1980s offered the prospect of a fundamental reshaping of the Ghanaian economy, and hence of the operating conditions for the country's private sector.

During the 1980s, these reforms had been implemented by government with almost no public debate, even with the most obvious

[186] Economist Intelligence Unit, *Ghana Country Profile 1990–91*, 12.
[187] Ernest Aryeetey, "Structural Adjustment and Aid in Ghana" (Accra, Ghana: Friedrich Ebert Foundation, 1996), 4.
[188] Anyemadu, "The Economic Policies of the PNDC," 29.
[189] Ayee, Lofchie, and Wieland, *Government–Business Relations in Ghana*, 4.
[190] Paul Nugent, *Big Men, Small Boys and Politics in Ghana: Power, Ideology and the Burden of History 1982–1994.* (Accra, Ghana: Asempa Publishers, 1996), 5–6.

constituency, namely business.[191] The business community had real concerns with the reforms but there were few avenues to communicate this sentiment in a helpful way to the government.[192] As one businessman described it: "If you open your mouth, you get cellotape on it."[193] It was not until February 1988 that the PNDC first agreed to meet publicly with private sector representatives.[194] The Government–Private Sector Dialogue, established at that time, did little to change the guarded nature of government–business interactions.[195] The suspicion was mutual although, once again, not uncomplicated. Nugent remarks[196]

that business remained ambivalent about the PNDC, while aspirant businessmen looked more kindly upon it. In view of the lengths to which the PNDC had gone to attract outside investment, the first half of this statement might occasion surprise. But there remained a legacy of suspicion towards the Rawlings regime that was born of the revolutionary phase and kept alive by Rawlings' periodic outbursts of populist hubris.

The opening of the 1990s brought with it an urgent need to broaden the debate about economic policy – particularly with the private sector, to ensure the sustainability of the reforms and the country's long-term economic recovery. The revival of economic activity associated with the ERP also "produced a different breed of elites. These entrepreneurs were, unlike many of their predecessors, neither linked to the state, nor dependent on its resources ... These elites began to serve as an important political counterweight to the state-based strata, thereby suggesting new bargaining possibilities absent in clientelistic frameworks."[197] Chapter 5 will assess the extent to which these possibilities were realized during the 1990s.

---

[191] Anyemadu, "The Economic Policies of the PNDC," 41.
[192] For example, Kraus records the unhappiness of the National Chamber of Commerce about the "draconian" interest rates. Jon Kraus, "The Political Economy of Stabilization and Structural Adjustment in Ghana," in *Ghana: The Political Economy of Recovery*, ed. Donald Rothchild (Boulder, CO: Lynne Rienner Publishers, 1991), 135.
[193] Phillip Y. Amakye, Personal interview with author, 26 March 2001.
[194] Ayee, Lofchie, and Wieland, *Government–Business Relations in Ghana*, 29.
[195] Unattributed, *People's Daily Graphic*, 22 May 1991.
[196] Nugent, *Big Men, Small Boys and Politics in Ghana*, 203.
[197] Naomi Chazan, "The Political Transformation of Ghana under the PNDC," in *Ghana: The Political Economy of Recovery*, ed. Donald Rothchild (Boulder, CO: Lynne Rienner Publishers, 1991), 29.

5 | State-dominant reform: Ghana in the 1990s and 2000s

The government kept saying that the private sector was in the driving seat but it was not. The private sector has been marginal all along.[1]

By 1990, the Ghanaian government was considered by some a model World Bank pupil. The first generation of neo-liberal reforms to restructure the Ghanaian economy had been completed successfully and the government was poised to introduce a second generation of reforms. The common wisdom among reform technocrats is that this second reform phase is difficult and, in contrast with the first phase of reform, that it requires high levels of cooperation from broader society and from the private sector in particular. There were thus strong incentives for the Ghanaian government to step up its consultations with business, and the World Bank urged it to do so. In addition, the business community in Ghana was slightly larger and more independent minded than its Zambian counterpart, or at least, much of it was. Despite all of these factors, business in Ghana had little influence on the course of economic policy in the 1990s. Why was this?

The answer, I will argue, lies in both the natures of the Ghanaian state and business sectors, and the character of their interactions. The Ghanaian private sector comprised elements that could be described as neo-patrimonial, as well as elements that were distinctively autonomous. The relationship between business and government in Ghana then was subject to a constant push and pull as a highly neo-patrimonial state sought to draw sections of business closer through patronage. Some businesspeople responded. Many others sought to retain some distance while still trying to win the government's ear for business' policy preferences.

---

[1] S. K. Apea, Deputy Secretary of the PNDC and Special Advisor to the Ministry of Finance, Personal interview with author, 20 March 2001.

The chapter opens with an outline of the shape of the Ghanaian economy and of the business sector in particular at the start of the decade. I then undertake a more thorough analysis of business' attempts to shape economic policy in the 1990s. Throughout the decade, management of the economy continued to be firmly lodged in the state and the impact of organized business on policy-making remained relatively low. In the conclusion I consider whether this may be changing.

The Ghanaian political economy: short on the middle

Ghana's economy provided a paradigmatic case of what the World Bank calls "the missing middle": it lacked a sizable, robust middle stratum of indigenous manufacturers and industrialists.[2] Instead, the Ghanaian economy was marked by the predominance of agriculture. The robustness of the services sub-sector was mostly due to the strength of, first, retailing, and, second, the state's involvement in the economy. In this sense, Ghana's development trajectory diverged significantly from the modernization model, which anticipated that societies would progress first from being agriculturally based to highly industrialized and would only then mature into economies dominated by services. In Ghana, much of the economy instead revolved around the state.

Despite fierce fighting between minor ethnic groups in the north during the 1990s, ethnicity did not play an overt part in the mainstream political process in Ghana – at least, outside Asante. Historically, Akan-speakers (associated with the Asante kingdom) tended to be the most prosperous sector within Ghana because of their prominence in cocoa, gold, and timber (see chapter 4). In the modern day, this translated into a large Akan presence within the business community. In the 1970s Garlick suggested that over 80 percent of the traders that he interviewed in Kumasi and Accra, the two largest commercial centers, were either Ashanti or Kwahu (both Akan-speaking groups).[3] This figure would probably be replicated by a similar study today. Given claims that the Rawlings regime tended to favor the

---

[2] Nugent eschews the use of the term "bourgeoisie" in Ghana. Nugent, *Big Men, Small Boys and Politics in Ghana*, 8.

[3] Garlick, *African Traders and Economic Development in Ghana*, 29.

political and economic fortunes of the Ewe, the ethnic identity of many in the business community reinforced their political estrangement from the Rawlings government.[4] Overall, however, ethnicity and ethnic conflict *per se* were not a prominent feature of Ghanaian politics.[5]

In the political terrain, the more important cleavages were expressed by personalized party affiliation. This significantly affected the relationship between business and the state – and here the contrast with Zambia is striking. While many Ghanaian businesspeople were politically active, relatively few were employed directly by the state, within either the civil service or the state-owned enterprise sector.[6] In addition, business in Ghana had long tended to be associated with Ghana's liberal political tradition (known there as the Busia-Danquah tradition, after two of its most famous local exponents) in direct political opposition to the mass-based Nkrumahist tradition.

While many in Ghana would contest Rawlings' assumption of Nkrumah's mantle, it was an identification that Rawlings and his supporters frequently made. There were attributes that the two leaders had in common. Like Nkrumah's Congress People's Party (CPP), Rawlings' Provisional National Defence Council (PNDC) frequently rested on charismatic appeals to the "common" person. The basis of political support in both cases was the urban-based working classes.

---

[4] This would, however, be less a factor than it was in either South Africa or Mauritius. See chapters 1–3.

[5] A survey of popular attitudes in July 1999 found that less than 3 percent of those interviewed "believed that a specific Ghanaian region had benefited from the Economic Reform Programme." There was, instead, a widely held belief that the country's economic elites had benefited disproportionately from the reform program. Center for Democracy and Development, "Popular Attitudes to Democracy and Markets in Ghana," in *Survey Report/CDD Research Paper* (Accra, Ghana: Center for Democracy and Development, 1999), 29–30. A similar view that ethnic conflict was not a particular problem in Ghana was found in a survey of elite attitudes, conducted in August 2000. Center for Democracy and Development, "Elite Attitudes to Democracy and Markets in Ghana," in *CDD-Ghana Research Paper* (Accra, Ghana: Center for Democracy and Development, 2000), 17–18.

[6] This may simply be a function of timing and generations. Given that Ghana attained independence in 1957, many of those originally employed by Nkrumah's government have since retired or passed away. By contrast, Zambia's more recent independence means that many of today's most prominent businessmen are precisely those "bright young things" who staffed that country's first post-colonial government.

This could be contrasted with the liberal and frequently elitist tone of the Busia-Danquah tradition and its contemporary incarnation, the New Patriotic Party (NPP). While figures on the funding of parties by business were impossible to come by, observers speculated that the NPP was generously supported by business.[7]

Ghana had a well-developed set of business institutions, many of which were sub-sector specific and many of which dated back only to the independence era. The oldest of these was the Association of Ghana Industries (AGI), founded in 1958 as the Federation of Ghana Industries. At the time of writing, it boasted 500 members, mostly small to medium-size industrialists.[8] In terms of policy preferences, the AGI pressed for stability of the exchange rate, and was often more protectionist than were other associations.

The Ghana National Chambers of Commerce and Industry (GNCCI or GNCC)[9] represented an overlapping if somewhat broader grouping. Established in 1961, the GNCC was an encompassing association whose membership included a high proportion of smaller indigenous businesses. The GNCC and AGI formerly had a competitive relationship and clashed on matters of policy. (The merchants, traders, and bankers who were members of the GNCC were more likely to be supporters of free trade and financial liberalization than their manufacturing colleagues in the AGI were.[10])

The Ghana Employers, Association (GEA) tended to represent the interests of larger firms. Like GNCC it drew membership from a range of sub-sectors of the economy. As the name suggests, the association's interaction with government tended to focus on labor issues.

The more recently established (1992) Federation of Associations of Ghanaian Exporters (FAGE) emerged in response to the new opportunities opened up by the liberalization of the previously moribund

---

[7] While certain businesspeople funded the ruling PNDC too, the level of support for the opposition NPP contrasted with the situation in Zambia where opposition parties found it difficult to attract any funding.

[8] Association of Ghana Industries (AGI, 2005 [accessed July 2007]) www. agighana.org/agi_info/about_us.htm.

[9] Commonly known just as the GNCC; this ellipsis betrays the extent to which the voice of the industrialists was muted in an association dominated by traders.

[10] See Elizabeth Hart and E. Gyimah-Boadi, *Business Associations in Ghana's Economic and Political Transition*, Critical Perspectives, no. 3 (Accra, Ghana: Centre for Democracy and Development, 2000): 9–10 for a discussion of the tensions between the AGI and GNCC.

export market. Accordingly, FAGE generally proposed further economic liberalization.

Overall then, Ghana had a private sector that was of more recent origin, less structurally powerful, and less internally diverse than that of South Africa or Mauritius. Much of business had neo-patrimonial ties to government, but the Rawlings government regarded liberal business as a political enemy. In terms of its levels of institutionalization, business in Ghana was probably in better shape than its counterpart in Zambia, but far weaker than in South Africa or Mauritius.

Economic policy-making in Ghana

Although there was probably more meaningful debate in the Accra legislature than in Lusaka, parliament in the Ghana of the 1990s was not particularly influential on economic policy matters. For his part, President Rawlings was also not preoccupied with these issues. This does not mean he was without influence. His broad preferences (and his suspicion of business) undoubtedly colored economic policy. Over time he developed strong patronage ties with particular businesspeople and these connections became important in the implementation of policy. When the PNDC first assumed power, an informal "kitchen cabinet" was where economic policy was cooked up. The 1990s started with the reformers still in a strong position in this cabinet. The section that follows examines particular policy areas of concern to business, beginning with a review of business–government relations.

The 1990s: one step forward, two steps back

By the 1990s, Ghana had successfully achieved much of the first generation of economic reforms: "getting the prices right," currency devaluation, and trade liberalization. The next generation of reforms would, business hoped, institutionalize economic recovery and boost the private sector's role in the economy.

Relations between business and government

I argued earlier that the Ghanaian political economy was marked by broad ideological differences between sections of the business community and the ruling P/NDC.[11] This affected both parties' attitudes:[12]

Government leaders point with pride to sixteen years of far-reaching economic reform and ask why their economic motives are still the subject of deep suspicion, while business leaders point to the anti-capitalist rhetoric of a few outspoken government leaders, as well as to the still incomplete reform agenda and incidents of past mistreatment as evidence that key governmental officials still view business in adversarial terms.

This distrust was reinforced by the political alienation of much of business from the NDC – although there were those who formed a close and profitable association with the ruling regime. Reform had opened up potentially lucrative new opportunities for the well-connected: "[b]y the early 1990s, it was possible to distinguish a stratum of *nouveaux riches* – people whose wealth had been acquired over a matter of years rather than decades. Whereas established wealth was orientated toward established political traditions, newcomers felt more comfortable within the embrace of the PNDC."[13]

The NDC established the Council of Independent Business Associations (CIBA) as a "government-friendly" alternative to existing business associations. It was supposed to represent twenty groupings of small entrepreneurs but, according to Sandbrook and Oelbaum, it was "a creature of government,"[14] dispensing patronage through tax-farming, and credit and resource allocations. Few business people regarded CIBA as representative of the private sector. Rather, they saw it as a cynical manipulation. According to the Director General of the Private Enterprise Foundation (PEF), "[the NDC] wanted to create their own forum; they wanted to create a new private sector from the

---

[11] The Provisional National Defence Council (PNDC) changed its name to the National Democratic Congress (NDC) in order to contest the 1992 elections but it was effectively the same party. To avoid confusion, I will generally use NDC; if I am referring only to the pre-1992 period I will use PNDC.

[12] Ayee, Lofchie, and Wieland, *Government–Business Relations in Ghana*, 4.

[13] Nugent, *Big Men, Small Boys and Politics in Ghana*, 204.

[14] Richard Sandbrook and Jay Oelbaum, *Reforming the Political Kingdom: Governance and Development in Ghana's Fourth Republic*, Critical Perspectives, no. 2 (Accra, Ghana : Centre for Democracy and Development, 1999): 20.

ranks of the NDC ... It was highly politicized and they used government funds to fund what was supposed to be the private sector."[15]

Patronage followed political contacts via licensing, divestitures, and government contracting practices,[16] and, as the decade progressed, allegations of irregularities were made in almost every commercial arena where the government interacted with business. (One newspaper described "mind boggling favouritism" in the award of government contracts.)[17] Given this background, it is not surprising that elections in 1992 and 1996 led to a hardening of attitudes. The government became more sensitive to criticism from the business community while business grew increasingly cynical about the government's commitment to market-based reform. Rather than viewing each other as partners in development, business and government came to see each other as political enemies.

In the 1996 elections, CIBA was once again used to shore up support for the NDC, distributing election paraphernalia and "gifts," including watches, sewing machines, and televisions.[18] At the same time, the NDC made a short-term effort to woo members of the business community. Leading newspapers carried advertisements explicitly directed at the Ghanaian business and professional classes, intended to assure them of the government's commitment to macroeconomic stability. The NDC sought to project itself as the party of responsible fiscal management – an image increasingly at odds with the reality, as I will outline below.

There was little evidence of significant financial support for the NDC from mainstream business; instead, the party's financial resources were widely seen as deriving from "kickbacks on government contracts, which were channelled into NDC coffers."[19] This period demonstrates a clear pattern in business–government relations: the NDC seeking the political support of businesspeople but alienating many legitimate businesspeople because of its partisan, corrupt behavior.

[15] Kwasi Abeasi, Personal interview with author, 6 April 2001.
[16] The *Ghanaian Chronicle* alleged that timber-export contracts were awarded to Mohammed Farouk on the basis of his "powerful connections at the Castle." Unattributed, *Ghanaian Chronicle*, 14–16 November 1994. Allegations were also made about government contracts for prisons procurement, lands, and cocoa.
[17] Unattributed, *The Statesman*, 26 February 1995, 1.
[18] Sandbrook and Oelbaum, *Reforming the Political Kingdom*, 14.
[19] Ibid.

In post-Rawlings Ghana, it is difficult to find a businessperson who will admit to having ever supported the NDC[20] but there *were* significant, reciprocal ties between elements of the state and sections of business. Certainly, all evidence is that levels of clientelism, patronage, and corruption climbed more steeply the longer the NDC was in office, and particularly after the return of party politics. I spoke to a member of one local family, prominent in the business community, who had formerly been associated with the opposition but had been forced to switch allegiance to the NDC in order to retain access to government contracts. He insisted that "[o]n paper, the [government's economic] policies were all the right ones, but behind the scenes there were all kinds of political maneuvering and shenanigans. At the absolute minimum, you needed to be politically neutral to be allowed to do business with the government."[21]

Finally, a word about probably the single most important employer in the country, Ashanti Goldfields (AGC). AGC had always had access to government that was the envy of other Ghanaian companies.[22] Partly, this derived from the size and importance of the company, but it also had to do with the warm personal relations that developed between the country's president, Jerry John Rawlings, and the CEO of AGC, Sam Jonah. Despite his neo-liberal reform credentials, Rawlings had never shaken his distrust of the Ghanaian business community. His reform program was intended to improve the capacity and productiveness of the private sector but that sector was barely consulted about how to accomplish this. Instead, the president tended to keep local businesspeople at arm's length – especially those associated with his political opposition.[23] Rawlings' relationship with Jonah seemed a striking exception to his relations with Ghanaian businesspeople generally; the two were regarded as friends and used to attend public sporting events together.

Atu Ahwoi, a beneficiary of the liberalization of cocoa marketing, summed up the impact of politics on the conduct of business in Ghana as follows:[24]

---

[20] Although clearly some firms did and individuals will happily report instances of others they know about who supported the NDC.

[21] Anonymous, Confidential interview with author, 14 March 2001.

[22] Samuel Dzotefe, Personal interview with author, 5 August 2004.

[23] Tangri, "The Politics of Government–Business Relations in Ghana."

[24] Atu Ahwoi, Personal interview with author, 5 April 2001.

[P]olitics permeates everything. We have not got a big private sector. Instead, the biggest supplier of contracts is the government. You have to know how to play your cards right. No matter what we say now, you had to deal with the fact that the government is everywhere. So, for example, to be able to buy cocoa, you have to register with COCOBOD and they have to approve your application. It is possible for government to pull the strings from behind in this regard. But it goes beyond that: because of the volume of money involved [in the purchase of cocoa], you will have to go to the banks for credit – and most of the banks are owned by government.

What was crucial was how the state shaped the behavior of business. Those businesspeople that associated with the opposition were castigated; by contrast, support for the regime was likely to prove remunerative. The situation was well described by Dr. Paa Kwesi Nduom in an after-dinner address: "When members of the opposition are denied business opportunities and seemingly successful people are assumed to be supporters of the ruling government, then we face a much bigger problem as a nation."[25]

In the discussion of policy cases that follows, when I speak of the preferences of the mainstream business community, I am referring to the policy preferences expressed by firms organized into formal business associations. After seven years of economic reform without consultation, their first demand was simply to be seriously consulted on matters of economic policy.

It's good to talk: policy consultation between business and government

Gyimah-Boadi and Hart argue that the reform process of the 1990s created two new challenges for business associations.[26] First, they had to deal with the decimation of their membership by the rigors of economic liberalization. Second, and perhaps more important, they had to negotiate a shift in their own organizational mandate. Previously an important function of business associations had been to "[m]ediat[e] negotiations between individual entrepreneurs and bureaucrats responsible for assigning import licenses and foreign exchange

---

[25] Quoted in Unattributed, *Ghanaian Chronicle*, 18–20 September 1995, 3.
[26] Hart and Gyimah-Boadi, *Business Associations in Ghana's Economic and Political Transition*, 5–8.

allocations."[27] Association membership had been "functionally required of almost any businessperson desiring access to government-controlled resources."[28] The dramatic shift in the regulatory environment wiped out this function.

Now associations had to carve out new raisons d'être. Increasingly, they shifted their attention to the overall policy environment, trying to influence that in the interests of their membership. Specifically, they sought stabilization of the macroeconomy, deepening of the financial sector and increased access to credit, a reduction in government spending, lower inflation, and some sought the divestiture of state assets. Business began to call for government to shift its focus, away from recovery to broad-based growth driven by more meaningful consultation with the private sector.

One of business' primary demands in the new decade was for institutionalized fora where it could press its policy interests with government. From 1983, despite the government's rhetoric about the private sector as the engine of growth, business had barely been consulted by government. When consultation did occur, it was generally the result of pressure from the IFIs. The World Bank in particular had come to regard the participation of a country's private sector in economic reform as key to its long-term success.[29] And so the government convened the Private Sector Advisory Group (PSAG) in February 1991.

The PSAG was a small, tightly knit grouping of some of the most powerful figures within the Ghanaian private sector, with similarly high-level representation from government, headed up by the reform-minded Finance Minister Kwesi Botchwey. It was closely associated too with the market-friendly P. V. Obeng, then Chairman of the Committee of Secretaries and *de facto* prime minister.[30]

The Group's mandate was tightly circumscribed: to examine the legal infrastructure that impeded the development of the private sector and recommend appropriate amendments. PSAG provided a prime opportunity for business leaders to speak directly with the government.

---

[27] Ibid.: 5.   [28] Ibid.: 5–6.

[29] For one of the best discussions of business–government consultations in Ghana, see Ayee, Lofchie, and Wieland, "Government–Business Relations in Ghana." I rely extensively on their analysis in this section.

[30] He had been in the private sector himself prior to entering the government.

They spoke clearly, and with effect. The government made a number of regulatory changes in 1992 to improve the environment for business, including the repeal of price-control laws and significant amendments to the Investment Code.

Nonetheless, perceptions persisted that the government was hostile to business. In 1993, for example, one of the president's speeches reportedly created "the impression that President Rawlings does not like Ghanaians who have been successful in private business."[31] The Chairman of Unilever, Ishmael Yamson, warned that the government's neo-liberal policy set would only succeed "if it is accompanied also by a fundamental change in the attitude of the bureaucracy in their new roles as economic facilitators rather than controllers."[32] In the same year, even Rawlings' one-time ally, the MD of Ashanti Goldfields, Sam Jonah, urged the creation of "an effective forum through which [well-meaning private sector people] can advance ideas for government's consideration."[33]

In an attempt to build on the success of the PSAG, the Private Sector Roundtable was set up in June 1993 and met on and off for a year. Private sector representation here was larger both in scope and in numbers than it had been in the PSAG, and business hoped that the Roundtable would prove as fruitful as the Group had been. Initial signs were promising. The Roundtable would be chaired by P. V. Obeng, the same Obeng who had been active in PSAG and had since been promoted to Presidential Advisor on Government Affairs.

However, the forum proved unwieldy and its mandate too generalized to succeed. Business was unable to agree on or articulate clear, easily achievable demands for government. Any prospects the Roundtable might have had were doomed when relations between the president and Obeng began to cool. In November 1993, the Roundtable issued a report to the government which was received and acknowledged, but the government never issued a substantive policy response to it. Obeng met with private sector representatives in 1994,

---

[31] Bradford Nyinah, "They Hate the Truth – President Rawlings," *People's Daily Graphic*, 19 June 1993.

[32] Faustina Ashirifie, "The Private Sector and Government," *People's Daily Graphic*, 27 October 1993.

[33] Sam Jonah, "The Private Sector in Ghana's Economic Development," *People's Daily Graphic*, 30 October 1993.

but little followed from these meetings.[34] Business leaders continued to call for ongoing consultation on both routine and urgent policy issues.

In 1994, key actors within the four major business associations (AGI, GNCC, GEA, and FAGE) decided to establish a vanguard to articulate their growing concerns about the macroeconomy.[35] They established the Private Enterprise Foundation (PEF) to "play a role in influencing policies and regulations of Government."[36] It was well placed to develop and articulate clear, economy-wide policy preferences and it quickly became the most important voice for business.

In March 1997, the new organization flexed its muscles, convening its own gathering at Akosombo. This was followed in June of the same year by a second conference in North Carolina in the USA. Both of these gatherings set out to "focus public attention on the recent poor fiscal performance of the Ghana government" and they succeeded in this. The two conferences highlighted the extent to which high levels of deficit budgeting were "impeding private sector growth."[37] The presence of Vice President Atta Mills was central to the success of these gatherings. Mills was both sympathetic to the private sector and on good terms with the president. Participants in these two conferences reported a growing, non-partisan sense of "Team Ghana" among the delegates, from the public and private sectors alike.[38] This may have been the high point of business' policy interactions with government.

Ayee, Lofchie, and Wieland argue that the PEF overreached itself with plans for a high-level follow-up summit in Ghana in September.[39] Having built consensus on the main economic problems, the PEF hoped to pin government down to concrete solutions. This provoked alarm at the Castle, home of the executive. Trenchant criticisms of

---

[34] Unattributed, "Government, Private Sector Hold Discussion," *People's Daily Graphic*, 12 March 1994.

[35] See reports in Unattributed, *People's Daily Graphic*, 26 January 1995.

[36] Unlike the other business associations, which are chiefly funded by membership subscriptions and in response to sector-specific concerns, the PEF derived the major share of its funding from international donors. This enabled it to develop a more organized secretariat, to rise above parochial or sector-specific policy problems, and to develop a broader vision of economic policy. However, this also raised questions about its legitimacy and the extent to which it truly represented local business. See Private Enterprise Foundation (undated pamphlet), 1. See also Unattributed, *Business and Financial Times*, 12–18 December 1994.

[37] Ayee, Lofchie, and Wieland, *Government–Business Relations in Ghana*, 36.

[38] Ibid.   [39] Ibid., 35–6.

government policy had emerged from the earlier fora; another such gathering, it was felt, could only be intended to embarrass the government. The Foundation's plans for a grand summit were downgraded to a lower profile "forum" to be hosted, not by the PEF, but by the government's own (politically marginal) Planning and Development Commission. The National Economic Forum, as it was called, met to no great effect. Government was simply not listening. Ayee, Lofchie, and Wieland conclude that "[t]he ability of Ghana's business community to use the policy dialogue to elicit a favourable policy response from the government remains very weak."[40]

Some blame might be laid at the door of the business associations. There appeared to be some hesitation about assertively confronting government, particularly as election-related political tensions developed. Certainly some criticized the PEF for being overly accommodationist: "The Abeasis of this world [Abeasi was then the Director General of the PEF] go out of their way to avoid confrontation with government. Despite the fact that they were not getting results, they continued to favor behind-the-scenes maneuvering rather than upfront confrontation. This perpetuates business' subordinate position vis-à-vis government."[41]

The situation worsened in the late 1990s. In his last eighteen months in office, Peprah, Rawlings' last Minister of Finance, did not meet once with business representatives. By the end of the decade, little progress had been made on bridging the gulf in the perceptions of organized business and the NDC. I now consider particular areas of policy reform.

The policy agenda

Access to finance
In my interviews, I asked a range of businesspeople, analysts, and business association officers what the greatest obstacle to private sector development was in the 1990s. Almost without exception, a single answer shot back: "lack of access to finance." However, on this, which was perhaps the single most important issue to the sector, the combined efforts of numerous associations and businesspeople had no discernible impact on the government policy.

---

[40] Ibid., 37.
[41] Professor E. Gyimah-Boadi, Personal interview with author, 13 March 2001.

Since the start of structural adjustment, business associations repeatedly petitioned government about the difficulties of accessing credit. In 1994, government set up the Business Assistance Fund (BAF). Funded by divestiture receipts, the fund was intended as a resource for troubled companies that had the potential to recover and compete in a liberalized environment. It was never clear just how that potential was to be judged, but the Fund was eagerly welcomed by business and, indeed, was rapidly oversubscribed. Anecdotal evidence suggests that, in at least some instances, disbursements from the Fund served as political patronage.[42] Certainly the repayment rate was pitiful.

While the BAF was welcomed by business, it did not address the root causes of the credit crunch, namely the government's fiscal and macroeconomic policies. Instead, government borrowing continued to have a "grievous" impact on private sector growth.[43] The government's crowding out of investment and the capital markets was to become the single most important policy issue for the private sector.

Getting and spending: government profligacy

On the revenue side, the Central Revenue Department achieved some success in increasing revenue collection.[44] Less successful was the plan to introduce VAT at 15 percent in 1993/4: the introduction of the new tax was badly bungled, resulting in rioting and deaths. Insufficient consultation with business was not least among the reasons for its failure. Businesspeople did not understand how the new tax was supposed to work, or its intended benefits for the economy.

On the expenditure side, there were even more serious problems, for which some blame the return to multipartyism. Under pressure from the IFIs, the PNDC had decided to return the country to multiparty rule in the early 1990s. Faced with an urgent need to build political

---

[42] Government was not solely to blame for this. The PEF also sat on the management committee of the BAF. In this respect, as in so many others, "irregular" practices were tolerated within both the public and private sectors.

[43] Institute of Statistical Social and Economic Research, *The State of the Ghanaian Economy in 1994* (Legon, Ghana: Institute of Statistical Social and Economic Research, University of Ghana, 1995), 14.

[44] Led by NDC lieutenant Atu Ahwoi, department investigations for tax evasion were used as a political weapon against opposition-minded professionals. See Eboe Hutchful, "Why Regimes Adjust: The World Bank Ponders its 'Star Pupil,'" *Canadian Journal of African Studies* 29, no. 2 (1995): 309.

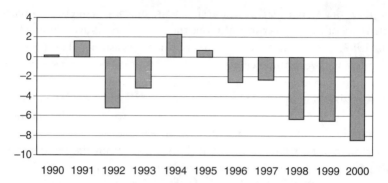

Figure 5.1 Ghanaian government fiscal balance (as % of GDP)
Source: Institute of Statistical, Social and Economic Research, University of Ghana, Legon

support, the Rawlings government acted as many others have done in such a situation, dramatically expanding government spending in the run-up to the election. The first big unbudgeted expense comprised wage increases for civil servants.[45]

Quite how badly fiscal discipline had slipped became evident only in the aftermath of the elections. Since 1986, Ghana had recorded almost continuous surpluses in the government budget. In 1992, however, a "substantial" deficit was recorded (see Figure 5.1).[46] The deficit, and

---

[45] The wage increases began with raises for staff at the Bank of Ghana and for lecturers at the country's tertiary institutions. This set off a "rush for the cake" as doctors, pharmacists, nurses, and staff of the railway corporation demanded similar treatment. Unattributed, *People's Daily Graphic*, 21 January 1993, 5. There has been some dispute about whether the wage increases awarded to civil servants in the run-up to the election were justified. There can be little doubt that wages in the civil service were appallingly low – so low indeed that they are widely regarded as a key explanation for corruption. Many would argue that there was a legitimate argument for reassessing wages. However, most agree that this should have formed part of a broader process of civil service reform that would have restructured the service as a whole. Needless to say, this broader reform did not occur and there is little evidence that the wage increases were anything more than a thinly disguised bid for political support. Center for Democracy and Development, "The Ghana Governance and Corruption Survey: Evidence from Households, Enterprises and Public Officials" (Accra, Ghana: Center for Democracy and Development, 2000), 17.

[46] Institute of Statistical Social and Economic Research, *The State of the Ghanaian Economy in 1992*, (Legon, Ghana: Institute of Statistical Social and Economic Research, University of Ghana, 1993), 10.

the government's emphasis on increasing its revenue rather than cutting its expenditure, became an ongoing bone of contention in business–government relations.

By 1995, the government's own past decisions had become a critical shaper of the budget. State spending was increasingly recurrent so that past budgetary decisions locked the government into future commitments. For some time, Finance Minister Kwesi Botchwey managed to mask spending trends and retain the confidence of the international community. However, these contradictions ultimately became too extreme for the Finance Minister to manage. He became increasingly frank about shortcomings in the government's management of the economy. In particular, he objected to the "woefully misleading and inadequate" projections that the government was setting for itself. He also publicly criticized the "gross abuse" of the procurement system, arguing that lack of transparency here was a major cause of government over-expenditure.[47] Needless to say, this criticism was regarded by many at the Castle as disloyal.[48] The minister was progressively sidelined in favor of such Rawlings loyalists as Tsatsu Tsikata. Botchwey resigned abruptly in 1995, allegedly over the profligacy of the Ghana National Petroleum Company (GNPC), headed up by Tsikata.[49] Business had regarded Botchwey as an ally and was alarmed by this turn of events.

1996 brought another round of elections and, to business' further dismay, another round of election spending and wage increases. The government appeared to have learnt nothing and none of the budgetary macroeconomic targets bar growth was met in that year.[50] The

---

[47] Unattributed, *The Ghanaian Chronicle*, 28–30 November 1994.

[48] "The Castle" is a reference to Christiansborg Castle (also known as Osu Castle), the seat of government in Accra.

[49] Regarded as wily, even brilliant, Tsikata appeared to lack the knack of profitably managing the country's petroleum resources. The company was hemorrhaging cash as a result of poorly judged investments, despite several sizable cabinet bailouts. Tsikata's closeness to the president rendered him unassailable, however, and his political fortunes prospered. He was invited to accompany the president on an investment-seeking trip to the UK, while the Finance Minister languished in Accra. Botchwey submitted his letter of resignation shortly after the delegation's departure for London.

[50] Institute of Statistical Social and Economic Research, *The State of the Ghanaian Economy in 1996* (Legon, Ghana: Institute of Statistical Social and Economic Research, University of Ghana, 1997), 1.

inducements to vote for the NDC went beyond handing out household appliances; they extended to the deployment of the budget. Government spending for that year was an increase of 40 percent on 1995 figures – which had in turn represented an increase of over 50 percent on 1994.[51] Wage increases to civil servants were only the most obvious part of the story. The government's capital expenditure program was designed to prove the NDC's commitment to politically important areas of the country. Perhaps the most cynical expression of this was articulated after the election in a disarmingly frank rebuke by Nana Rawlings, at Bonwire's Kente festival: "You people want to have development projects from us but you do not vote for us. How do we develop your area? You must know that the left hand washes the right hand whilst the right hand also washes the left hand."[52]

While there was a reduction in lending to the government by the Bank of Ghana in 1997, it was replaced by a sixfold increase in the rate of lending to the government by commercial banks! Government spending spiraled upwards as new commitments piled on top of past purchases that had yet to be paid for.[53] Government spending quickly began to impede the ability of firms to conduct business via its effects on interest rates, inflation and the financial sector or, in short, the broader macro-economy.

Macroeconomic management and inflation

The impact of government spending on broad macroeconomic indicators was not long in coming. In 1993, the annual rate of inflation almost doubled, precipitating a sustained debate about the root causes of the problem. Inflation created a number of problems for business, namely dollarization of the economy, depreciation of the cedi, and high interest rates. And, in order to protect themselves, businesspeople responded in ways that were often damaging for the economy, for

---

[51] Ibid., 29.

[52] Quoted in Unattributed, *Ghanaian Chronicle*, 14–15 January 1998.

[53] The problem was so serious that in early 2001 the incoming NPP government was unable to present a complete budget statement on Budget Day; they had no idea just what the government still owed by way of arrears. Institute of Statistical Social and Economic Research, *The State of the Ghanaian Economy in 1999* (Legon, Ghana: Institute of Statistical Social and Economic Research, University of Ghana, 2000), 35.

example by holding their assets in a foreign currency, thus exacerbating exchange rate depreciation and accelerating inflation.[54]

The impact of this macroeconomic climate and, in particular, high interest rates on the private sector should not be underestimated. In a submission to the vice president, the AGI gave the following example of the impact of the current interest rates: "a company which borrowed an equivalence of 200 million cedis in 1987 had an amount of 820 million cedis outstanding in 1993 after having paid a total amount of 404 million cedis in interest and principal payments. This firm did not only suffer from high exchange risk, it has also been exposed to an exorbitant domestic interest rate."[55]

Botchwey's successor as Finance Minister, Richard Kwame Peprah, had previously served as Minister of Mines. He lacked Botchwey's intellect and charisma. Crucially, he also lacked Botchwey's dogged determination to stick to the reform course, and the NDC's economic policy became fractured and directionless. Economic policy-making came to rest by default with its implementers (senior civil servants) and with self-interested interjections from various ministers and the president's wife.

In 1996, in response to the concerns of the Trades Union Congress, the government hosted a meeting on inflation with a variety of stakeholders, including business, at Akosombo.[56] The meeting attributed the high rate of inflation principally to the government's fiscal deficit[57] – but all of the debate and prognostication had little impact on government behavior. In the aftermath of Akosombo, the government's domestic debt continued to grow and the government made increased use of treasury bills that restricted the access of the private sector to credit.

The problem was not macroeconomic policy on paper. It was how the government chose to conduct the day-to-day management of its

---

[54] Institute of Statistical Social and Economic Research, *The State of the Ghanaian Economy in 1995* (Legon, Ghana: Institute of Statistical Social and Economic Research, University of Ghana, 1996), 40.

[55] Association of Ghana Industries, "Problems and Constraints Facing Industry in Ghana" (Accra, Ghana: Association of Ghana Industries, undated), 42.

[56] This should not be confused with the PEF's 1997 meeting at Akosombo.

[57] Institute of Statistical Social and Economic Research, *The State of the Ghanaian Economy in 1996*, Strategic African Securities, "Ghana's Economic Performance, 1990–1999: Lessons from the Analysis of Key Macro-Economic Indicators" (Accra, Ghana: Strategic African Securities, 2001).

finances. In his response to the government's 1995 budget, Ishmael Yamson, Chairman of Unilever Ghana and President of the GEA, argued that:[58]

[that] year's budget [would] be able to address the short term economic problems of the economy. "What is needed is that the government should stick to those measures without any deviation," he stressed. Commenting on some aspects of the budget in Accra yesterday, he said the budget will only be good *if the government will do what it has promised* with commitment.

Like the consultative meetings that preceded it, the Economic Forum in 1998 identified inflation as the most serious weakness of the Ghanaian economy and similarly argued that this resulted from government spending. Again, these observations had little effect. The continued upward trend in interest payments reinforced the government's shift away from capital spending and toward recurrent expenditure.[59] At the end of the 1980s, Ghana had been applauded for the improvement in its macroeconomic figures. By the early 1990s, it seemed that the much-vaunted reduction of the budget deficit had been achieved, at least in part, by cutting capital expenditure.[60]

The 1990s were supposed to be the decade in which Ghana would move from economic recovery to accelerated growth. Business had looked forward to higher levels of investment and a period of expansion and consolidation. Unfortunately this was not to be the case. Instead of the hoped-for improvement, "[v]irtually all macroeconomic indicators of a move toward accelerated growth were decidedly poorer [in the 1990s] than in the period before 1992."[61]

---

[58] Quoted in Unattributed, *People's Daily Graphic*, 11 February 1995, 1. My italics.

[59] Institute of Statistical Social and Economic Research, *The State of the Ghanaian Economy in 1997* (Legon, Ghana: Institute of Statistical Social and Economic Research, University of Ghana, 1998), 8.

[60] As Armah argues, "[s]uch trends are cause for concern since capital expenditure is a key indicator of investment expenditure. Investment in turn is imperative for growth since it expands the productive resources of the economy." Bartholomew K. Armah, *Reflections on the State of the Economy of Ghana in 1999*, Legislative Alert 6, no. 3, (Accra, Ghana: Institute of Economic Affairs, 1999), 3.

[61] Institute of Statistical Social and Economic Research, *The State of the Ghanaian Economy in 1993* (Legon, Ghana: Institute of Statistical Social and Economic Research, University of Ghana, 1994), 1.

Divestiture

The decision to "privatize" may represent a key moment in the relations between a government and its business community, between a country's public and private sectors respectively. After all, such a decision is, at the level of publicly stated policy at least, intended to take assets – and the power and influence in the economy that those assets represent – out of the hands of the state and put them into the hands of the private sector. Yet all too often, the intended diminution of the state's role in the economy does not occur. Privatization may instead reinforce the power of state-based political elites (when the sale, for example, is made to someone who is a client of key political figures). Whatever the outcome, a close examination of how privatization proceeds can tell us much about the overall relationship between business and government in any given country.

While sections of business in Ghana sought to make divestiture part of government policy, to the extent that there was any progress on this, it was won more by pressure from the IFIs. The PNDC was not instinctively supportive of privatization but the government's desperate need for revenue ensured that sales began and continued.[62] Divestiture receipts and the financial support of the IFIs were about the only thing keeping the government solvent as state spending continued to increase throughout the 1990s.[63] And so, the divestiture process did move forward, albeit slowly and clouded in controversy.

There is some disagreement as to where the idea of selling off some of the government's shares in the giant mining company AGC originated. The government had been casting about for ways to make up the massive budgetary shortfall it was anticipating. It was also looking for a success story for its privatization program. For its part, the AGC was seeking an injection of capital and hoping to develop a more international profile. Whatever the case, both sides agreed that they should proceed to sell off a portion of the shares that the government held in the company by a public offering of those shares, and preparations for the listing commenced.

---

[62] Roger Tangri, "The Politics of State Divestiture in Ghana," *African Affairs* 90, no. 361 (1991): 526.

[63] Divestiture proceeds went straight into the government budget as regular revenue. Institute of Statistical Social and Economic Research, *The State of the Ghanaian Economy in 1994.*

The company had been performing strongly and was well positioned for a flotation; it had effectively tripled gold production from 244,000 ounces in the mid-1980s to 770,000 ounces in the early to mid-1990s.[64] Through astute management and the use of new technology, Ashanti had increased both its output and its earnings every year since 1988.[65] Not only was this flotation a big deal in Ghana's small economy, it was a significant sale in global capital markets. This did not make it universally popular, however.

The international listing was opposed by those Ghanaians who did not want to see a national asset being bought by foreign investors. Because of these political tensions, the divestiture team devised a parallel listing on the Ghanaian Stock Exchange so that locals could acquire shares in the company and imposed a ceiling of 1 million cedis per person to ensure that the offering would be available to a large, diverse number of local shareholders. Prominent newspaper advertisements and public seminars publicized the share offer, and explained the workings of the stock market and how to buy shares. In addition, the government and AGC devised schemes to facilitate the acquisition of shares by company workers.

Finally, in March 1994 the London and Accra offers opened. The then Minister of Mines and Energy, Kwame Peprah, argued that the flotation would prove that "government is not paying lip service to its privatization and divestiture programme" and professed that the government would do "everything possible to ensure that the private sector really drives the national economy."[66] Few in business believed the latter claim, but those who could afford to took the opportunity to invest in their economy's behemoth. Both the local and international share issues were oversubscribed.[67] It was a triumph and, two years later, AGC was the first African company ever to list on the New York Stock Exchange.

[64] Unattributed, "Golden Shares: African Privatisation," *The Economist*, 19 March 1994.

[65] Priscilla Ross, "Ashanti Gold Glistens Again," *African Business*, March 1995, 27.

[66] Edwin Lloyd Evans, "21.4m AGC Shares for Sale," *People's Daily Graphic*, Tuesday 15 March 1994.

[67] Unattributed, "AGC Shares Oversubscribed by 0.4m," *Ghanaian Times*, 11, no. 452, 1994.

At this time, relations between AGC and government – or to put it more precisely and accurately, between AGC's head, Jonah, and President Rawlings – continued to be cordial in public. At a meeting of potential investors in London in March 1994, Jonah had, for example, praised the government, attributing the company's good performance to the enabling environment put in place by the Ghanaian government.

For its part, the government had every reason to be grateful to Jonah and his management team. The Ashanti divestiture had attracted great interest from international investors, enhancing the image of Ghana abroad. Domestically, the sale had broadened Ghana's financial markets and deepened its financial instruments. It had also netted the government $454 million, plugging a substantial hole in the 1994 budget.

The listing undoubtedly raised the profile of Sam Jonah. Already a public figure, he now became ubiquitous. He was regarded in many circles as an NDC protégé and had been, by some accounts, Rawlings' first choice for running mate in the 1992 poll. He is alleged to have turned the offer down, however. In addition, he began to display an unsettling independence, for example hosting fortnightly breakfasts for the media. The Castle began to fear that he might have his own political aspirations:[68]

Rawlings operated on one basic principle: if you are not with us, you are against us. The notion of an independent source of power was truly intolerable. As Jonah's status grew both nationally and internationally, the PNDC grew afraid of him; they came to see him as a political threat that could not easily be contained. The [forthcoming] conflict between government and Jonah at the AGC was about clipping Jonah's wings.

The president's relationship with Sam Jonah illustrates some of the dynamics that characterized the NDC's relationship with much of the Ghanaian business community. So long as Rawlings perceived a businessperson to be supportive of him, he would take some pains to ensure that that business prospered. For those who opposed him, however, he could be ruthless.

---

[68] Gyimah-Boadi, Interview. It is striking that some of the president's most fraught interactions with businesspeople were those with *Ghanaian* businesspeople. By contrast he seemed to rather relish meeting international business figures.

The 1999 hedging debacle

It is ironic that AGC's troubles in the late 1990s arose, not because of a drop in the gold price, but rather because of a steep rise in its price. This seems incredible until you take a closer look at the company's finances – and its hedge books in particular. Hedging is a strategy intended to reduce the uncertainty associated with international commodity price fluctuations. It "spreads" a company's risk by forward selling a share of the company's production at a particular, agreed-upon price. The strategy is effectively a form of protection against a drop in gold prices and it served the company well for several years, allowing it to maintain high levels of profitability despite a lackluster gold price. Over time, however, the company's financial team came to hedge an ever larger proportion of the company's future production. In 1996, 17 percent of AGC's reserve position was hedged; two years later, 46 percent of AGC's reserve position was hedged.[69]

What few anticipated was that the price of gold might actually rise – and that this would propel AGC into financial trouble. Gold production for 1999 had been hedged at around $380 per ounce. And then, unexpectedly, the price of gold soared in late September and early October, climbing a giddy $86 in just eleven trading days. The valuation of AGC's hedge book was transformed from a healthy credit of $290 million to a sickening debit of $570 million.[70] The company's liquidity problem was exacerbated by costs incurred from a strike at the Obuasi mine and by poor weather conditions at the Siguiri mine in Guinea. Suddenly the company faced margin calls for $270 million, money which it did not have to hand.

The company's financial crisis rapidly took on the dimensions of a political crisis when it became clear that the upper management of the company – and Jonah in particular – no longer enjoyed the support of the government. Indeed, it soon became apparent that Rawlings saw this as an opportunity to oust the beleaguered CEO.[71]

---

[69] Ashanti Goldfields Company, "Annual Report 1998" (Accra, Ghana: Ashanti Goldfields Company, 1998), 32.

[70] Ashanti Goldfields Company, "Annual Report 1999" (Accra, Ghana: Ashanti Goldfields Company, 1999), 5.

[71] Chris McGreal, "Gold Crisis Exposes Seam of Suspicion," *Daily Mail and Guardian*, 4 November 1999.

Confronted with this crisis, Jonah pursued a number of potential solutions. He unsuccessfully sought loan guarantees from the government, perhaps the first public indication of how far the relationship had soured. He also approached senior lending banks with no immediate success and pursued various merger or takeover options, the most promising of which was with Lonmin. This provoked fierce opposition from the government of Ghana. The government did not clearly articulate the grounds for its opposition, but they seemed to include a concern that the timing of the sale would not secure a good selling price, and some discomfort with selling a national asset to foreigners.[72]

There was another, undeclared reason for government obduracy, however: the relationship between Jonah and Rawlings had faltered some time before the hedging crisis broke. This rupture was exacerbated by the crisis which, by all accounts, Rawlings did not fully understand. He was not alone in this. Hedges are extremely complex financial instruments and most of the business community in Ghana was quite lost as to exactly why the crisis had arisen. Nonetheless, the president did not respond kindly to those of his advisors who tried to explain the mechanics of the crisis to him. The president may in addition have felt betrayed by his representatives on the board; he felt that they were ganging up with AGC executives to sell the company to foreigners and he dismissed them from the board.

With the merger option closed off, AGC entered a period of uncertainty when it was not clear whether the century-old firm would survive. The uncertainty was not good for business or for shareholders. AGC's shares fell from $9 per share in October 1999 to $2 at the end

---

[72] The government was joined in its opposition to the sale by a minority shareholder. A French director, acting on behalf of Adryx Mining and Metals, initiated legal proceedings to block any potential sale. Three prominent Ghanaians, Kwamena Essilfie Adjaye, Dr. Jones Ofori Atta, and Prof. Jonas Mawuse Dake, acting as members of the general public, also sought an injunction through the Ghanaian courts to halt the sale on the grounds that "the sudden, unjustifiable decision of government to sell part of the shares to Lonrho constitutes a grave breach of trust which will injure the interest of the beneficiaries who are the people of Ghana." They argued further that, should there be a compelling need to sell the shares, they should first be sold to Ghanaians. The court was not persuaded, however, and their application was dismissed with costs. Unattributed, "AGC Suit Fixed for Feb 22," *People's Daily Graphic*, Friday 18 February 1994.

of March 2000.[73] Before the crisis was resolved, the shares dropped further to $1.40 and a million shares were sold.[74] The tension between Rawlings and Jonah resurrected old concerns that the NDC was, at heart, still a radical populist government that might attempt to renationalize the company. However, Jonah doggedly pursued his options and the outlook began to improve for the company in mid-February as AGC negotiated an agreement with its creditors.[75]

The emergency AGM at which Jonah's opponents had planned to try to oust him from the leadership of the company was abandoned; instead, planning proceeded for the regularly scheduled annual meeting, under the firm grip of its CEO. With the support of key shareholders, Jonah would retain control of the company. Not everyone survived the process, however. In February, the chairman of the board, Kwame Peprah (then serving as Minister of Finance) resigned, and in March, the two remaining government representatives on the board, Kofi Ansah and Fred Ohene Kena, were replaced.

Jonah's survival was secured by a patchwork of deals at the center of which was support from the company's counterpart banks. These banks had already agreed to a rollover of the deadline by which AGC was to pay up for the derivative contracts. Now they gave AGC access to a $100 million loan.[76] The support of the banks appears to have been crucial to Jonah's survival. One local newspaper featured the headline: "'Lord' Jonah Walks: 20 Banks Reject His Resignation."[77] (AGC also had to raise cash through the sale of the profitable Geita mine in Tanzania for $335 million to a South African firm, AngloGold.)

Given that this was a regime that was historically hostile to business, one might have expected many in business to regard the attempt to remove Jonah as an attack on the private sector more broadly, and

---

[73] Ovid Abrams, "The Troubles of Ghana's Ashanti Goldfields," *African Link Magazine* 9, no.1 (2002) (accessed 19 September 2002) www.africanlinkmagazine.com.

[74] Unattributed, "'Lord' Jonah Walks: 20 Banks Reject His Resignation," *Ghanaian Chronicle*, 18 February – 20 February 2000.

[75] The court application brought by the minority shareholder Adryx Mining and Metals was resolved out of court.

[76] Unattributed, "Ashanti Sighs but Has One More Hurdle to Clear," *Ghanaian Chronicle*, 21 February – 22 February 2000.

[77] Unattributed, "'Lord' Jonah Walks: 20 Banks Reject His Resignation."

to rally behind Jonah. This was not the case. Instead, private sector representatives revealed a surprisingly mixed set of responses to the AGC affair and little sense of the collective interests of business.

This ambiguity can be explained in a number of ways. First, it was clear that Ghanaian businesspeople, simply by virtue of being in business, were no less prone to economic nationalism than anyone else. If anything, some of them were even more vociferously nationalistic. There was no significant constituency for divestiture. Granted, of 212 divestitures, 169 were sold to locals, but the firms sold to locals were overwhelmingly the smallest, least valuable firms and, in terms of value, may have comprised only 10 percent of the total.[78] In reality, few Ghanaians were able to buy privatized firms, mostly because they were struggling to stay afloat in the risky liberalized environment and were unable to mobilize the necessary capital.[79] While business organizations continued to support privatization, many individual businesspeople opposed the sale of Ghana's economic assets to foreigners.

In addition, for a small but significant minority in the business community, it was a matter of partisan politics. The majority of the business community supported the liberal NPP, but there were some businesspeople who owed their profitability to the ruling party and whose political loyalties thus lay with that party. The latter would not openly criticize the government.

Further, one cannot discount the possibility that jealousy of the CEO motivated business responses. Jonah was a prominent and successful figure, but he was not regarded as a "team" player in the Ghanaian private sector. Outside of the Chamber of Mines, AGC did not play an active role in corporate organizations; instead, the company and its CEO tended to hold themselves apart from the rest of the business community.

Not surprisingly AGC received a rather more sympathetic reaction from the mining sector. Here, many did see the attempt to depose him as an assault on the broader industry; they felt that the government's behavior had damaged the image of the sector, both in Ghana and internationally.

---

[78] Kojo Appiah-Kubi, "State-Owned Enterprises and Privatisation in Ghana," *Journal of Modern African Studies* 39, no. 2 (2001): 218, 222.
[79] Ibid.: 209.

Happily for AGC, the strained relations with Rawlings would not be a factor for much longer. On 28 December 2000, in the country's third multiparty election since its return to democracy, Ghanaians voted for a change of government.

The policy outcomes

Toward the end of the 1990s, a series of shocks demonstrated the continuing fragility of the economy. An energy crisis in late 1997 was exacerbated later by fallout from the Asian financial crisis and by declines in gold, timber, and coca prices. Inflows from Ghana's international development partners reached their lowest level since the introduction of the ERP. Crude oil prices increased by almost 100 percent.[80] The economy's extreme vulnerability to these developments raised questions over the extent to which the economy had been successfully restructured.

Some of the policy preferences expressed by businesspeople varied depending on the sub-sector in which they operated. At first glance, it looked as though some sub-sectors of the economy won more than others. The industrial and manufacturing sub-sectors' recovery of the late 1980s wavered in the 1990s.[81] By contrast, the construction sub-sector flourished.[82] However, it must be remembered that the construction sub-sector's primary client was the state, and state spending on roads, for example, remained robust throughout the decade.[83] On closer examination then, what seem to be sub-sectoral unevennesses can be accounted for by particular sub-sectors' political relationship with the state.

What of the policy areas that business mostly agreed on? Structured policy consultation between business and government was intermittent

---

[80] Institute of Statistical Social and Economic Research, *The State of the Ghanaian Economy in 1999*, 14.

[81] Manufacturing, which had grown strongly in the early days of the ERP (growing at 11 percent between 1984 and 1988) slowed to 4.7 percent between 1989 and 1993. Institute of Statistical Social and Economic Research, *The State of the Ghanaian Economy in 1993*, 103.

[82] The construction sub-sector's growth rate in the 1990s averaged 6.1 percent. Institute of Statistical Social and Economic Research, *The State of the Ghanaian Economy in 1999*, 120.

[83] There was also construction by government in the health, education, and housing sub-sectors.

and often the result of pressure from the IFIs. Any time that it looked as if this consultation would threaten the interests of government leaders, it was shut down. Instead, the government tried to build patronage ties to select elements of the business community.

Beyond consultation, what business really cared about was its lack of access to finance; business associations lobbied the government continuously and largely unsuccessfully on this issue. Causes of business' credit crunch were complex, but were undoubtedly connected to the government's spending patterns and overall management of the economy. The government was prepared to make gestures that might win it some political support – such as setting up the BAF – but was not prepared to amend its spending behavior.

Divestiture was an important policy area because it could potentially have reduced the overwhelming dominance of the government in driving the economy. This was a mixed story, with some successes but marred by allegations of patronage and personalism.

Why business won so little

There is no straightforward explanation for Ghana's policy outcomes of the 1990s. Business in Ghana was both stronger and more autonomous from government than its counterpart in Zambia, but the Ghanaian state, for its part, was also stronger and more neo-patrimonial than Zambia. The result was a state-driven reform program, dominated by rent-seeking and patronage despite the efforts of business to shape policy.

Some fifteen years after the start of the economic reform program, far from the state's involvement in the economy decreasing, almost the reverse had occurred. Having reviewed the public expenditure patterns of the 1990s, Wetzel concludes that "public expenditures are playing an increasingly important role in the economy. As in the early days of independence, it seems that the government is looking toward public expenditures to catalyse the country's economic growth in the absence of a strong private sector."[84] Aryeetey similarly argues that "[w]ith the rather slow growth of private investments, continued growth

---

[84] Deborah Wetzel, "Promises and Pitfalls in Public Expenditure," in *Economic Reforms in Ghana: The Miracle and the Mirage*, ed. Ernest Aryeetey, Jane Harrigan, and Machiko Nissanke (Oxford: James Currey, 2000), 126.

is having to depend on public investments and other expenditures, more than is desirable."[85]

Instead of privileging the role of the private sector in the economy, the ERP and related policies were part of a *state-led* economic program. One of the former economic advisors to the Rawlings government expressed it as follows: "All along, the program that we ran was a *government* program. The private sector was not involved. It was not until 1995 that they started involving the private sector ... and even then, it was reluctant consultation because they did not bring them fully into it."[86]

Throughout, it was public expenditure that was central to the government's economic recovery program, and yet the private sector was expected to play its apportioned role as the engine of growth, without any of the necessary financial and macroeconomic preconditions having been secured. According to Aryeetey[87]

it is now generally acknowledged that one of the most severe drawbacks to the Economic Recovery Program was its failure to generate adequate private sector response. The growth potential was lost due to tardiness in giving positive signals to the private sector, and by the contradictory nature of signals that were given. Some have delayed investment decisions while others have perceived an anti-private sector or anti-profit bias, resulting in low levels of savings, investment and capital flight.

The style of macroeconomic management, levels of state spending, divestiture – these policy areas turned out as they did because these outcomes suited the ruling PNDC. Throughout the 1990s, those policy areas which would improve the access of the government to international or local finance were privileged. Policy rents were secured by selective compliance with the IFIs' most urgent demands, such as for consultation or divestiture.[88] The NDC was clearly aware that business was a potential source of financial and political support, but the NPP seemed to have secured the support of this constituency so the NDC resorted to more limited, patronage-based attempts to win particular support.

[85] Aryeetey, "Structural Adjustment and Aid in Ghana," 4.
[86] Apea, Interview.
[87] Aryeetey, "Structural Adjustment and Aid in Ghana," 39.
[88] Hutchful, "Why Regimes Adjust."

Throughout the decade, far from the state being reformed in a neo-liberal direction, the economic reform program confirmed the neo-patrimonial nature of the Ghanaian state. A survey of popular attitudes conducted in July 1999 found, for example, that an "overwhelming 84.9 percent of Ghanaians thought that bribery was common among public officials."[89]

Some analysts are inclined to blame these developments on the pressures associated with democratization. It is a tempting explanation: not only do the dates of the slide in policy performance and the restoration of multiparty politics coincide neatly, but there is also evidence that much government spending was directly related to the NDC's desire to win elections. Of course, there are a number of ways to win political support. Faced with elections, the political elites associated with the executive could have chosen to build a political support base the hard way, by actually addressing the long-term needs and interests of their constituents. Instead, the neo-patrimonial system within which they were embedded presented an easier solution: bolstering their support by means of patronage.

This was not inevitable. Sandbrook and Oelbaum argue that in fact there were two simultaneous responses to democratization:[90]

On the one hand, democratization since 1992 has stimulated the resurgence of neopatrimonial institutions under the guise of liberal democracy – to the extent that the Rawlings regime in the mid-1990s resembled the regime of Kwame Nkrumah which Rawlings had once decried. Pervasive clientelism in 1992 predictably undermined macroeconomic stability as the government opened up the sluice gates of patronage to win the election ... On the other hand, beneath the surface, and in tandem with the strengthening of middle-class civil associations, important institutional changes were underway that ran counter to the logic of neopatrimonial traditions.

An examination of economic policy-making in the 1990s demonstrates two modes of interaction between business and government: hostility or patronage. Hostility was easily secured by an identification with the liberal tendency or opposition parties. Patronage was more hit and miss. If a firm was big or important enough, it could usually get an audience with the minister. Access to the president seemed to be

---

[89] Center for Democracy and Development, "Popular Attitudes to Democracy and Markets in Ghana," 3.
[90] Sandbrook and Oelbaum, *Reforming the Political Kingdom*, 6–7.

much more idiosyncratic:[91] family connections or long-standing friend-ship with either the president or his wife appeared to open sesame. This was entirely consistent with the political and economic insti-tutions that had historically developed in Ghana.

Business had limited input into economic policy-making, and much of the input it had was selective and uninstitutionalized. This was widely understood both by elites themselves and by the broader population.[92] The challenge in Ghana was to regularize business–government interactions – and this would require a change within the state as much a change within business. Recent developments point to some possibilities in this regard.

Ghana: the waning of neo-patrimonialism?

After ruling the country for nineteen years the NDC was rejected by Ghanaian voters in 2000 in favor of the NPP under the leadership of John Agyekum Kufuor. The ballot was important for a number of reasons. For a start, the elections themselves were considered among the fairest ever conducted in Ghana.[93] Moreover, they seemed to consolidate the status of competitive elections as the primary legiti-mate mechanism for changing the government in Ghana. As Morrison and Jae Woo Hong point out, Ghana's new constitution "has [now] survived through three election cycles and also witnessed a peaceful alternation in power ... the first time this feat had been accomplished since independence."[94]

Political developments in the succeeding seven years of NPP rule have been broadly positive. According to one observer, "Kufuor's major achievement ... has been in the area of human rights and personal freedoms. The police and military now know their places and

---

[91] Hart and Gyimah-Boadi, *Business Associations in Ghana's Economic and Political Transition*, 21.

[92] Center for Democracy and Development, "Elite Attitudes to Democracy and Markets in Ghana," 10, Center for Democracy and Development, "Popular Attitudes to Democracy and Markets in Ghana," 29.

[93] Edward Briku Boafu of the Friedrich Ebert Foundation, cited in Klaas van Walraven, "The End of an Era: The Ghanaian Elections of December 2000," *Journal of Contemporary African Studies* 20, no. 2 (2002): 186.

[94] Minion K. C. Morrison and Jae Woo Hong, "Ghana's Political Parties: How Ethno/Regional Variations Sustain the National Two-Party System," *Journal of Modern African Studies* 44, no. 4 (2006): 626.

roles in society."[95] Under the NPP, the media have continued to be extremely vocal on the political issues of the day, and there appear to be few barriers to their holding – and expressing – a range of views. According to NEPAD's peer review of political governance in Ghana, "competition for power is robust and open."[96] Indeed, the government's willingness to subject itself to potentially negative assessments was evidenced also in the government's decision to submit itself to that peer review process, the first member state of NEPAD to do so. Ghanaian democracy remains far from perfect but Gyimah-Boadi of Ghana's Center for Democratic Development observed that this experience of political freedom was "the best we have had so far."[97]

On paper, the economic policies of the NPP and the NDC looked very similar. Once in government therefore, the NPP sought to differentiate itself from its predecessor in terms of how those stated policies were put into practice. Confronted with rapidly growing debts at the Tema oil refinery, for example, the NPP slashed its subsidies to the refinery, almost doubling the price of fuel. In an attempt to draw the political sting from this move, MPs relinquished their fuel allowances and accepted a freeze in their salaries for that year.[98] Moreover, under the NPP, Ghana's economic reform program was considered to be back on track. The macroeconomic stabilization this engendered has been favored by – and favorable to – Ghanaian business.[99]

Because of its liberal orientation, the NPP had presented a firmly pro-business face when it was the chief opposition party. In government, the party sought to further consolidate this reputation.[100] In his inaugural address, for example, President Kufuor announced the creation of a special ministry to focus on private sector development,[101]

[95] George Asmah and Tom Mbakwe, "Ghana: So Far, So Good?," *New African*, January 2003, 15.
[96] African Peer Review Mechanism, *Country Review Report of the Republic of Ghana* (Midrand, South Africa: The New Partnership for Africa's Development, 2005), 23.
[97] Unattributed, "International: Black Star Tries to Rise, Again," *The Economist*, 24 June 2006, 72.
[98] Neil Ford, "Ghana," *African Business*, June 2003, 48.
[99] George Frank Asmah, "Ghana," *African Business*, December 2004.
[100] Unattributed, "Ghana: Economy Turned Around?," *Africa Research Bulletin*, 16 November – 15 December 2004.
[101] Peter Arthur, "The State, Private Sector Development and Ghana's 'Golden Age of Business,'" *African Studies Review* 49, no. 1 (2006): 32.

and shortly thereafter, his government launched the President's Special Initiative to "[identify and develop] potential business opportunities in the country."[102] In May of the same year, the government hosted a National Economic Dialogue to solicit the views of various constituencies, among them business, as to how to grow the economy.[103] In 2002, working with the World Bank's Private Sector Group, Kufuor launched the Ghana Investors' Advisory Council (GIAC) to identify and remove obstacles to higher levels of private investment in the economy.[104] The following year, the NPP government issued a Private Sector Development Strategy[105] whose focus was again on improving the investment climate as well as the broader environment for doing business.

The NPP government sought to distinguish itself from its predecessor also in terms of its commitment to rooting out corruption and to following the rule of law. Alleging that the process had been marred by political favoritism, the new government reexamined how many of the former state-owned enterprises had been disposed of. Although undoubtedly motivated by a desire to discredit the NDC, there did seem to be valid grounds for this exercise.

The net effect of these developments were hints that the highly personalized relationship between the state and business might, over time, be gradually replaced by a more formal, institutionalized relationship. In a discussion with the author about the privatization of Ashanti Goldfields, a senior official with the Minerals Commission commented as follows:[106]

Yes, you could extrapolate from how [the NPP government] dealt with this matter to its views more broadly. Whatever lapses came, they came through the formal operation of government and parliament. There was no attempt [on the part of the NPP] to circumvent procedures to make things easier for themselves. This shows that relations with [the NPP] government have

---

[102] Ibid.: 37.
[103] Musah Ibrahim and Alhassan Y. Babal-waiz, "Economic Recovery Steps in Ghana," *West Africa*, 30 September – 6 October 2002.
[104] Africa Private Sector Group, *Presidential Investors' Advisory Councils in Africa: Impact Assessment Study* (Washington, DC: World Bank, 2005), 17.
[105] Government of Ghana, "National Medium Term Private Sector Development Strategy 2004–2008" (Accra, Ghana: Government of Ghana, 2003).
[106] Personal interview with author, 11 August 2004.

formalized; they are not personal anymore. This generates [bureaucratic and procedural] delays but it is still preferable to the highly personal interactions which occurred under the NDC.

Arthur too draws the contrast between the two governments: "The difference [between the two regimes] ... is one of attitude; while the Rawlings administration was somewhat ambivalent and sometime openly hostile to the private sector, the NPP government seems to be showing greater commitment to helping local entrepreneurs spearhead the economic development process."[107]

Having said all that, there were still high costs for doing business in Ghana;[108] Ghanaian businesses continued to feel constrained by lack of access to finance, unreliable and expensive energy supplies, what they saw as excessive government regulations and red tape, and the continuing poor state of the infrastructure. Moreover, the Ghanaian business community still faced structural impediments to its ability to shape policy: it was still not able to wield financial resources (and hence policy influence) equivalent to those of the IFIs. Nonetheless, there was some evidence that neo-patrimonial behavior on the part of the Ghanaian state might be waning in the 2000s – with important implications for business too.

Conclusion

Ironically, for most of the neo-liberal era in Ghana, economic reform was, first and foremost, a state-driven affair. In the end, perhaps the most devastating failure of the ERP under Rawlings was its inability to generate a robust private sector response. Throughout the 1980s and 1990s, the economy continued to be driven by increasingly partisan infusions of public investment and spending. Private investment, by contrast, remained paltry. The impact on the business environment was twofold, restricting access to the credit markets, and rewarding certain modes of economic behavior and accumulation. These constraints did not vanish under Kufuor, but they did seem to loosen.

---

[107] Arthur, "The State, Private Sector Development and Ghana's 'Golden Age of Business,'" 40.

[108] African Development Bank, *Ghana: Country Strategy Paper 2005–2009* (African Development Fund, 2005), 14.

The new NPP government promised a "golden age" for business. From the experience of their predecessors in government, the NDC, it was evident that this would require more than a rhetorical commitment to market-oriented reform. This would need to go beyond improved public–private sector dialogue, to a transformation of the way that both the public and private sectors do business. It is too early to tell whether such a transformation is underway but it does suggest, at least, that it might be possible.

6 | *Business and government in Zambia: too close for comfort*

Big business [in Zambia] is quasi-parastatal. You're supplying government and lending money to government. A huge proportion of the private sector milks the government for a living.[1]

After decades of economic decline in Zambia, the transition to multiparty democracy in 1991 presented Zambians with an opportunity to redraw their political and economic landscape. Despite an auspicious start to the reform process, however, by the end of the decade there had been no fundamental revision of the role of business in economic policy-making. The puzzle that this chapter seeks to solve concerns this surprisingly low level of input by business into the policy-making of a government that had embraced, apparently fervently, an extensive role for the private sector in the economy. In particular, why was it that, despite a high level of influence in the formation of the Movement for Multi-Party Democracy (the MMD) as a party and in the early days of the MMD as a government, the business sector as a corporate entity rapidly lost this level of influence in that decade?

The proximate answer is twofold. First, despite the apparent political revolution represented by the return to multiparty politics and the conversion to neo-liberal economics, government by the MMD rapidly reverted to an older, neo-patrimonial mode of governance in which the access of business to the state was personalized. Second, the voice of organized business weakened over the course of the decade. This was due to the emergence over time of doubts within the business community about how economic reform was being implemented, to the centralization of political power around President Frederick Chiluba, and to the overwhelming influence of the World Bank and

---

[1] Guy Scott, former Minister of Agriculture, MMD, Personal interview with author, 2000.

IMF. Ultimately, however, these are proximate causes. A more comprehensive explanation of the weakness of the private sector and its lack of autonomy can be found by tracing the origins and emergence of the indigenous business community in Zambia. In particular, I argue that the Zambian business community has long been connected to the state and to the political incentives emerging from the state (indeed, it was largely created by the state), and was not able to establish a market-related economic sphere outside of the ambit of the state.

This chapter begins with an account of the creation of the modern Zambian state and its role in forging an indigenous business class. After reviewing the nature of the Zambian economy, the Zambian business sector, and economic policy-making by the late 1980s, I proceed to the core question, namely the ability of the business sector to successfully press its policy preferences with government during the 1990s. Here I consider a number of business' policy demands, principally privatization, the liberalization of trade, and deregulation. The chapter concludes with an assessment of what business won and lost, and why this was so.

The emergence of a political elite in Northern Rhodesia

In the pre-colonial era, the territory that was to become Zambia was governed by kingdoms of various sizes and with different forms of political organization. Many of these societies were characterized by a close connection between political and economic power and it was common practice for civilians to pay tribute to their chiefs, who were also responsible for the allocation of economic assets. In pre-colonial Bulozi, for example, "all land and basic natural resources [were] owned by the state, in the custody of the king" and leadership figures used their position, "not only to distribute commodities to the citizens in need, but also to subsidise their own needs and wants."[2]

The advent of white minority rule did not uncouple political power from the extraction and deployment of economic resources. Indeed, one of the curiosities of Zambia's history is that from the 1890s to mid-1920s, the territory was administered not by a government but by

[2] Akashambatwa Mbikusita-Lewanika, *Milk in a Basket! The Political Economic Malaise in Zambia* (Lusaka, Zambia: Zambian Research Foundation, 1990), 46–7.

a commercial firm, the British South Africa Company (BSAC). A royal charter authorized the company to operate as "a colonial state as well as a business"[3] – perhaps the ultimate fusion of public and private sectors.

At this time, there had been no significant mineral finds in Zambia that could be profitably exploited with the then available technology. There was therefore no explosion of economic activity similar to that occurring in the diamond fields and gold-mining areas of South Africa. This did not mean that the BSAC had no economic interest in the territory. Rather, Posner argues that the company profited from the royalties associated with small-scale mining and from the sale of land to settlers.[4] Consequently, the interests of the Company did not lie in facilitating either a broader process of capitalist development or the emergence of a flourishing business community. They lay instead with inducing self-sufficient peasant farmers to leave their lands for badly paid, back-breaking work on the mines further south and on settler farms.

The mechanism employed to this end was the imposition of taxes on Zambia's people, taxes that had to be paid in cash and therefore earned with wage labor. The company subcontracted revenue collection out to local indigenous political authorities where they existed, and created them where they did not. This revenue collection system formed the basis for a more elaborated model of Native Authorities when the British government assumed control of the territory in the 1920s. The Native Treasuries in particular provided the material base for an emergent Boma (governing) class as local elites discovered that a centrally organized state was a potentially lucrative source of income.

Chipungu argues that civil service salaries enhanced the capital accumulation of the Boma class; in turn, "Native Authority personnel ... showed remarkable interest in investing much of their earnings in productive ventures while they were in employment,"[5] ventures such

---

[3] Kenneth P. Vickery, *Black and White in Southern Tonga: The Tonga Plateau Economy and British Imperialism, 1890–1939* (New York: Greenwood Press, 1986), 39.

[4] Daniel N. Posner, *Institutions and Ethnic Politics in Africa* (Cambridge University Press, 2005), 41.

[5] Samuel N. Chipungu, "Accumulation from Within: The Boma Class and the Native Treasury in Colonial Zambia," in *Guardians in Their Time: Experiences of Zambians under Colonial Rule 1890–1964*, ed. Samuel N. Chipungu (London: Macmillan, 1992), 82.

as fishing, hunting, or agriculture. Thus, even in these early days of the Zambian state, both individuals and spheres of economic activity in what may otherwise have become the "private sector" were being drawn into a relationship with the state.

The benefits for those involved went beyond salaries and tax collection. This new bureaucratic structure granted important political responsibilities to the chiefs, including the authority to provide loans to individuals in their jurisdiction, control Native Courts, and allocate access to land. The chiefs also consolidated their influence over service provision:[6]

> By controlling the Native Treasuries, chiefs controlled where ... services [such as wells, schools, court buildings, roads, and dams] were sited. This allowed them to transform what were originally public goods into quasi-private goods ... The patronage powers that chiefs derived from their control over the siting of such projects gave their subjects incentives to cultivate close relationships with them.

Consequently, the Boma class became an important economic class in its own right; most commonly, its members became property owners, consolidating their authority over the distribution of economic resources. From the start then, the emergence of an indigenous economic elite was linked to the formal structures of political authority. By contrast, in the so-called private sphere, indigenous entrepreneurship was constrained by the racially skewed nature of policy-making. Sklar describes the "overwhelming reality of racial discrimination" in almost every sphere of life including racially skewed provision of education, restrictions on where locals could trade, and limited access to capital and credit.[7]

The opening of the copper mines in the late 1920s and subsequent mining boom presented opportunities for a more thorough capitalist transformation of the economy. However, African entrepreneurship continued to be hampered by a legal and social system in which "business was the preserve of whites in the first place and Indians in

---

[6] Posner, *Institutions and Ethnic Politics in Africa*, 32.
[7] Richard L. Sklar, *Corporate Power in an African State* (Berkeley, CA: University of California Press, 1975), 13–14. See also Yona Ngalaba Seleti, "Entrepreneurship in Colonial Zambia," in *Guardians in Their Time: Experiences of Zambians under Colonial Rule 1890–1964*, ed. Samuel N. Chipungu (London: Macmillan, 1992), 157.

the second place."[8] Indigenous Zambians were restricted to small commercial and transport-related ventures.[9] In addition, much of the wealth of the territory, instead of being harnessed for the development of that region, was being channeled south, to Southern Rhodesia with which it was then yoked in a federation. Still, at this point, one might be tempted to observe that the Zambian political economy resembled that of South Africa – were it not for some crucial differences.

The germinal private sector in Zambia was tiny in relation to the state; moreover, it remained centered on the emerging mining sector. Biermann argues that even though profit rates in Zambia were relatively high, industrialization was hampered by the monopolistic economy structured by mining capital.[10] This was permitted by the British colonial government, which had every reason to favor a mining economy dominated by expatriate capital.[11] The economy's dependence on copper was thus structured by colonialism.[12]

One can contrast this situation with the early days of the modern South African economy; there, Afrikaner interests pushed the state to deliberately foster other sectors of the economy, notably industry and manufacturing, to offset the power of mining and the English economic elite which dominated that sector. The South African state thus sought to nurture the development of countervailing economic sectors, while at the same time having to negotiate these policies with an already established and powerful set of private interests. By contrast, the embryonic private sector in Zambia was much smaller than that of South Africa, less powerful, and much less diversified. Moreover, there were no urgent political incentives for the state to actively pursue economic diversification. On the contrary, the economic and

[8] Seleti, "Entrepreneurship in Colonial Zambia," 160.
[9] Chileshe cites the Musango Brothers and Mwenso Brothers as key examples of this grouping. Jonathan H. Chileshe, *Third World Countries and Development Options: Zambia* (New Delhi, India: Vikas Publishing House, 1986), 86.
[10] Werner Biermann, "The Development of Underdevelopment: The Historic Perspective," in *Development in Zambia: A Reader*, ed. Ben Turok (London: Zed Press, 1979), 134.
[11] Parpart writes that "[t]he dependence upon copper revenues shaped Northern Rhodesians' government and Colonial Office policies." Jane L. Parpart, *Labor and Capital on the African Copperbelt* (Philadelphia, PA: Temple University Press, 1983), 26.
[12] Peter Meyns, "The Political Economy of Zambia," in *Beyond Political Independence: Zambia's Development Predicament in the 1980s*, ed. Klaas Woldring and Chibiwe Chibaye (Berlin, Germany: Mouton Publishers, 1984), 8.

political interests of the state were best served by a flourishing if somewhat monopolistic mining sector.

This setup was not cost-free. The drain of labor away from peasant agriculture into the mining economy did not lay a solid basis for the development of an industrial capitalist economy. Instead, prospects for the emergence of a more diversified economy, and a robust indigenous business class, were distorted by the impact of the mines, the barriers to the entry of black Zambians into other sub-sectors of the economy, and the presence of a well-established alternative route to economic security: the offices of the state.

The result of all of this was a set of economic stratifications which, superficially, resembled South Africa's: "Europeans on top and in command of the country's major economic sectors ... in between Asians and other non-African minority communities who control most medium-level industry and commercial activities ... and, at the bottom the indigenous African population who were engaged in selling their cheap labor to the two economically powerful groups or were living simply as peasant farmers or small-time traders."[13] Crucially, however, South Africa's white settlers were able to effect a more thoroughgoing transformation of that economy, driven by internal political struggles. In addition, there were simply far larger numbers of settlers in South Africa (in Zambia white settlers comprised barely 2 percent of the overall population).[14] As a result, while the private sector was effectively restricted to the ranks of the white community in both countries, the larger size of that population in South Africa and its political dynamics resulted in a more numerous and diverse business community.

Three elements stand out from the colonial period: first, the tendency for the state to serve as the primary source of income for an indigenous political and economic elite and the related tendency for influence derived from or via the state to become a source of economic opportunity; second, the overwhelming dominance of mining and the lack of incentives pushing the state to diversify the economy beyond that; third, and consequently, policy-making that was directed at furthering the interests of that state-associated class of actors and of mining. After Zambian independence in 1964, these same three

[13] Chileshe, *Third World Countries and Development Options*, 57.
[14] Vickery, *Black and White in Southern Tonga*, 140.

elements would continue to shape relations between business and the new political elite.

Independent Zambia: "humanist," not capitalist

If anything, the dominance of the state and mining respectively grew in the first decade of independence. In the first six years after independence, copper contributed 60 percent of the government's revenues and 95 percent of the value of its exports;[15] it also employed around one-seventh of the labor force.[16] The strength of copper meant that the new political leadership could – and did – envision the economic development of the country being funded by copper revenues, funneled via the state. There was, in this view, little need for private sector investment or for the fostering of an autonomous capitalist class. Indeed Zambia's new president, Kenneth Kaunda, publicly declared that "as humanists we cannot allow Zambians to develop into capitalists at all."[17]

He and his government were remarkably successful in achieving this goal. While the United National Independence Party (UNIP) was not vehemently anti-private sector at the outset, over the course of the decade, political battles within the ruling party pushed policy in a direction that excoriated the private sector and promoted the role of the state. One high-level state official described the milieu: "In the First and Second Republics, capitalism was the devil, shunned as a greedy system with no human face. This did a lot to prevent the emergence of capitalism. It also promoted the development of speculative business because you had to have good relations with the government and the party."[18]

In this way, a new business class was fostered in the shadow of the state and operating within a politically directed economy. A number of expatriate businesses withdrew at independence; of those who remained, many slotted neatly into this paradigm.[19] And a new

[15] Sklar, *Corporate Power in an African State*, 24.
[16] Meyns, "The Political Economy of Zambia," 8.
[17] K. D. Kaunda, "Zambia's Economic Revolution," Address by the President (Lusaka, Zambia: Zambian Information Services, 1968).
[18] Jacob Mumbi Mwanza, Personal interview with author, 17 August 2000.
[19] Sardanis, for example, alleges that there was an ongoing and mutually lucrative association between UNIP and Tiny Rowland, the head of Lonrho. Andrew Sardanis, *Africa: Another Side of the Coin: Northern Rhodesia's Final Years and Zambia's Nationhood* (London: I. B. Tauris, 2003), 141.

generation of indigenous businessmen benefited from – or arguably was created by – indigenization and nationalization decrees.

Beginning in the late 1960s, the Zambian state extended its control over the economy by buying up existing firms, creating new ones, and establishing parastatals. Following the Mulungushi reforms of 1968, the Zambia Industrial and Mining Corporation (ZIMCO) and the Industrial Development Corporation (INDECO) under the leadership of Andrew Sardanis were set up to oversee the state's vast holdings.

In this endeavor, however, the public sector faced the same problem as the private: Who would staff and manage enterprises? Following decades of under-education, there was a desperate shortage of human capital. At independence, the country had only 109 university graduates and very few Zambians with any managerial, technical, or business skills. Of the small number that existed, most were snapped up by the state and would come to comprise what Sklar calls the "managerial bourgeoisie" of Zambia.[20] Many young Zambians were happy to provide this service, motivated by the nationalist project and by relatively high public sector salaries. According to one such former manager, "[t]he parastatals were a breeding ground for transforming civil servants into managers. They offered us very good opportunities, for example of training at Harvard. Large numbers of the current generation of businessmen came through that system."[21] The state essentially created the country's managerial and business class.

Over time, however, the performance of those recruits suffered as a result of growing political pressure. While they were initially granted some degree of autonomy, increasingly the workings of the parastatals and SOEs were shaped by political incentives and infighting.[22] Political imperatives were imposed from on high, often in the form of a note from Kaunda himself. Parastatal managers were transferred frequently, rotated among very different enterprises, with their appointments subject to political considerations.[23] President Kaunda

---

[20] Sklar, *Corporate Power in an African State*, 199.

[21] Abel Mkandawire, Personal interview with author, 11 August 2000.

[22] Marcia Burdette, "Were the Copper Nationalisations Worth-While?," in *Beyond Political Independence: Zambia's Development Predicament in the 1980s*, ed. Klaas Woldring and Chibiwe Chibaye (Berlin, Germany: Mouton Publishers, 1984), 49–50.

[23] Muna Ndulo, "Domestic Participation in Mining in Zambia," in *Development in Zambia: A Reader*, ed. Ben Turok (London: Zed Press, 1979), 63.

directed government ministers to "make parastatals an organic part of the body politic," impressing on their chief executives that they were "an extension of the Party and its Government."[24] The head of INDECO, for example, described how "[p]olitical pressures started building up on loan applications ... the UNIP faithful would not countenance rejection of their applications and demanded instant decisions in their favour."[25] The parastatals were thus drawn into a web of patronage, the allocation of rewards and censure via appointments, the award of state contracts, and the placement of factories.

In addition to shaping the individuals who were active in the economy, the predominance of the parastatal sector conditioned the incentives within that economy. One businessman attributed the weakness of the Zambian private sector directly to this period: "At a time when it [the private sector] should have developed," he argued, "the predominant environment was parastatal. Supply and demand dynamics were thus targeted at building up relationships between parastatals."[26]

Nationalization of the economy was accompanied by Zambianization. Access to certain classes of trading licenses, for example, and government contracts below a certain level were restricted to indigenous Zambians. Crucially, however, these limitations were not imposed within an already existing and flourishing private sector; nor were they intended to produce such a sector. Indeed, as Meyns argues, "[i]t was not Kaunda's intention to 'create capitalism' in Zambia. Were Zambian companies to grow beyond a certain size, they would be taken over by the state. The dominant position in the national economy was reserved for state capital."[27]

In lieu of a healthy private sector then, Zambia's economy was directed by a series of ambitious developmental plans. The government was eager to tackle the developmental deficit inherited at independence and authorized a ramp-up in state spending on education, healthcare, and housing, and to finance the acquisition and creation of Zambian enterprises.[28] At first, revenues from the then-flourishing

---

[24] Ben Turok, "The Penalties of Zambia's Mixed Economy," in *Development in Zambia: A Reader*, ed. Ben Turok (London: Zed Press, 1979), 74.

[25] Sardanis, *Africa*, 183–4.

[26] Muna Hantuba, Personal interview with author, 19 July 2000.

[27] Meyns, "The Political Economy of Zambia," 16.

[28] Chileshe, *Third World Countries and Development Options*, 62–64.

copper industry easily financed this spending.[29] Accordingly, government investment for the first development plan period (1966–70) represented a 100 percent increase over the figures for 1965/6.[30]

A large injection of capital into the economy, judicially targeted and scrupulously managed, would have done the Zambian economy a world of good. However, many of these early investments were poorly targeted and managed. The returns were slow to arrive and costs mounted in the interim. This created an economic milieu in which political and state-driven incentives were rewarded more directly than one's ability to compete or transact efficiently in a broader marketplace. Burnell notes, for example, the popular attitude toward paying back (or not – as the case may be) state loans: "Zambians were encouraged to treat loans as free gifts, offered in exchange for support to the former ruling party."[31] This shaped a very particular kind of economic transaction, even for those economic actors who were not formally part of the structures of government. Businesspeople cultivated political connections "because it was easier to use party ties to circumvent rules than to change the system."[32] The party slogan, "[i]t pays to belong to UNIP," thus took on a more sinister meaning.[33]

Over the course of the late 1960s and early 1970s, the Zambian state consolidated its position as the dominant actor in the economy. Nationalization "effectively ended" FDI in the industrial sub-sector[34] while public investment tripled.[35] By the end of that decade, parastatals were contributing half of the country's GDP[36] and, by the middle of the next decade, the state was employing just over a third of

[29] Indeed in the 1960s the state's biggest fiscal headache was actually spending all the money allocated in the budget each year.

[30] Office of National Development and Planning, "First National Development Plan 1966–1970" (Lusaka, Zambia: Republic of Zambia, undated), 11.

[31] Peter Burnell, "Does Economic Reform Promote Democratisation? Evidence from Zambia's Third Republic," *New Political Economy* 6, no. 2 (2001): 198.

[32] Lise Rakner, "The Pluralist Paradox: The Decline of Economic Interest Groups in Zambia in the 1990s," *Development and Change* 32 (2001): 529.

[33] Bornwell C. Chikulo, "Elections in a One-Party Participatory Democracy," in *Development in Zambia: A Reader*, ed. Ben Turok (London: Zed Press, 1979), 202.

[34] Lise Rakner, *Political and Economic Liberalisation in Zambia, 1991–2001* (Uppsala, Sweden: The Nordic Africa Institute, 2003), 45.

[35] Per-Ake Andersson, Arne Bigsten, and Hakan Persson, *Foreign Aid, Debt and Growth in Zambia* (Uppsala, Sweden: Nordiska Afrikainstitutet, 2000), 13.

[36] Turok, "The Penalties of Zambia's Mixed Economy," 75.

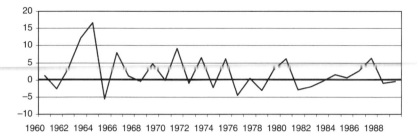

Figure 6.1 Zambian GDP growth (annual %)
Source: World Development Indicators, World Bank Group

the formal sector workforce.[37] As the size and prominence of the state in the economy grew, "the government became both a leading supplier and competitor to business."[38]

Granted, manufacturing did expand significantly in the 1960s and 1970s and growth was intermittently good (see Figure 6.1). However, as Seidman warns, this rapid expansion did not increase productivity.[39] Even Turok, no friend of private sector business, cites "glaring cases of failure" among the SOEs.[40] "[Q]uestionable" investments made on the basis of "ad hoc criteria,"[41] along with significant maladministration contributed to a severe lack of profitability in the SOE sector. By 1980, state subsidies and credit to the parastatal sector swallowed up a staggering 80 percent of the government's revenues.[42]

While INDECO had originally been instructed to operate on a business basis, over the course of the 1970s management authority was undermined by increasingly specific and political directives, and the objectives that directors were instructed to pursue proliferated bewilderingly.[43] A number of analysts point to battles between managerial

---

[37] Roger Tangri, "Public Enterprise and Industrial Development: The Industrial Development Corporation of Zambia," in *Beyond Political Independence: Zambia's Development Predicament in the 1980s*, ed. Klaas Woldring and Chibiwe Chibaye (Berlin, Germany: Mouton Publishers, 1984), 113.

[38] Rakner, *Political and Economic Liberalisation in Zambia*, 46.

[39] Ann Seidman, "The Distorted Growth of Import-Substitution Industry: The Zambian Case," *Journal of Modern African Studies* 12, no. 4 (1974): 601.

[40] Turok, "The Penalties of Zambia's Mixed Economy," 73.

[41] Tangri, "Public Enterprise and Industrial Development," 120.

[42] Andersson, Bigsten, and Persson, *Foreign Aid, Debt and Growth in Zambia*, 17, Mbikusita-Lewanika, *Milk in a Basket!*, 81.

[43] Tangri, "Public Enterprise and Industrial Development," 120.

technocrats and politicians "who act[ed] more in accordance with their own political survival and [did] not appear so bound by the legalistic traditions of western capitalism [as the technocrats were]."[44]

Given the structure of the Zambian economy and its dependence on the revenue and foreign exchange generated by copper, it was perhaps inevitable that the state should seek to tighten its control over that sub-sector. In the early years of independence, the state had entered into a partnership with the two largest mining corporations but as the broader program of nationalization was unrolled, there was pressure within the state to further increase its control.

The timing of this move was unfortunate. The state's purchase of a controlling share of the mines came only years before a dramatic reversal in the international terms of trade, specifically a hike in the price of oil and imports (including the crucial components for ISI manufacturing), and a steep decline in the copper price.[45] Government, assuming that these shifts were temporary, did little to curb its ambitious investment program which was funded, increasingly, by borrowing. The result was a shortage of foreign exchange and a rapid build up of debt, from 40 percent of GDP in 1975 to 400 percent just eleven years later.[46] The copper industry, organized by now into the Zambia Consolidated Copper Mines (ZCCM), was starved of the foreign exchange it needed to invest in production. The already limited autonomy of the parastatals – and especially of ZCCM – was further eroded as foreign exchange applications were granted on the basis of political connections.[47]

Years of economic mismanagement and under-investment in the mines began to take their toll, resulting in lower output and compounding the effect of depressed international prices.[48] Nationalization "transformed ZCCM from a respectable mining group into a mindless conglomerate encompassing all sorts of irrelevant businesses."[49] At

[44] Burdette, "Were the Copper Nationalisations Worth-While?," 52.

[45] Sardanis, *Africa*, 273.

[46] Roger Young and John Loxley, *Zambia: An Assessment of Zambia's Structural Adjustment Experience* (Ottawa, Canada: The North–South Institute, 1990), 4–6.

[47] Sardanis, *Africa*, 292.

[48] The costs of production also increased dramatically as the mines grew deeper, all of which meant that the mines, previously a source of profit, became a drain on the economy.

[49] Sardanis, *Africa*, 297.

independence, the intention had been to use the revenues from copper to drive Zambia's economic development. In the end, this strategy killed the copper goose, and the economy crashed to the ground along with it.

The Zambian political economy by the late 1980s

By the mid-1980s, international terms of trade were still calamitous for Zambia, growth was uneven (see Figure 6.1) and the country was ensnared in a debt trap. Whatever private sector there was had shrunk and been forced to make a living by manipulating opportunities created by state intervention. Domestic manufacturing and industry were uncompetitive, living standards had plummeted, and Zambia's traditional mainstay, the mines, were unproductive and costly to run. Kenneth Kaunda began and then abandoned a set of IMF-sponsored reforms, only to find that "no one else would lend."[50] By the 1990s, Zambia was in a state of political and economic crisis. Following the failure of a home-grown economic reform program, calls for political and economic reform mounted.

Membership of Zambia's business community at that time cut across all of the country's seventy-odd ethnic, linguistic, and racial groups. Under UNIP, President Kenneth Kaunda, regarded as an astute manager of ethnicity, had been careful to balance ethnic considerations in his appointments to the state's parastatal empire. As a result, business in Zambia in the 1990s was not excessively dominated by any one ethnic grouping, unlike South Africa or Mauritius.[51]

On the face of it, race might have been a more salient issue for the business community. As outlined above, Kaunda had set out to indigenize ownership and management of the Zambian economy. Despite these efforts, there were still small numbers of white and Asian businesspeople active in the business community. Yet, while the business community was characterized by ethnic and racial plurality, these factors did not appear to be a major source of tension between

---

[50] Margaret Hanson and James J. Hentz, "Neocolonialism and Neoliberalism in South Africa and Zambia," *Political Science Quarterly* 114, no. 3 (2002): 485.
[51] There were allegations that President Frederick Chiluba's government favored northerners (Chiluba is himself a Bemba from the north). There was, however, little evidence that this shaped the business community in significant ways.

business and government.[52] Rather, because those appointed by Kaunda after independence owed their positions and their affluence to political favor, this had bound entrepreneurs to the state.

In this sense then, Zambia resembles Ghana more closely than it does South Africa or Mauritius. As in Ghana, the primacy of individual or firm-level connections to the state was the more important characteristic of the business community. As one businessman observed, "the whole framework of doing business is doing deals with government."[53]

The dependence of business in Zambia on the state was unusually one-sided, in part because of the structure of the economy. The government had long received its revenue directly from copper and from its control of that sub-sector through ZCCM. It was thus not reliant on the fortunes of the broader business community.[54] For its part, indigenous business in Zambia was unusually small and weak, and depended on the state for its survival, rather than the reverse. With the patronage power conferred by its purchasing and contracting budget, the government could dominate the market as a consumer of goods and services. And because of its control of the communications and energy sub-sectors, the government also determined many of the input costs that business faced. Finally, and more difficult to quantify, was the influence that the government had in shaping the overall milieu within which business was conducted. As one businessman told me: "If you are a businessman and you choose to go against government policy, you are on a highway to nowhere."[55]

Two business associations represented business in its formal and public interactions with government during the 1990s.[56] The Zambia Association of Chambers of Commerce and Industry (ZACCI) was an

---

[52] Scott Duncan Taylor, "Beyond Business as Usual: Business Associations, the State and Liberalization in Zimbabwe and Zambia" (Ph.D. Dissertation, Emory University, 1998), 147.

[53] Anonymous, Confidential interview with author, 14 July 2000.

[54] The prominence of a single large mining corporation which is largely owned by the state is another important similarity between Ghana and Zambia, and a clear contrast with the South African case where mining assets remained largely in private hands.

[55] Mark O'Donnell, Personal interview with author, 20 June 2002.

[56] While there are other sub-sectoral representatives, such as the Tourism Council and a board that deals with the insurance sub-sector, they were not nearly as high profile and barely featured in economic policy discussions.

encompassing national body composed of local chambers of commerce. Since its founding in 1938, the chamber movement collapsed and reemerged several times and was renamed ZACCI in 1992.[57] As is typical of chamber movements, ZACCI represented a spread of businesses, large and small and from all sub-sectors of the economy. In the 1990s, around twenty corporate firms (some of the largest in Zambia) were direct members of ZACCI. On the whole, however, ZACCI relied for its legitimacy and funding on the membership and reach of local chambers.[58] Membership dues were paid on an honors system and this revenue was not reliable, forcing ZACCI to rely on donor support for many of its programs.

ZACCI exemplified the broader Zambian business community. While many of its members and office bearers were legitimate businesspeople, many also had close connections with government. For example, Ronald Penza (later Finance Minister) and Alex Chikwanda (later Presidential Chief of Staff) occupied leadership positions in ZACCI before the political transition and their subsequent involvement in government. MMD MP and one-time Minister of Foreign Affairs Vernon Mwaanga was also a ZACCI trustee until 1994.[59]

The Zambia Association of Manufacturers (ZAM) was founded in 1985 to address the specific needs of manufacturers. It was thus more targeted in its policy demands than ZACCI. While there was significant policy overlap between the two organizations, ZAM was more inclined to seek such policies as reduced VAT rates or protection for manufacturers.

ZAM was both smaller and less well institutionalized than ZACCI. Unlike ZACCI, it had no permanent office or full-time secretariat.[60] ZAM's membership was more homogeneous (in addition to members generally coming from the same sub-sector of the economy, ZAM's member firms tended to be Zambia's slightly larger enterprises).

As in many highly centralized polities, the National Assembly and members of parliament were marginal to the making of economic

---

[57] Taylor, "Beyond Business as Usual," 133.
[58] As it was a coalition of chambers, most individual firms were members first of their local chambers, which were in turn members of ZACCI.
[59] Taylor, "Beyond Business as Usual," 138.
[60] Rather, ZAM was usually just run out of the office of whoever headed the Association up at the time. As a result, the Association had low overhead costs but its effectiveness varied, depending on the leadership.

policy in Zambia, and the transition to multiparty democracy in 1991 did little to change this. Accordingly, business continued to direct its lobbying efforts at the executive and the relevant ministries.

Because of Zambia's level of indebtedness, World Bank and IMF officials also had vital input into policy-making, especially following the change of government in 1991. This did not mean, however, that select Zambians were unable to shape the way that structural adjustment was actually implemented in their country – but they frequently did so in order to secure personal advantage rather than to advance an alternative ideological approach.

Economic reform in the 1990s

By the end of the 1980s, Kenneth Kaunda's UNIP appeared unable to resolve Zambia's political and economic crisis. Business, dissatisfied in particular with the exchange control regime and high levels of inflation, concluded that economic recovery required political change.[61] It looked, at first, as if they just might get both.

The business of political reform

In July 1990, a number of leading businesspeople played a key role in founding (and funding) a new opposition movement, the MMD. Weary of years of economic mismanagement and decline, the private sector quickly aligned itself with the demand for change in both the political and economic sphere. According to Burnell, "[t]he MMD leadership believed that economic and political reform would be mutually beneficial. It saw that in the Second Republic powers of social control ... were underpinned by state ownership and control of most of the modern economy."[62] Business was thus closely associated with the MMD from the start, and the party aligned itself with a market-friendly set of policies.

The basis for the MMD's economic reform agenda was developed in a number of informal settings outside of the state. Perhaps the most effective of these was the Economics Association of Zambia (EAZ). This discussion forum provided an opportunity for reform-minded

[61] Meyns, "The Political Economy of Zambia," 19.
[62] Burnell, "Does Economic Reform Promote Democratisation?," 192–3.

individuals from within government, the University of Zambia, research institutions, and business to explore ideas for reforming the economy. Toward the end of the 1980s as UNIP-led reform efforts faltered, EAZ discussions turned in a business-minded and even neo-liberal direction and many of these ideas would inform the MMD's economic policy platform.

The manifesto of the MMD proposed a dramatic transformation of the governance of Zambia. Politically, it committed the new party to moving away from the centralized, personality-driven nature of UNIP-style politics. Economically, the document proposed a radical over-haul of the commandist economy.[63] Instead, a rejuvenated private sector would drive economic recovery via the privatization, liberal-ization, and deregulation of the economy. The vision was a distinctly neo-liberal one: "MMD believes that economic prosperity for all can best be created by free men and women through free enterprise … with the Government only creating an enabling environment whereby economic growth must follow."[64] Organized business was not for-mally represented in the drawing up of the manifesto,[65] but it seemed that it did not need to be. MMD activists were intent on moving away from a failed commandist model toward precisely the set of free market models that the major business organizations would have pressed for.

Despite the oppositional nature of the new MMD's platform, in practice the party did not represent a complete departure from UNIP-style politics, or personalities. In the elections that followed, a number of the MMD candidates for the National Assembly had previously served as UNIP MPs, including a handful who had served either in cabinet or on the party's Central Committee.[66] Nonetheless, embody-ing (as it appeared to do) the popular demand for change, the MMD swept to power in 1991, in Zambia's first multiparty elections in decades. The new government, under the leadership of the former

[63] Dipak Patel, Personal interview with author, 2 August 2000.
[64] From the MMD manifesto, quoted in Hanson and Hentz, "Neocolonialism and Neoliberalism in South Africa and Zambia," 488.
[65] Although one of the key authors was Emmanuel Kasonde, a prominent businessman who would go on to be the MMD's first Minister of Finance. Ibid.: 489.
[66] Julius O. Ihonvbere, *Economic Crisis, Civil Society, and Democratisation: The Case of Zambia* (Trenton, NJ: Africa World Press, 1996), 65–70, Rakner, *Political and Economic Liberalisation in Zambia*, 104–7.

trade unionist Frederick Chiluba, embarked upon a radical program of economic liberalization. Business hoped to be a partner in that process.

In the early years of the new regime, the urgency of the economic crisis provided an opportunity for a small number of key reformers within the cabinet and civil service to push through a far-reaching and breathtakingly rapid program of economic liberalization. From the start, business was enthusiastic about the new government and what it was attempting. At the time, business' interests were in accord with the prescriptions of the IFIs, and it seemed that the government sought to please both these sets of actors.

It was during this period that Zambia earned its reputation as a star pupil of the World Bank. The MMD worked hard to establish the credibility of both the political and the economic reform process and largely succeeded in this; in fact, Zambia's reformist reputation would ultimately outlast the reality as, over time, this commitment to a set of economic principles began to erode from within.

The MMD gets personal

In 1993, the MMD government imposed its first State of Emergency. The party defended the move as a response to a "subversive coup plot" hatched by elements within UNIP, but many saw the imposition of emergency measures as an indictment of a party that had come to power opposing precisely such tactics.

In April of the same year, President Chiluba reshuffled his cabinet, ejecting a number of reform-minded ministers including Emmanuel Kasonde (finance), Guy Scott (agriculture), Humphrey Mulemba (mines), and Arthur Wina (education). The reshuffle was significant not so much for the way it shifted the balance of power between economic reformers and non-reformers[67] but for what it indicated of what lay ahead. Those who were axed were independent-minded and vocal about a creeping tendency to revert to the toadyism that had prevailed under Kaunda. Three other party stalwarts, including founder members of the party (Baldwin Nkumbula, Akashambatwa Mbikusita-Lewanika, and Katongo Main), were also forced out of the MMD at this time as Chiluba and his supporters sought to consolidate

---

[67] There were neo-liberals who remained in cabinet and a number of the new appointees or promotions were also reform-minded.

their power.[68] A generational struggle within the MMD was settled in favor of the old guard in March 1995 when Chiluba launched a public attack on the younger politicians and fired two deputy ministers associated with the "Young Turks," namely Derek Chitala and Dean Mun'gomba. Chiluba came to surround himself with supporters who were "absolutely ruthless" in pursuit of their own interests, according to a local businessman.[69]

By 1996, Zambian politics had become dangerously partisan and personalized. These tendencies were reinforced by the weakness and disorganization of opposition parties. In that year, elements close to Chiluba passed a constitutional amendment intended to bar Kaunda from running again for president. In the same year, unknown political forces detonated a series of bombs in the capital, and the state brought treason charges against the UNIP leadership.[70] ZACCI became increasingly concerned about the impact of political repression on business confidence, investment, donor support, and the economy more broadly. These reservations were discreetly expressed, however. Organized business did not endorse the opposition, intervene directly in elections, or make any statements that could have been construed as politically partisan.[71] The personalization of politics was not only bad news for political liberalization but for economic reform too.

Specific policy demands

As the economic reform program unfolded,[72] business' policy preferences moved beyond support for the broad outlines of reform, to engage with the details of implementation. While ZACCI and ZAM

---

[68] Bizeck Jube Phiri, *A Political History of Zambia* (Trenton, NJ: Africa World Press, 2006).

[69] Anonymous, Confidential interview with author, 11 July 2000.

[70] Hanson and Hentz argue that "[t]he ruling MMD party treated its rivalry with the former ruling UNIP party as a fight to the death, rather than a competition with the loyal opposition." Hanson and Hentz, "Neocolonialism and Neoliberalism in South Africa and Zambia," 490–1.

[71] The Zambia National Farmers' Union (ZNFU), by contrast, was more assertive. See Taylor, "Beyond Business as Usual."

[72] Cf. Catherine B. Hill and Malcolm F. McPherson, eds., *Promoting and Sustaining Economic Reform in Zambia* (Cambridge, MA: Harvard University Press, 2004), Rakner, *Political and Economic Liberalisation in Zambia, 1991–2001.*

did not publish a definitive list of business' emerging policy preferences, these can be imputed from in-house documents, association
publications, and the statements of the associations' office bearers.
Given the extent and inefficiency of state ownership in the economy,
and how important the recovery of the mining sector was to the
overall recovery of the Zambian economy, the call for privatization
was foremost among business' demands. The deregulation and liberalization of trade, prices, and the currency followed closely thereafter.

Privatization

While it was a key constituency in support of the overall economic
reform program, Zambia's business community was not universally
pro-privatization. The best explanation for this is the bifurcated
nature of the Zambian business community: a small number of private
sector entrepreneurs and a larger class that rose to prominence
through the state-owned industrial sector. Business associations,
forced to consider the best interests of the private sector as a whole,
understood the potential benefits to the economy of privatization.
Individual actors were more inclined to hunt for individual profit-
making opportunities, and these did not always lie with a quick,
efficient sell-off of state assets. Some resented the fact that few
Zambians could afford to purchase these assets. Abel Mkandawire,
then chair of ZACCI, put it as follows: "No one was able to buy
[privatized] companies as there are few Zambians coming from a
business background with capital. Most of us have a background in
the parastatal industries and we have no capital."[73]

Further, while ZACCI and ZAM were consistently pro-privatization
throughout the 1990s, they quickly came to oppose the way in which
this was being pursued. Specifically, business associations were per-
turbed by growing allegations of improper tendering procedures and
of assets being sold to political insiders.

Even without these neo-patrimonial elements, however, it is likely
that areas of disagreement would have emerged between business and
government on how to pursue privatization. Privatizations can be
technically complex and many different choices are available at each
step of decision making. It is not surprising then that there was some
dissension about how the overall program was undertaken. Business

---

[73] Quoted in Rakner, *Political and Economic Liberalisation in Zambia*, 93.

argued that the process should inject new ownership, investment, and higher levels of efficiency into the Zambian markets and into the Copperbelt. What was disturbing for the associations was how, instead, a neo-patrimonial logic began to dictate the course of the process.

The government began its privatization program slowly.[74] Technocrats argued that it was important to start with smaller sell-offs in order to prepare for the more important privatizations that lay ahead. Mostly, however, this seemed to provide opportunities for bureaucrats in ZIMCO, the state's holding company, to sabotage the process.[75] President Chiluba, under pressure from the IFIs to show results, ultimately transferred the responsibility for privatization away from ZIMCO to the Minister of Commerce, Trade and Industry.

Privatization subsequently picked up speed and, by the end of 1997, 213 out of a potential 331 entities had been privatized. However, the privatized entities were mostly small companies[76] that netted the state a paltry $70 million.[77] The really important privatization, that of ZCCM, still lay ahead.

It was obvious to all that ZCCM would be the centerpiece, not only of the privatization program, but of any potential economic recovery for Zambia. Business hoped that the sale would revive the mining sub-sector and, in turn, rejuvenate the many firms that served this sub-sector. All three of the major, private sector organizations, ZACCI, ZAM, and ZNFU, were vocal in criticizing the delay in the privatization of the mines, and with good reason. Over the course of the 1990s, the condition of the mines had continued to decline while the international terms of trade for copper had worsened.

In preparation for its privatization, the giant corporation was restructured into ten packages that were offered for individual sale.[78] The most important of these was the Nkana/Nchanga package, which

---

[74] John Craig, "Putting Privatisation into Practice: The Case of Zambia Consolidated Copper Mines Limited," *Journal of Modern African Studies* 39, no. 3 (2001).

[75] Tactics included personal attacks on the leadership of the Zambia Privatisation Agency (ZPA), lobbying various ministers, leaking sensitive information to the press, providing illegal retrenchments benefits to selected managers, and asset stripping.

[76] Zambian Breweries and the Zambian Sugar Company were notable exceptions.

[77] Taylor, "Beyond Business as Usual," 239–42.

[78] Craig, "Putting Privatisation into Practice," 399.

accounted for over half of ZCCM's copper production and 80 percent of its cobalt production, and there was initially great interest in its sale. Serious negotiations began with the Kafue Consortium, made up of Moranda, Phelps-Dodge, Avmin, and the Commonwealth Development Corporation.

Chiluba personally appointed Francis Kaunda[79] to head up the government's negotiating team and at first Kaunda's role was a positive one. Initially, he succeeded in significantly improving the Consortium's offer, in terms of both the cash price and the proposed investment in the mines, but he may ultimately have overplayed his hand. Officially, he continued to insist that the price being offered was still too low. Unofficially, rumors were that the kickbacks being demanded were too high to be seriously considered. Either way, by early June 1998 the deal was off. The Consortium backed away and the mines were left begging a buyer.

To quote *Africa Confidential*, "[t]he timing could hardly have been worse."[80] The price of copper dropped dramatically almost immediately after the collapse of the Kafue negotiations. Eventually, another deal was patched together with the South African-based mining giant, the AAC. It was, however, worth a scant 40 percent of the previous offer made by the Kafue Consortium.[81] Even at this price, AAC was not able to turn the mines into a profitable concern and the company pulled out of Zambia in 2002.[82] The Copperbelt's rejuvenation would have to wait.

Throughout the 1990s, although there were a number of allegations made about irregularities in the privatization process (in particular the

---

[79] Kaunda (no relative of Kenneth Kaunda) had been prominent under the previous UNIP regime. He had fallen from grace with the advent of the new MMD government but, by the time of the ZCCM privatization, had been resurrected under the personal stewardship of President Chiluba.

[80] Unattributed, "Zambia: Copper Crunch," *Africa Confidential*, 1999, 5 February 8.

[81] The Kafue offer was for 88 percent of the assets for $160 million in cash plus the assumption of $150 million of ZCCM's outstanding debt. By contrast, AAC ultimately purchased 80 percent of the assets for $90 million in cash, and, critically, it assumed none of ZCCM's debts. South African Institute of International Affairs, "Zambia: A Shining Example of Privatisation?," in *Intelligence Update* (Johannesburg, South Africa: South African Institute of International Affairs, 1999), 2.

[82] Greg Mills, "Chile or Zambia? Anglo's Choice Shows What Africa Must Do," *Business Report, Sunday Times*, 30 June 2005.

sale of privatized companies to government ministers) ZACCI made little public criticism of such practices.[83] The costs of such direct criticism may have been deemed too high – and prominent members of that organization may have benefited from such practices.

Trade liberalization

In the early days of the MMD, business participated in external negotiations alongside the government concerning regional trading regimes such as those for the Common Market for Eastern and Southern Africa (COMESA) and the Southern African Development Community (SADC). However, this was both the beginning and the end of such discussions. After the initial spate of meetings, the government barely consulted with business on how best to prepare firms for a liberalized economy.

There were a number of areas where input from business could have made the process more constructive. First, while there was significant liberalization of imports, government support for exports was "sporadic and badly designed."[84] Second, a more nuanced and staggered timetable of trade liberalization could have been negotiated with ZAM. While business commended the overall trend of trade liberalization, the process was not designed to salvage potentially viable Zambian manufacturers. Duties that were lower for the import of finished articles than for raw materials, for example, devastated Zambian manufacturing, leading to the closure of a number of concerns including Dunlop Tyres. After decades of protection, much of the Zambian manufacturing sector was inefficient, indeed unviable. However, the speed of the reforms, their indiscriminate application, and the fact that Zambia's trade liberalization was not matched by equivalent measures from its trading partners in the region (such as South Africa) destroyed even those industries that could successfully have restructured themselves.

Finally, ZACCI was concerned that liberalization was undertaken in such a hurry that few of the macroeconomic conditions necessary for its success had been secured. Of particular concern to industrialists and manufacturers, the government never significantly lowered interest rates and inflation. As Taylor argues, "Zambia has liberalization without stabilization, the results of which decimated manufacturers

---

[83] Taylor, "Beyond Business as Usual," 309.   [84] Ibid., 219.

while disproportionately (but certainly not universally) benefiting traders."[85] The result – a flood of imported goods – was popular with consumers and with politically influential traders (not coincidentally, a number of government ministers had invested in trading concerns), but it was not so positive for manufacturers and exporters.

Business argued that the government could have taken measures to improve business' access to credit and to reasonably priced electricity, services, fuel, and transport. As it was, the particular combination of reforms implemented meant that the production costs of Zambian manufacturers and industries in the 1990s were disproportionately high (at least, again, in relation to those of their major trading partners and rivals) such that it became cheaper to import processed goods than to produce them locally. This was good news for South African exporters and, again, for traders in Zambia but not for the broader Zambian business sector. One businessman commented as follows: "The MMD is focusing on trading not manufacturing, on trade liberalization without industrialization ... These politicians, they live for the day, not for long-term development."[86]

Business was divided over trade reform with some firms calling for protection and subsidies but the business associations did not demand an end to the liberalization program. A good example was ZACCI's support for regional trade liberalization and integration processes. Bilateral trade relations with South Africa and Zimbabwe were a particular source of concern to the business associations; ZACCI argued that Zambia's openness was being exploited by the South Africans. Nonetheless, ZACCI's response was not to demand protection but to argue the need to more effectively promote exports and to control smuggling. Indeed, both ZAM and ZACCI consistently opposed bans on imports and advocated working within the framework of the WTO. There is evidence then that the business associations were doing their job: aggregating their members' preferences and forcing the debate toward policy positions that were long term and broad-based in outlook.

In short, government and business in Zambia could have cooperated to ensure that Zambian firms were equipped to compete with other economies in the region. Instead, the government implemented a doctrinaire program, intended more to satisfy the loan conditions of

[85] Ibid., 180.   [86] Mkandawire, Interview.

the IFIs and the trading interests of MMD stalwarts than to build up a viable private sector in Zambia.

Deregulation

The deregulation of the Zambian economy that occurred in the 1990s demonstrated that tariffs could be cut and regulations lifted in such a way that very particular advantage would accrue. The 1996 budget provides some good examples of this. On the face of it, the budget seemed to address the major planks of economic reform, authorizing substantial reductions in tariffs for example. Neither was business absent from this process. On the contrary, certain people in business undoubtedly influenced the level and nature of tariff reductions – but these individuals were generally in the business of politics too. A number of those in the MMD cabinet owned commercial trading companies, and government officials "had the inputs needed for their own companies ... reclassified at a lower rate of duty even though they are predominantly finished, consumer-ready goods that should attract the *highest* tariffs."[87] The "highly individualized" policy response that Taylor points to undermined the business associations and cynically exploited deregulation.

Developments were not unremittingly negative. Business associations successfully lobbied on two fronts on an issue always close to business' heart, namely taxation. First, they applauded the establishment of the Zambia Revenue Authority (ZRA) in 1996. The ZRA's attempts to cast the tax net wider and reduce smuggling were welcomed by organized business.[88] Second, ZACCI and ZAM championed the move toward VAT. The former tax regime had encouraged the consumption of imported goods and VAT was thus welcomed by domestic manufacturing firms.

The pattern in the area of the deregulation and promotion of investment was similar to that found in other areas of economic policy: lots of input from the business associations in the early 1990s, but after the first three years of MMD rule, a cooling of relations and a diminution of their institutional influence in favor of personalism.

---

[87] Taylor, "Beyond Business as Usual," 229.
[88] While business worldwide is inclined to bemoan its tax burden, in Zambia this may have been a legitimate grievance. Because of the narrowness of the national tax base, the formal business sector was in practice heavily taxed.

In the early 1990s, individual businesspeople (including ZACCI and ZAM delegates) participated at their own expense in investment missions abroad. ZACCI and ZAM also pushed successfully for reform of the investment framework and the Zambia Investment Centre (ZIC) was set up, alongside the Zambia Privatisation Agency (ZPA).[89] The ZIC was initially well regarded but did not live up to its early promise, largely because of subsequent amendments to the legislative framework.

Deregulation more broadly included loosening licensing and exchange controls. While the broad outlines of this policy were welcomed by business, the implementation received somewhat more mixed reviews.[90] Currency devaluation, for example, was certainly necessary and was something business lobbied for but, given high interest and inflation rates, the overall impact of the move was neutral or perhaps even negative. It turned Zambia into an *entrepôt* for South Africans and Zimbabweans to exchange their own beleaguered currencies for US dollars. In addition, deregulation of currency markets opened up lucrative new opportunities for bureaus de change, seized by a number of those within government.

There was a significant level of deregulation of the economy including the freeing of prices across the economy. Much of this was in accord with the Washington consensus and with what Zambian business associations prescribed, but much of it also served the partisan agenda of the new MMD government.[91] In this early stage, the interests of the new ruling party coincided with the interests and demands of both the IFIs and business as a whole. This happy accord did not hold for long as the ruling party discovered new ways to do as its predecessor had done, namely to use economic policy to secure patronage resources.

One of the most blatant instances of this occurred in 1993 in the financial sector, with the executive's treatment of the ailing Meridien

---

[89] For an account of the structure of the ZPA, see Kenneth Kaoma Mwenda, *Zambia's Stock Exchange and Privatisation Programme: Corporate Finance Law in Emerging Markets* (Lewiston, NY: The Edwin Mellen Press, 2001), 243–8.

[90] O'Donnell, Interview, 8 July 2000.

[91] Lise Rakner, "Reform as a Matter of Political Survival: Political and Economic Liberalisation in Zambia 1991–1996" (Dr. Polit Dissertation, Christen Michelsen Institute, 1998), 110.

Bank. Andrew Sardanis, the owner of Meridien, was an influential businessman who had previously headed up the government's parastatal empire (see above). A key associate of Kenneth Kaunda, he had developed a network of loyal associates through his directorship of ZIMCO and continued to be a successful (and politically well-connected) businessman after the 1991 transition.

When Meridien ran into financial trouble, highly placed individuals within the cabinet attempted to save the ailing bank. Despite a negative internal assessment of Meridien's operations, State House instructed the Central Bank of Zambia (BOZ) to rescue the bank. Having failed to convince other commercial banks in Zambia to cooperate in a bailout, BOZ itself poured millions into Meridien to try and restore the confidence of the bank's clients and the financial markets.[92] The attempt failed, and Meridien was placed under receivership.

The government's handling of the collapse of Meridien Bank signaled a decisive shift in the relationship between business and government. As the group of politicians that centered on the presidency strengthened their hold on power, the voice of the legitimate business associations was muted.

Business' interactions with government on policy questions

In the early 1990s, both business associations and key figures in the MMD had agreed on the need to restructure their interactions to be more regular and institutionalized. Dipak Patel, then Minister of Commerce, Trade and Industry, instituted monthly meetings between ZACCI and his ministry. Business and government met in a number of public fora and businesspeople were invited to sit on government boards. This did not last. The monthly ministerial meetings with ZACCI first became quarterly meetings and then were dropped entirely. By the end of the decade, organized business was marginal to policy-making.

Two proximate developments explain this shift. First, confronted with the reality of how reform was being implemented, the business

---

[92] Andersson *et al.* claim that the total amount spent by the state to support the bank equaled 1 percent of the national GDP. Andersson, Bigsten, and Persson, *Foreign Aid, Debt and Growth in Zambia*, 28.

community itself fractured. Second and simultaneously, other voices were being strengthened, in particular those of associates of the president, and the IFIs.

In the early 1990s both ZACCI and ZAM postulated strong support for the MMD and for economic reform including privatization, deregulation, and trade and forex liberalization. Within a couple of short years, however, this approbation began to fracture. One reason for this was the diversity of ZACCI's membership which meant that members would be affected in very different ways by trade liberalization.

Business also began to differ with government on the course of the reforms. Obstacles to private sector development in Zambia by the end of the decade included a crippling lack of access to medium- and long-term finance, the high cost of electricity and fuel, and the lack of local government services.[93] These concerns were not the focus of the IFIs nor, crucially, did they coincide with the particular interests of the political elites. The result was that business' institutionalized input into economic policy-making became increasingly restricted.[94] By the year 2000, one businessman remarked that "[t]his government fancies itself as the government of dialogue but it does not understand the meaning of the term."[95] While representatives of government and business continued to meet, these meetings were regarded as empty talk.[96]

During the course of the decade, economic policy and its implementation increasingly privileged political considerations in a way that did not advance the restructuring process but rather benefited selected individuals. From 1993 on it became evident that interest coalitions located within government and the bureaucracy or closely associated with them were becoming more influential than broad-based independent interest associations such as business.

The neo-liberal model optimistically predicts that, after an initial period of hardship, an economy that has undertaken the necessary reforms will see a revival of growth and the emergence of new opportunities for entrepreneurship. What transpired in Zambia was less happy. Business opportunities continued to be monopolized by

[93] Peter Armond and Moses Simamba, Personal interview with author, 22 June 2000.
[94] Rakner, "The Pluralist Paradox."
[95] Anonymous, Confidential interview with author, 3 July 2000.
[96] Taylor, "Beyond Business as Usual," 124–5.

those with access to political power. A prominent Zambian businessman argued that "[a]gain we are making a mistake to let a small clique of government ministers get into business … I have been in business for twenty years and I have never seen the benefits these guys [in government] are now reaping. I simply cannot penetrate the market as all business opportunities are crowded out by government ministers monopolizing business with government."[97]

By the end of the 1990s organized business was, at best, marginal to economic policy-making. It was also marginal in the economy – and this was a key part of its political weakness; Rakner points out that the private sector employed less than one-fifth of the Zambian workforce and "constituted neither an electoral threat nor a useful political ally for MMD."[98] It could therefore be easily dismissed.

The policy outcomes

There can be no doubt that the MMD introduced significant changes in economic policy and in the overall way in which private enterprise was regarded in Zambia. According to one Lusaka businessperson, "[t]he MMD deserves praise for changing public perceptions of wealth creation. While … [wealth creation] is still not sufficiently understood by the broader public, it is at least no longer a dirty word. K. K. [Kenneth Kaunda] only conceived of getting rich as negative and inherently exploitative."[99]

Having said that, business *qua* business had little success in shaping economic policy-making. This is not obvious at first glance; there were, after all, significant levels of privatization, trade liberalization, and deregulation in Zambia.[100] According to the Chair of ZAM, business associations had the greatest impact on policy in the areas of trade tariff reductions, cross-border trade issues, the reduction of duties and increasing competitiveness, and, in the early days, limiting the number of bureaucratic hurdles. But in policy-making, as in so much else, the devil is in the detail, and here business did not have any meaningful impact. Unable to maintain its early level of influence, it

---

[97] Quoted in Rakner, "Reform as a Matter of Political Survival," 150.
[98] Rakner, "The Pluralist Paradox," 536.
[99] Theo Bull, Personal interview with author, 3 July 2000.
[100] O'Donnell, Interview, 2000.

may be that business' biggest failure in the end was its inability to halt Chiluba's "abandonment" of the reform program.[101]

While government privatized the lion's share of its holdings, the bungling of the ZCCM privatization cost the Zambian government millions of dollars and, potentially, the rejuvenation of the Copperbelt.[102] The brutal and rushed nature of the trade liberalization program provided much in the way of the harsh winds of competition for Zambian enterprises but very little constructive support to enable potentially viable firms to build their regional competitiveness. Deregulation, technically probably the simplest area, had more successes. However, deregulation of the financial sector was overshadowed by the scandal surrounding Meridien Bank.

Why business lost what it lost

The 1990s demonstrated the weakness of both the public and private sectors in Zambia, with a government characterized by a high level of neo-patrimonialism, and a business community deeply scarred by these neo-patrimonial forms of behavior. The outcome is strikingly similar to Ghana's over the same period. According to a former MMD Minister of Agriculture, "[i]n terms of impact there is little positive to show for structural adjustment [in Zambia], even if many fiscal and monetary benchmarks have been met, many state industries privatized and many restrictions on the free market abandoned."[103]

At the beginning of the MMD's first term in office, it seemed possible to marry the interests of three groups: government, business, and the IFIs. They all agreed on the broadly neo-liberal nature of the reform process. According to one local observer, the MMD's first Minister of Finance Ronald Penza "epitomized MMD policy as well as formulated it. He did actively formulate policy. He also built his own fortune. Mostly this was done quite legally and adroitly. They [the MMD elites] are masters at creating economic opportunities – and then taking them."[104] It was not that neo-patrimonial behavior

---

[101] Ibid.
[102] The parallel here with the costliness of the *nationalization* of the mines under Kenneth Kaunda is striking.
[103] Guy Scott, "Zambia: Structural Adjustment, Rural Livelihoods and Sustainable Development," *Development Southern Africa* 19, no. 3 (2002): 406.
[104] Anonymous, Confidential interview with author, 3 July 2000.

among the political elite was absent in the early 1990s but rather that it did not, at first, obscure the voice of legitimate business or damage the quality of economic policy-making.

As the reform program unfolded, however, differences began to emerge between all three actors. Disagreements also began to emerge within the business community itself on how reform should proceed. These divisions, alongside its own structural weakness, damaged business' ability to win its policy preferences as these diverged from those of the IFIs and the governing elites.

The government's agenda also split between those genuinely committed to neo-liberal reform and those seeking personal gain from the process. The latter group won. While the government had to, at least appear to adhere to the broad outlines of the neo-liberal agenda, in the small details and the implementation economic policy-making was driven by the need to secure new sources of funding for those elites. Such sources were found sometimes in the stripping of assets from soon-to-be-privatized entities or from the acquisition of those entities themselves. They were found in the government contracts that were now awarded to private sector firms. They were found too in areas where the state continued to play a dominant role in the market, notably the energy sector.[105]

It is striking that those reforms that were technically easy and did not harm the interests of important actors within the state were most swiftly accomplished.[106] In addition, those reforms that could win the president and his allies political support were also implemented.[107] However, those reforms that would damage the interests of key individuals and politically important constituencies were impeded at every turn.[108]

This neo-patrimonial behavior on the part of state-based elites required the active cooperation of some in the private sector. Business' historical entanglement with political elites compromised its capacity to defend a distinct set of institutional interests. Instead, individual

---

[105] Specifically the regulation of the Zambia Electricity Supply Commission (ZESCO) and National Petroleum Company.

[106] Indeed, reforms that affected the living standards of the poor and vulnerable such as the lifting of maize and fertilizer subsidies seemed most easily effected.

[107] For example the sale of municipal housing to individuals.

[108] Such as privatization of the mines, the wrangle over the sale of the state-owned electricity supply commission, and reform of the public sector.

businesspeople sought opportunity where they could find it, and, given the overwhelmingly neo-patrimonial nature of their environment, this frequently lay in a personal relationship with those close to political power.

This is not to argue that there were not market-minded members of the business community or that the business associations did not attempt to represent their views. Ultimately, however, because of their marginal political and economic status, these views could be safely ignored, whereas those of the IFIs could not. During the course of the 1990s, the business associations often came to want more detailed or qualified interventions than the IFIs required. After welcoming the first wave of reforms, businesspeople became concerned with a number of lower order obstacles to broader economic recovery that were not being attended to. My interviews with large numbers of businesspeople revealed broad consensus across the private sector on what these obstacles were, and an inability to win this view with government.[109]

Neo-liberal reforms were intended to shut down access to illicit rents via the state's involvement in the economy. Van de Walle has argued instead that the resumption of international financing by the IFIs in Africa opened up huge new potential streams of revenue for neo-patrimonial states in Africa.[110] This was certainly true in Zambia as the World Bank and IMF rewarded Zambia's initial progress with renewed access to international financing. This incentive privileged the voice of the IFIs in economic policy-making as governmental elites were forced to continue to reform just enough to ensure continued funding.

A leftist explanation for the low level of impact by business might point to the overweening role of the IFIs. As a simple review of the flow of funds from and to Washington DC suggests, the role of the IFIs was substantial – but popular perceptions overplay their influence. For its part, business had no illusions about who was most important in shaping policy implementation. While the business associations had intermittent discussions with the resident IFI representatives over the course of the 1990s, business did not seek to

---

[109] I conducted interviews with a range of business people and business associations in Lusaka and on the Copperbelt in 2000 and 2002.

[110] Van de Walle, *African Economies and the Politics of Permanent Crisis 1979–1999*.

structure regular meetings with these officials.[111] Instead, business focused its lobbying energy on government, especially the Finance Minister and the executive as the authors of economic policy.

Reform then, did not succeed in transforming the overall milieu within which economic actors traded, earned their income, and invested. Instead, Burnell argues, allocative decisions continued to be made "through such informal practices as cronyism, ethnically-rooted clientelism and corruption."[112]

The overall ideological outlines of economic policy in the 1990s then do not help us to understand the dynamics of business–government interaction in Zambia. What are crucial are the specific details of how reforms were effected as well as the implementation that actually followed. In turn, a dense personalistic network of keenly defended, overlapping economic and political interests affected that implementation and confounded the ability of organized business to articulate its sector-wide policy preferences. The origins of these features lay in the historically constructed nature of the Zambian state and its business community.

Conclusion

Zambia has a long history of entrepreneurial-minded individuals being drawn to careers located in or around the state. Certainly, the racially exclusive pattern of economic activity set up under the colonial regime restricted economic opportunities for indigenous Zambians outside of the state. Post-independence nationalization, the state's access to copper rents, and the reliance on state-led industrialization further reinforced this tendency.

Nonetheless, 1990 presented an opportunity to reorder the relationship between business, government, and economic policy-making. A number of developments seemed to indicate that the new MMD government would seize that opportunity. These included the transition to multiparty rule which promised greater access for a range of interest groups to policy-making; the overwhelming level of support from the local business community for the MMD that presumably would render that community an important constituency for the new

---

[111] O'Donnell, Interview.
[112] Burnell, "Does Economic Reform Promote Democratisation?," 209.

ruling party; and the rigorously neo-liberal nature of the policy advocated by the new MMD government, again which presumably would incline government to be receptive to input from the business sector.

In the early 1990s, business associations reported themselves satisfied with both the level of access that they enjoyed to key government officials and the way in which their views were incorporated into policy-making. However, during the course of the decade, two factors came to mute the input of the business sector as a whole into economic policy.

First, the impact of the business associations was weakened as business began to fracture over how implementation should proceed and, on occasion, to part company with the IFIs on the details. Instead, the particular voices of certain well-connected individuals rose above the sector-wide hum of business.

Second, in a related process, power was increasingly centered on the presidency. Political power became more concentrated and rigid, and political rationale triumphed over economic rationale in the government's economic policy-making. This resulted in the reassertion of long-standing clientelist relationships between individual businesspeople and government, the symptom of a society in which political and economic power had long been fused and where there were few incentives to change this.

The Third Republic thus resembled its predecessors in important ways. A former high-level government bureaucrat made the following observation about business–government relations and economic policy-making in the independence era under Kenneth Kaunda: "The policy environment gave rise to particular allegiances between individuals within the public and private sectors that became crucial to the survival of a business. Economic policies in turn then became influenced by those allegiances."[113] This description could be applied, verbatim, to Chiluba's economic policy-making too. Zambian economic and political life continued to be dominated by a small number of elites who moved easily between business and government, between the "public" and "private" sectors in a context in which success in one sphere was dependent on success in the other. As before, "politics led ... the economy rather than vice versa."[114]

---

[113] Mike Soko, Personal interview with author, 2000.
[114] Troy Damian Fitrell, Personal interview with author 2000.

In short, more than a decade after the launch of a political project that seemed to hold out the promise for a revolution in relations between the state and the private sector and their respective roles in the economy, this observer was struck by the apparent triumph of old-style, Zambian "business as usual." However, this set of practices and associations had less to do with "business" as the World Bank and neo-liberal theorists understood it, and more to do with a mode of transacting characterized by the drearily familiar practices of clientelism and patronage.

Conclusion: the business of economic policy-making, comparatively speaking

An ambitious shopkeeper class, urban homogenization ... and intense minority group problems on the one side give a quite different picture than ... a fusion of political and economic elites ... and the confinement of business activities to a small percentage of the population give on the other.[1]

In a classic study, Clifford Geertz reflects on the differences between two very different Indonesian towns, one dominated by peddlers, the other by princes. Modjokuto, on the one hand, is a market-centered society with an extraordinarily energetic commercial life characterized by "vigorous competitive interaction."[2] The Muslim traders are somewhat marginal to the political life of the town but their industry forms the dynamic core of its economic life. By contrast, in Tabanan, "it has not been the bazaar but the palace which has stamped its character upon the town."[3] Here the political elites are dominant, and they would like to parlay their political power into economic power too. The danger is that "Tabanan's firms can become easily politicized in modern terms and this is ... extremely dysfunctional to further growth or even to continued solvency."[4]

The same phenotypes are evident in the griot's account of two sons of a Malian king: "the younger preferred fortune and wealth and became the ancestor of those who go from country to country seeking their fortune" while "the elder chose royal power and reigned."[5] Similarly, my four case studies divide into two distinct groups, one in which there is a thriving and sizable commercial class, and another in

---

[1] Clifford Geertz, *Peddlers and Princes* (Chicago, IL: University of Chicago Press, 1963), 146. Geertz is comparing the two Indonesian towns of Modjokuto and Tabanan.

[2] Ibid., 13.   [3] Ibid., 17.   [4] Ibid., 123.

[5] D. T. Niane, *Sundiata: An Epic of Old Mali*, trans. G. D. Pickett (London: Longman, 1965), 3. Cited also in Wilks, *Forests of Gold*, 2.

242

which it is instead the political elites that dominate the economic milieu. This Conclusion contrasts the outcomes of the four case study countries and considers the comparative implications of these outcomes. It opens with a review of the country studies before reflecting on the implications of these findings for broader developmental prospects.

The country studies

Much of the explanation for business' influence in Ghana, Mauritius, South Africa, and Zambia lies with the capacity and power of the indigenous business community and state respectively. The cases reviewed in this book demonstrate that we understand the modalities of neo-liberal reform by first examining the relationship between business and the state in question. In what follows, I will review the contours of my four country studies before considering those findings alongside related events and interactions elsewhere in the developing world.

Mauritius and South Africa differ in important respects but they also share a number of suggestive similarities, perhaps most strikingly the way that ethnicity had historically separated out their respective political and economic elites. In each case, as in Modjokuto, the ethnic group that dominated the economy was distinct from that which dominated the polity. In direct and indirect ways, this accorded the business community room to develop apart from the state. As a result, local businesspeople were not able to rely principally on patronage from the state for their profit making. They were instead forced to rely on more conventional market mechanisms.

In neither South Africa nor Mauritius was the state highly neo-patrimonial. Moreover, while the two states were very different from each other, they had each created a more or less market-driven context in which business could operate. In each case, business was long-standing, structurally powerful within the economy, internally diverse, and highly institutionalized. The conjunction of these factors and the impact of ethnicity, as in Modjokuto, informed business' significant political and organizational capacity. The result? In both countries, business had a significant impact on policy-making, the content of which was generally economy-wide, although in each case there was a bias toward certain sub-sectors.

In Zambia and Ghana, by contrast, politics served to bind business closely to states that were highly neo-patrimonial. In both cases business was structurally weak and uninstitutionalized with low levels of autonomy. It is not that there was no ethnic differentiation between economic and political elites in these two cases but that it was significantly less important to their relationship than political connections.

The result was a low level of business capacity as significant numbers of businesspeople were drawn into a patronage-based relationship with the state. In both countries, despite the adoption of two of the most rigorous neo-liberal reform programs on the continent, business associations were marginal to economic policy-making. Business people were not entirely without influence, however. Over the course of the reform programs in both countries, a stratum of business that owed its existence and profitability to its connections with the state emerged or was rejuvenated. These businesspeople enjoyed influence, but it was personal and designed to secure very particular advantage. As in Geertz's Tabanan, the political princes dominated.

Contributions of this study

To what extent do these findings fit with the state of business–government relations elsewhere in the developing world? And what contributions to the broader literature on that subject does this study make? The contributions may be clustered in four areas.

Business disaggregated

Business is, of course, not a homogeneous category. One of the most important set of intra-business distinctions is structured by the various sub-sectors of the economy that a particular firm may operate within, and the literature predicts that the content of business' policy demands will vary along this dimension.[6] In my four cases, the various sub-sectors generally behaved as leading theories would have us expect. Traders, for example, were consistently more pro-liberalization than manufacturers, who tended to demand more protectionist measures.

---

[6] See, for example, Helen Milner, *Resisting Protectionism: Global Industries and the Politics of International Trade* (Princeton, NJ: Princeton University Press, 1988).

(Significantly, this also tended to be the sub-sector most easily colonized by the political elites.) Exporters, predictably, were the most liberal-minded. Encompassing business associations generally succeeded in adopting broader and longer-term views while sub-sector-specific associations served narrower interests.

This study addresses also a second, influential set of arguments concerning the determinant role of factor or sub-sectoral endowments:[7] Looking beyond policy preferences, this literature argues that the politics and behavior of the private sector (and the state) depend on which economic sub-sector dominates the economy. The politics of a mining-dominated economy, for example, will look very different to that of a well-diversified manufacturing economy. This group of writers focuses on the structure of the economy and in particular which sub-sector of the economy predominates, arguing that this will decisively shape the character of business and of its political interactions. In particular, Shafer's argument seems a good explanation of the policy outcomes in Zambia, which are collusive and not in the interests of the economy more broadly. Shafer accurately predicts, for example, that there will be very little autonomy evident in the relationship between the political leadership and those managing the mining sub-sector.

Crucially, however, this model presents little prospect for dynamism or change. While it would presumably predict that business–government relations would change in nature as an economy diversifies, it is silent on why or how that diversification might take place. It therefore cannot explain how Zambia and South Africa, both originally mining-based economies, came to look so different over time. An understanding of the broader institutional politics at play better explains why some states – like South Africa and Mauritius – are able to escape the policy strictures imposed by sub-sectoral domination, and others are unable to do so.

I have argued, for example, that other internal and structural characteristics of business are at least as important as its factor and sub-sector endowments, inasmuch as they affect the capacity of business as a whole to lobby government on specific policy issues. The extremely selective incentives provided by a neo-patrimonial state to its kin

---

[7] See Jeffry A. Frieden, *Debt, Development, and Democracy: Modern Political Economy and Latin America 1965–1985* (Princeton, NJ: Princeton University Press, 1991), Karl, *The Paradox of Plenty*, Shafer, *Winners and Losers*.

operating in the putatively "private sector" predict more accurately the behavior of African business than the sub-sectoral profile of its economy. My country studies demonstrate that the ability of business to influence policy has less to do with the asset base or product cycle of that community and more to do with the way in which the character and stature of both the state and business – and in two cases in particular, ethnicity – shape the political capacity of the business community. In short, while there is some evidence that such features as asset base can shape the business community, I conclude that ultimately it is the nature of the state itself that decisively shapes the private sector.

Business as institutionalized contestation

Reflecting further on the four-country comparison of this study allows us to locate the real importance of a rather fuzzy variable: the existence of some degree of "hostility" between business and government. While in two of my cases, business–government hostility seems to be correlated with state and business capacity, this is by no means always the case. Rawlings exhibited high levels of hostility toward liberal Ghanaian businesspeople, for example. Crucially, however, Rawlings' hostility took on a highly personalized form; indeed, the impact of his animus on policy-making demonstrates that the Ghanaian state was prey to a personalistic and patronage-based form of politics and helps us to specify more clearly the conditions under which state hostility to capital may be constructive. For much of the period under review, business–government relations in Mauritius and South Africa were not about infelicitous personalistic relations but about conflicts between institutionalized sets of interests. What was crucial in the development of a discrete business community in South Africa and Mauritius then was not so much the hostility of the state *per se*. Rather, what was crucial was how the incentives created by that institutionalized hostility facilitated the emergence of a separate sphere in which business could develop a set of interests that were distinct from those of the state.

A comparative review reinforces these findings. In his study of neo-liberal reforms in Brazil and Venezuela, Schneider, for example, finds that there is real value in contested policy processes. He contrasts the slower, negotiated course of neo-liberal reforms in Brazil with the much faster, "reform by decree" process of Venezuela, concluding that "[t]he tortoise bests the hare once again: resolute governments that push policies diligently *through multiple veto points* are better at consolidating reform than decisive ones."[8] He could just as easily have been contrasting the more methodical, consultative reforms of the leftist governments of South Africa and Mauritius with the initially zealous neo-liberal reform programs that stumbled in Ghana and Zambia.

Institutionalized consultation with business can solve two key problems that reforming states face: the significant transaction costs of dragging unwilling social actors along in a reform process, and imperfect information about what is really going on in the market (a problem for technically weak states with few means of effectively penetrating their societies).

The importance of contestation, however, is also in the way that it, in turn, shapes the state itself.[9] Historically, contestation and the establishment of private spheres of autonomous economic activity have been central to the emergence of a broadly based and responsive state. Acemoglu *et al.* link the rise of constitutional monarchy in England and the Netherlands to the inability of those states to dominate their nationals' involvements in the Atlantic trade. (In England, for example, most of the Atlantic trade was carried out by individuals, private citizens, and firms. By contrast in Portugal and Spain the royal households maintained tight control over explorations and trade.) Limited constitutional rule created a more effective state, which could better pursue further economic development.[10]

Moreover, political estrangement from the state can provide strong incentives for private sector actors to invest in institutionalization. In an argument that parallels my findings for Mauritius and South Africa, Schneider argues that business in Mexico was motivated to invest in business associations precisely because it was excluded from the politics of the ruling party; the lack of personal connections

---

[8] Ben Ross Schneider, "Organizing Interests and Coalitions in the Politics of Market Reform in Latin America," *World Politics* 56 (2004): 466. Italics mine.

[9] It is significant that in both Mauritius and South Africa organized labor also contested policy-making with the government.

[10] Daron Acemoglu, Simon Johnson, and James A. Robinson, "Institutions as a Fundamental Cause of Long-Run Growth," in *Handbook of Economic Growth*, ed. Philippe Aghion and Steven N. Durlauf (Amsterdam, The Netherlands: Elsevier North-Holland, 2005), 452–7.

between businesspeople and the state – an apparent weakness – forced the business community to invest in organizational strength, rather than in personalism. Indeed he argues that it was the hostility of the Mexican state, its love–hate relationship with business, which motivated business to organize effectively to defend its long-term interests.[11] A similar pattern was evident in the relationship between successive Chilean governments and business, and in the relationship between the Korean government and the Federation of Korean Industries. In all of these instances, however, animus alone was insufficient. It was crucial too that business enjoy some structural power in the economy, so that it could not easily be swept aside by a hostile government. Equally, it was important that access to government remained institutionalized.[12]

For that matter, the quality of both public and private sector institutions counted. Peter Evans argues that "having a public counterpart that is organized and predictable makes it much more likely that the business community moves from merchant-capital strategies of 'buying cheap and selling dear' to a more developmentally desirable Schumpeterian strategy of confronting risk and making long-term investments."[13] A certain kind of state can foster a politically and economically effective capitalist class; while another shapes a very different outcome.

Mobutu Sese Seko once remarked that in Zaire "holding any slice of public power constitutes a veritable exchange instrument."[14] As the president of that country and chief plunderer of its coffers, he knew of what he spoke. His remarks can be read in two ways and they would be equally true for both. The most obvious interpretation is that public office equals a license to seek rents. A second reading is that the public sphere (the state) molds and generates ("constitutes") markets and other sorts of economic and exchange institutions.

---

[11] Ben Ross Schneider, "Why is Mexican Business so Organized?," *Latin American Research Review* 37, no. 1 (2002): 87.

[12] Ben Ross Schneider, *Business, Politics and the State in Twentieth-Century Latin America* (Cambridge University Press, 2004), 16, 199.

[13] Peter B. Evans, "State Structures, Government–Business Relations, and Economic Transformation," in *Business and the State in Developing Countries*, ed. Sylvia Maxfield and Ben Ross Schneider (Ithaca, NY: Cornell University Press, 1997), 66.

[14] Quoted in Hutchcroft, *Booty Capitalism*, 51.

However, the nature of the private sector institutions in and of themselves is important too. Latin America is generally in a stronger position in this regard than much of Africa although there is of course variation on both continents. For the most part, however, in Latin America private businesses form a larger share of the national economies and they exhibit higher levels of political capacity than their African counterparts.[15] Doner *et al.* argue that three key characteristics of public–private institutions produce better policy outcomes: "They operate on functional or industry-wide criteria; their private sector participants tend to be 'encompassing'...; and their operations tend to be transparent, at least to government and business, and to proceed according to explicit and consistent rules and norms."[16]

The role of peak and/or encompassing institutions is particularly important: Doner and Schneider argue that Chile's peak associations were decisive in that country's reform process because of their ability to coordinate and harmonize the preferences of all the subsectors of business.[17] Business' political and organizational capacity then has implications for the state's ability to make economic policy unilaterally.[18]

In addition to contestation (especially institutionalized contestation), there are other processes and features that may provide a check on neo-patrimonialism, even in situations without optimal private sector capacity. The example of Mauritius considered alongside the recent history of certain East Asian cases suggests the importance of production for export markets in orienting private sector firms toward efficiency rather than rents, as Amsden argues.[19] An export market provides an objective means to assess which firms are producing efficiently; a developmentally minded state could then choose to reward

---

[15] Schneider, *Business Politics and the State in Twentieth-Century Latin America*.

[16] Richard F. Doner, Bryan K. Ritchie, and Dan Slater, "Systemic Vulnerability and the Origins of Developmental States: Northeast and Southeast Asia in Comparative Perspective," *International Organization* 59 (2005): 334.

[17] Richard F. Doner and Ben Ross Schneider, "Business Associations and Economic Development: Why Some Associations Contribute More Than Others," *Business and Politics* 2, no. 3 (2000): 264–5.

[18] Schneider, *Business Politics and the State in Twentieth-Century Latin America*, 203.

[19] Alice Amsden, *Asia's Next Giant* (Oxford University Press, 1989). Cited also in Doner and Schneider, "Business Associations and Economic Development."

high-performing firms, as the Korean state did.[20] This is a very different approach from that adopted by the Ghanaian and Zambian states, whose subsidies to firms increased even as those firms continued to fail, but it is not far from the spirit of what the Mauritian government undertook. Similarly, an economy like South Africa's which was highly internationalized with a large number of international linkages – of a certain kind – can send important signals about the types of policies and modes of production that are likely to prove internationally competitive. Moreover, the "veto" power of international markets may restrict the capacity of the state to make policy as it wishes.

Business as ethnicized "other" (or when bad ethnic relations make good political economy)

The particular cases of South Africa and Mauritius suggest that a strong dose of ethnic differentiation in the right place might have a beneficial economic policy-making outcome. This runs counter to the conventional wisdom of new institutional economists who argue that higher levels of ethnic diversity are correlated with poorer economic outcomes.[21] This more conventional literature is both intuitively appealing and strongly borne out by a large-n regression analysis, both for Africa and more broadly. The argument, however, fails to engage a number of questions crucial to the overall relationship between ethnic diversity and economic outcomes. First, while it utilizes a broad measure of ethno-linguistic diversity (ELD)[22] it does not consider a more finely calibrated measure: what this means for the power or influence of each respective group. Ratios and the weight of numbers matter here. It is crucial to consider not simply the number of ethno-linguistic groups in any one society, but the ability of a single group or likely coalition of groups to dominate political power.[23]

---

[20] Amsden, *Asia's Next Giant*.
[21] See most especially Easterly and Levine, "Africa's Growth Tragedy." That ethnic diversity is correlated with ethnic conflict is also a common assumption in political science literature. For an example of this argument applied to ethnic minorities in the business community, see Chua, *World on Fire*.
[22] Calculated as a figure between 1 and 0 that indicates the likelihood that any two randomly selected members of a population will come from different ethno-linguistic groups.
[23] See Posner, *Institutions and Ethnic Politics in Africa*.

This brings me to a second point, more pertinent to my argument. The ELD score throws very little light, in and of itself, on how power (both political and economic) is parceled out, and whether this accords with ethnicized demarcations. What was crucial in Mauritius and South Africa was not simply that the ethno-linguistic group that dominated the economy was one of four or eleven ethnic groups respectively. Rather, what mattered was a) whether the group that dominated the economy was different from and historically in opposition to the group that dominated the polity, b) the balance of power between the two, and hence c) what political incentives this established for the state. All of my cases were ethnically diverse, but they differed substantially in terms of these three dimensions. In the end what was determinant, more than any ELD score or even the presence or absence of ethnicized hostility, was how these factors interacted with the overall character of the state and business and the relationship between the two. This contradicts much common-sense thinking about the deleterious effects of ethnic diversity.[24]

There are obvious dangers in extrapolating the implications of this finding on ethnicity too widely or carelessly. Ethnicized hostility can all too easily tip into devastating social conflict as it has, on occasion, in both South Africa and Mauritius. Likewise, the expulsion of Asian traders from a number of African countries in the early post-independence period reminds us of the potential costs to a politically conspicuous – but in every other respect weak – ethnic minority.[25] In addition, there is some evidence that ethnicity lends itself to the politics of exclusion and "pork,"[26] a significant danger in states that may already be leaning in a neo-patrimonial direction.

---

[24] I am not alone here. Collier and Gunning argue that "the negative growth effect of ethnic diversity only applies in societies lacking political rights." Paul Collier and Jan Willem Gunning, "Explaining African Economic Performance," *Journal of Economic Literature* 37 (1999): 67. Fearon and Laitin assert that the literature systematically overestimates the tendency for ethnic diversity to result in conflict. Cf. James D. Fearon and David D. Laitin, "Explaining Interethnic Cooperation," *American Political Science Review* 90, no. 4 (1996).

[25] Paul Kennedy, *African Capitalism: The Struggle for Ascendancy* (Cambridge University Press, 1990), 71.

[26] James D. Fearon, "Why Ethnic Politics and 'Pork' Tend to Go Together" (paper presented at the "Ethnic Politics and Democratic Stability" conference, Wilder House, University of Chicago, 21–23 May 1999).

Nonetheless, advantages accrue from a business class that has a coherent sense of its own identity, whether that is ethnically defined or defined in some other way: Doner and Schneider argue, for example, that "ascriptive or ethnic linkages can make the potential group more homogenous and hence ... easier to organize." A strong sense of group identity can foster trust and hence assist in compliance with organizational policy, consolidating effective private sector associations,[27] and augmenting their capacity.

Moreover, it is clear from my case studies that ethnicity in Mauritius and South Africa historically served as a crucial political cleavage, separating out political and economic power, restricting access to patronage and permitting the emergence of a healthier, more robust strain of capitalism. Of course, it is entirely conceivable that other, less destructive mechanisms could perform the same function at least as well, if not better. The Ghana case offers some clues in this regard. It is early days yet, but under President Kufuor, the NPP government in Ghana appears to be taking steps to institutionalize business and its relations with government. On the face of it, this would present an alternative separation mechanism, one potentially more compatible with a liberal state form. Of course, the highly neo-patrimonial nature of the Ghanaian state for much of its modern history warn us of the difficulty of redirecting institutional pathways, but a careful reading of both the history of Ghana and more recent developments in that country suggest also more hopeful possibilities.

Zimbabwe might be presented as an unhappy counter to South Africa's outcomes, as an example of the obvious dangers of ethnic hostility. The comparison is important. Both countries had a "vocal, sophisticated, and diversified economic elite, which was predominantly white, and whose interests potentially conflicted with those of the newly enfranchised majority."[28] However, I will argue that after majority rule in Zimbabwe in 1980, that state rapidly developed neo-patrimonial traits and that the imperatives this generated ultimately revealed the limits of business' capacity.

Because of the relative strength and diversity of the white private sector in Zimbabwe, after the first democratic election that brought a

---

[27] Doner and Schneider, "Business Associations and Economic Development," 273.
[28] Carolyn Jenkins, "The Politics of Economic Policy-Making in Zimbabwe," *Journal of Modern African Studies* 35, no. 4 (1997): 578.

(black) majority government to power, economic elites could exploit fears that redistribution would damage production output.[29] In the decade after majority rule, the concern over white flight in Zimbabwe also restrained the state from appropriating economic assets. Business and government appeared to cohabit quite cozily for much of the decade that followed. A similar argument could have been made for South Africa just after democratization. At this point it was difficult to see what separated the two countries out, and this continued to be true for some time. As Brautigam *et al.* point out, "if we were to stop the Zimbabwe case in 1990, we would have a story of business associations effectively promoting largely growth-oriented policies, forging a nascent 'growth coalition' with technocrats and political elites in the Zimbabwe government."[30] Unfortunately, that is not where the story ends.

After the attainment of majority rule in Zimbabwe and the entrenchment of the ruling ZANU party in power, a state-based black elite developed rapidly, many of whose members moved into the formerly white suburbs and began to identify with these lifestyles. What occurred then was the by-now-familiar story of a political elite that came to occupy significant strata of economic power too, and to wield political power in their own interests. "Increasingly," Jenkins argues, "the interests of the old white and new black elites began to converge."[31] The interests of the business community came to be associated with those of the political elite, rather than with the fortunes of the country more broadly.

During the 1990s, the Zimbabwean state grew corrupt and undemocratic, and the fortunes of business came to be ever more closely tied to the decisions of the state. Power was personalized around the president and his wife, and Zimbabwe began to look increasingly neopatrimonial. Now the business community's ethnic makeup rendered it vulnerable to populist harangues – and worse. Because the interests of the business community had come to be aligned with those of the political elite rather than with a broader constituency, the business community (and the white population generally) enjoyed little popular

---

[29] Ibid.: 581.
[30] Brautigam, Rakner, and Taylor, "Business Associations and Growth Coalitions in Sub-Saharan Africa," 535.
[31] Jenkins, "The Politics of Economic Policy-Making in Zimbabwe," 594.

support or legitimacy. It also lacked the structural power of its South African equivalent: both the business community and the white population in Zimbabwe were far smaller than their counterparts in South Africa, as was their share of the national economy. (Whites in Zimbabwe comprise about 1 percent of the overall population. In South Africa, whites make up around 15 percent of the overall population.)

The case of Zimbabwe then demonstrates at least two things. First, it points to the obvious dangers for a structurally weak but ethnically distinct economic elite. While ethnicity historically may have functioned to carve out an independent sphere for business in Zimbabwe, there was no guarantee that it could safeguard that sphere indefinitely. What is vital for the maintenance of private sector capacity is the ability of business to bolster its political power. This may be done either by developing alliances with other ethnic groups or by being identified with the broader social good. Business elites could also achieve structural economic power sufficient that to threaten business would do immediate, obvious, and significant harm to the functioning of the broader economy. Of course, even these safeguards are insufficient in the face of a radically neo-patrimonial state, determined to pursue its own survival at all costs. Zimbabwe does not, however, refute my argument for South Africa. Indeed, it bolsters my assertion of the dangers inherent in a fusion of the narrow interests of political and economic elites. What the Zimbabwe case does underline is just how precarious the position of an ethnically distinct business community may be, and the real dangers posed by a slide toward neo-patrimonialism.

Malaysia is another interesting and important case to think about in this context. As in South Africa, an ethnic minority has long dominated economic power in Malaysia, while the indigenous majority won control of the state. In Malaysia it was the economically dominant Chinese, who number just under a quarter of the population, who dominated the economy.[32] The Malays and the indigenous population,[33] known collectively as the Bumiputera, were for the most part shut out of the economy. With the advent of independence, however, the Bumiputera came to dominate the sphere of government and

---

[32] As in South Africa therefore, we are talking about a sizable minority.
[33] Just over 50 and 10 percent of the population respectively.

political power. For its part, Chinese business flourished both under colonialism and in its immediate aftermath.[34] As with the private sector in South Africa, therefore, the structural power of Chinese business made it a force to be reckoned with in Malaysia.

There is a second important similarity with the South African private sector: In Malaysia, the position of Chinese businesspeople was, ironically, strengthened by the fact that they were "pariahs"; this meant that they could not assume a benevolent state and that, consequently, "the financial networks and business relationship which they developed did not rely greatly on state enforcement."[35]

Democracy of course came a little quicker to Malaysia than it did to South Africa, and the new Malaysian government embarked on the New Economic Policy (NEP) in 1970, which set out to address the imbalance of economic power. The ruling party, the United Malays National Organization (UMNO), resolved to create a Malay business class using all the means available to the state, and it achieved some success. Malay ownership of the economy rose from 2.4 percent in 1970 to 17.8 percent in 1985.[36] Arguably, however, this imposed some productive costs as "the bases for new business ventures in Malaysia have tended to be political and speculative rather than economically rational and productive."[37] Observers pointed to a proliferation of patronage networks under UMNO[38] and the way in which "[g]reen-field entrepreneurship has been virtually replaced by the acquisition of proven businesses."[39] State-owned enterprises suffered from poor management and not insignificant amounts of political patronage. Privatization in particular provided many ways to reward those who

---

[34] McVey, "The Materialization of the Southeast Asian Entrepreneur," 20.

[35] Ibid., 21.

[36] Heng Pek Koon, "The Chinese Business Elite of Malaysia," in *Southeast Asian Capitalists*, ed. Ruth McVey (Ithaca, NY: Cornell Southeast Asia Program, 1999), 130. Notably, it did not climb much thereafter, reaching 19.1 percent by 2000. E. T. Gomez, "The Perils of Pro-Malay Policies," *Far Eastern Economic Review* 168, no. 8 (2005): 36.

[37] Sieh Lee Mei Ling, "The Transformation of Malaysian Business Groups," in *Southeast Asian Capitalists*, ed. Ruth McVey (Ithaca, NY: Cornell Southeast Asia Program, 1999), 125.

[38] E. T. Gomez and K. S. Jomo, *Malaysia's Political Economy: Politics, Patronage and Profit* (Cambridge University Press, 1999).

[39] Sieh, "The Transformation of Malaysian Business Groups," 106.

were loyal to the ruling party.[40] Despite all of this, however, it does appear that "crony" practices in Malaysia were contained to reasonable levels and, at least, they did not seem to interfere with healthy growth rates.

Malaysia does suggest then that there are and should be strong grounds for concern whenever ethnic identifications are made significant for the apportionment of political or economic power. Nonetheless, where such cleavages can provide the right incentives to both government and business, they can play a positive role in boosting private sector capacity.

Business, context, and timing

In the Introduction I previewed an important competing explanation, viz. that the influence of business in Mauritius and South Africa in the neo-liberal era was greater than that in Ghana and Zambia simply because there was a higher level of economic development in the two former cases. My response to this is twofold. First, there can be little argument that the economies of Mauritius and South Africa are more industrialized and diverse than those of Zambia and Ghana. However, this begs the even larger question of why that is (I deal with this more fully in the Introduction). I have therefore been at some pains to provide a more historical account of business–government relations and of the emergence of the business class in each case.

Second, the logic of this argument suggests, in a manner reminiscent of modernization theory's linear assumptions, that the political influence of business increases neatly alongside economic development. This is not so. In any one country business influence may vary over time for a wide variety of reasons. Rather than evidence of a "higher" level of economic development, high levels of business influence on policy-making could, for example, be evidence of the weakness of the state and of other social interests such as labor. I have stressed that business' political capacity cannot be assessed in isolation from the capacity of

---

[40] Anita Doraisami, "The Political Economy of Capital Flows and Capital Controls in Malaysia," *Journal of Contemporary Asia* 35, no. 2 (2005): 253. This is an ongoing danger for attempts to redress the ethnicized control over the economy both in Malaysia and elsewhere, as with South Africa's Black Economic Empowerment (BEE) program.

the state. In both the South African and Mauritian cases, while it was true that business was stronger than it was in Zambia or Ghana, so too was the state. Therefore there was nothing predetermined about the outcome of a tussle between these two actors except that they would need to reckon with each other.

Also in the Introduction, I argued, *a la* Gerschenkron, that it was important to consider when a business class emerged in relation to the broader context, including both a country's own stage of development and that of the broader global economy. This wider context continues to be important for the subsequent development of that class too. McVey argues, for example, that the timing and modalities of Southeast Asian development helped to shape a particular kind of political economy in that region. The economic upsurge of the Pacific Rim meant that there "was money to be made but it involved opening out to the greater capitalist world."[41] She stresses the importance of the international environment, of "the incentives offered by available investment." Pressures in the international environment helped in South Africa and Mauritius too to nudge those countries away from rent-seeking toward adopting the outward form at least of embedded autonomy.[42] Mauritius chose to embark on an ISI strategy at a moment when Southeast Asian exporters were being locked out of lucrative European markets and were seeking new places to invest. For its part, South Africa had, from business' point of view, the good fortune of democratizing in the aftermath of the fall of the Berlin Wall, when socialism and economic policies such as nationalization had been widely discredited. Of course, it is well and good to point to timing and the international context, but this provides no road map for those countries where market pressures are very weak and are mediated through personalized political networks.

However, timing is important in at least two other respects: When and how a private sector consolidates its role in the economy (as opposed to when the state does this) can shape its economic and political capacity. We have already seen how in South Africa and Mauritius, the private sector came of age before the state. The same was true in

---

[41] McVey, "The Materialization of the Southeast Asian Entrepreneur," 30.

[42] South Africa's first black government came into power in an international environment that was extremely intolerant of a significant level of government involvement in the economy, particularly by an African government.

India[43] and in much of Latin America.[44] Obviously there are variations within both the Indian and Latin American subcontinents[45] – but the size and relative political capacity of the business communities in these regions is typically larger than those of most African states. Timing can give the private sector a head start in a development game which is otherwise stacked solidly on the side of the state.

Business as contingent capitalists?

Whether Malaysia is regarded as more developmental or more prone to crony capitalism seems to depend a little on who is writing and at what precise moment.[46] This ambiguity may reflect more than just the prejudices of those doing the looking; it may demonstrate the evanescence of the economic milieu. Political and economic actors can and do shift their shapes. In Africa, one need consider only Côte d'Ivoire and Kenya,[47] which seemed to offer promising grounds for politically capacitated indigenous business classes, but later turned neo-patrimonial. By contrast, early analyses of Mauritius seemed to predict a neo-patrimonial outcome and yet from the 1960s the country took a developmental turn. Businesspeople are "contingent capitalists";[48] their preferences shift as the state changes and so too do their nature and capacity.

---

[43] Aditya Mukherjee, *Imperialism, Nationalism and the Making of the Indian Capitalist Class, 1920–1947* (New Delhi, India: Sage Publications, 2002).

[44] Iliffe, *The Emergence of African Capitalism.*

[45] In Mexico, for example, Schneider describes how the private sector in Monterrey embarked on private sector-driven industrialization before the adoption of state-sponsored industrialization programs. The result there was an assertive and powerful business association. Schneider, "Why is Mexican Business so Organized?," 83.

[46] William Case, "Malaysia: New Reforms, Old Continuities, Tense Ambiguities," *Journal of Development Studies* 41, no. 2 (2005).

[47] Iliffe, *The Emergence of African Capitalism*, 81–3, Paul M. Lubeck, *The African Bourgeoisie: Capitalist Development in Nigeria, Kenya and the Ivory Coast* (Boulder, CO: Lynne Rienner Publishers, 1987), Nicola Swainson, *The Development of Corporate Capitalism in Kenya 1918–77* (Berkeley, CA: University of California Press, 1980).

[48] This usage is derived from Eva Bellin's phrase "contingent democrats," used to describe how business' political preferences change in response to the nature and behavior of the state. Cf. Eva Bellin, "Contingent Democrats: Industrialists, Labor, and Democratization in Late-Developing Countries," *World Politics* 52 (2000).

Ghana in particular seems to offer evidence of fluidity. If one looks at Ghana's state, it closely resembles a neo-patrimonial model. The picture shifts slightly, however, if one chooses to look instead at Ghana's business community, portions of which have some limited capacity. Both business' ethnic origins and its traditional liberal (oppositional) political loyalties pushed it away from the state. For much of its recent history, however, the Ghanaian state succeeded in pulling a section of the business community into a patronage-based relationship.

These two apparently contradictory tendencies (the state pulling in one direction and some of business pulling in another) make Ghana an important country to study. By contrast with Zambia, in Ghana there did appear to be some basis for a potential indigenous business class that was not closely linked to the state. While much of the business community had historically sought some autonomy from the state, this was undermined by a series of economic policies post-independence that gave the state a dominant role in directing the economy. In addition, the weakness of the business community (reflecting more broadly the weakness of the economy) meant that business was not in a position to demand anything of government. With the infusion of capital that came from the IFIs from the early 1980s, the government continued to hold the upper hand and sections of the business community succumbed to the neo-patrimonial lure of the state. Recent developments offer some hope that the state of the state – and hence of its relationship with business – is not immutable.

Implications and prospects

For some time, those concerned with development in Africa recognized the weaknesses and deficiencies of the African public sector. We have perhaps not considered fully the weaknesses too of the private sector. What is striking about African economies is how often there is no significant indigenous private sector that has the political and economic capacity to constructively engage the state on economic policy issues.

This dearth of capacity affects how the interests of the dominant classes are conceived of and pursued. It rewards those entrepreneurs who seek profit by means of a relationship with the state and may penalize those who try to push the state to lay the institutional basis for the long-term development of capitalism. What does this mean for the prospects of any developmental policy-making compact between business and government in Africa? At the very least it warns us that the path to development may be even more difficult than we had anticipated.

This study does offer some clues, however, to a way forward. To start, we should proceed with an awareness of the dangers of reifying the existing state of business–government relations. Because a relationship is currently dysfunctional for economic development does not mean it will necessarily remain so. It is not inevitable that all African states will remain (or become) neo-patrimonial. Botswana is a frequently quoted example of an African state that has successfully pursued a broadly developmental role and a higher level of involvement in the economy than many neo-liberals would be comfortable with.[49] New scholarship also suggests that neo-patrimonialism can wane as well as wax. Recent literature on Tanzania, for example, while cautious about its findings, does suggest that even a state with a much more checkered history than that of Botswana could achieve some success at reforming itself.[50]

Assuming that there is a way out then, in what direction should we look? There are at least two paths suggested by Geertz's Indonesian villages. One potential solution would be to take the Modjokuto road, attempting to reform the political economy in a more liberal direction. This route would de-emphasize the role of the state and instead focus on creating space for the private sector to develop a distinct sense of its interests. If we are to avoid the oversights of the neo-liberals, however, we need to recognize that business may be as flawed as the state – indeed, that the two actors may resemble each other closely both in how they understand their interests and in how they behave. The challenge here is to uncover incentives and constraints that will force businesspeople to shift their focus away from the state and a particularistic set of interests, and to engage with and negotiate a broader set of interests. This could occur in a number of ways including

[49] Francis Owusu and Abdi Ismail Samatar, "Industrial Strategy and the African State: The Botswana Experience," *Canadian Journal of African Studies* 31, no. 2 (1997): 289.

[50] Mike Stevens and Stefanie Teggemann, "Comparative Experience with Public Sector Reform in Ghana, Tanzania and Zambia," in *Building State Capacity in Africa*, ed. Sahr Kpundeh and Brian Levy (Washington, DC: World Bank Publications, 2004).

building up the organizational capacity of business; institutionalizing internal forms of contestation; structuring business' interactions with the state (so that they take place in formal, regularized, and publicly accountable ways); and strengthening the voice of other actors in the society, such as labor and those who represent the interests of the poor and the unemployed.

Strikingly, in many African economies, there already exists a commercial class that lies "outside the state,"[51] viz. informal sector entrepreneurs who run their businesses with little help from the state, indeed often despite the state. MacGaffey explicitly contrasts those who obtained their wealth through political connections, and entrepreneurs situated in what she calls the second economy. She recognizes how their distance from the state forced the latter to adopt a different way of doing business: "Since they [the informal sector entrepreneurs] do not have the benefit of state position and its opportunities to increase wealth through pillage and appropriation, their possibilities for wealth and advancement lie in the development of their business concerns." She points in particular to differences in how these two groups use any wealth that they manage to accumulate: "The political aristocracy ... have plundered rather than expanded their acquisitions." By contrast "[t]he nascent bourgeoisie ... displays true capitalist spirit: these entrepreneurs are concerned with good management and reinvestment of profit."[52] MacGaffey points us to the possibility that a more capacitated business community may emerge organically from this quarter.

However, we should not underestimate the challenges here. For all their energy and self-reliance, informal sector entrepreneurs will have to also build up the more muscular component of business capacity, viz. their financial and structural power in the economy. When business does not have the protection of preexisting size or power, the hostility of the state might be too overwhelming to contest. There are a legion of difficulties too in translating the success of small firms, often reliant on the energies and talents of a single proprietor, into larger, more institutionalized concerns.

The second potential way out is to head in a more developmental direction, namely to try to fix the state. Given how important the

---

[51] Janet MacGaffey, *Entrepreneurs and Parasites: The Struggle for Indigenous Capitalism in Zaire* (Cambridge University Press, 1987), 111.
[52] Ibid., 90.

state is in establishing the milieu within which business must operate, this may be a more rewarding avenue. What is absolutely vital here is to maintain – or introduce – some compulsory form of policy contestation from a broad range of economic and social interests. Otherwise the constant danger is that an unchecked developmental state could slide into crony capitalism as it did in East Asia in the late 1990s.

Finally, what are the options where the neo-patrimonialism of the state appears to be already entrenched? Are there conditions under which the rent-seeking of those in the state can evolve into something more likely to facilitate the conditions for productive capitalism? Ruth McVey suggests one means: the self-interested behavior of civil servants.[53] She argues that the uncertainty of having to rely on volatile politics may lead bureaucrats to diversify into business in an attempt to spread their risk. The same may be true for MacGaffey's political aristocracy, and in chapter 2 I described how a number of South Africa's political princes have moved into private business. It is not yet clear whether, in so doing, these political actors are laying the basis for the development of a more broadly based capitalist class, or whether they are instead crossing the line between close business–state relations and neo-patrimonialism. To be sure, there are dangers in going the Tabanan route, as Geertz's description makes clear. However, there is also the possibility that as the creatures of the state move into business, they will want to secure their investments there and that this might require, for example, measures to protect private property and the rule of law, measures that would safeguard and promote the interests of a politically and economically influential business community.

As South Africa and Mauritius demonstrate, African states and businesses can negotiate a relationship that is characterized by constructive contestation. Indeed, one of the best descriptions of the dynamic comes from Meillassoux's account of "merchant society" in pre-colonial West Africa, where:[54]

entrepreneurs knew that their productive activities, the commercial organization they controlled and the economic institutions they dominated, were

---

[53] McVey, "The Materialization of the Southeast Asian Entrepreneur."
[54] Claude Meillassoux, *The Anthropology of Slavery: The Womb of Iron and Gold*, trans. Alide Dasnois (Chicago, IL: University of Chicago Press, 1986), 254–5.

necessary to the general acquisition of wealth, and the princes knew it too. The wealth of the merchants did not consist of accumulated treasures which could be seized, once and for all. It was built on a constant process of production of consumer goods and on the uninterrupted flow of exchanges ... They knew that the warrior classes had no choice but to "protect" them, they could sometimes tax them or extract them, but they could never destroy them without depriving themselves of the benefits of this wealth.

The challenge for African businesspeople today is to negotiate a similarly productive interaction with their modern-day states. As with the sons of the ancient Malian king, the secret may lie not in forsaking either the merchant prince or his more politically minded brother, nor in ignoring the differences between them, but in constructing a relationship in which they each understand their distinct roles and each one can push the other to consider a wider set of interests than their own.

Bibliography

Primary sources

Newspapers and magazines

Africa Confidential, UK
Africa Research Bulletin, UK
African Business, UK
African Link Magazine, Canada
Business and Financial Times, Ghana*
Business Day, South Africa
Daily Mail and Guardian, South Africa
The Economist, UK
Engineering News Online, South Africa
Finance Week, South Africa
Financial Mail, South Africa
Financial Times, UK
Ghanaian Chronicle, Ghana
Ghanaian Times, Ghana
Industry Focus, Mauritius
Mail and Guardian, South Africa
Mauritius Times, Mauritius
New African, UK
News on Sunday, Mauritius
People's Daily Graphic, Ghana
The Star, South Africa
The Statesman, Ghana
Sunday Independent, South Africa
Sunday Times, South Africa
West Africa, UK

* Note that the *Daily Mail and Guardian* is a daily, online version of the weekly *Mail and Guardian*.

Government documents

African National Congress. "Constitutional Guidelines for a Democratic South Africa." South Africa: African National Congress, 1988.

"Ready to Govern: ANC Policy Guidelines for a Democratic South Africa Adopted at the National Conference." African National Congress, 1992, www.anc.org.za/ancdocs/history/readyto.html (accessed July 2007).

Black Economic Empowerment Commission. "Black Economic Empowerment Commission Presentation Prepared for the Portfolio Committee on Trade and Industry, South Africa," 2000, www.pmg.org.za/docs/2000/appendices/000913BEE.htm (accessed July 2007).

Bunwaree, Vasant K. "Budget Speech 1997–1998." La Tour Koenig, Mauritius, 9 June 1997.

Department of Trade and Industry. "South Africa's Economic Transformation: A Strategy for Broad-Based Economic Empowerment." Pretoria, South Africa: Department of Trade and Industry, 2003.

"Structure of South African Trade." In *South African Trade Statistics*, Government of South Africa, 2005, www.thedti.gov.za/econdb/raportt/rapstruc.html (accessed July 2007).

Government of Ghana. "Investment Code." Accra, Ghana: Government of Ghana, 1985.

"National Medium Term Private Sector Development Strategy 2004–2008." Accra, Ghana: Government of Ghana, 2003.

Government of Mauritius. *The Present State of the Economy*. Port Louis, Mauritius: Government of Mauritius, 2000.

Government of South Africa. "The Reconstruction and Development Programme: A Policy Framework." Government of South Africa, www.polity.org.za/govdocs/rdp/rdp.html (accessed July 2007).

Kaunda, K. D. "Zambia's Economic Revolution." Address by the President. Lusaka, Zambia: Zambian Information Services, 1968.

Ministry of Economic Planning and Development. "Mauritius Economic Review 1992–1995." Port Louis, Mauritius: Ministry of Economic Planning and Development, 1996.

Office of National Development and Planning. "First National Development Plan 1966–1970." Lusaka, Zambia: Republic of Zambia, undated.

Rawlings, Jerry John. *A Revolutionary Journey: Selected Speeches of Flt. Lt. J. J. Rawlings, Chairman of the Provisional National Defence Council, December 31 1981 – December 31 1982*. Vol. 1. Tema, Ghana: Information Services Department, Ghana Publishing Corporation, undated.

Sithanen, Hon. Ramakrishna, Minister of Finance. "Budget Speech 1994–1995." Port Louis, Mauritius, 20 June 1994.

South African Reserve Bank. "Annual Economic Report 1990."
    Johannesburg, South Africa: South African Reserve Bank, 1990.
    "Annual Economic Report 1996." Johannesburg, South Africa: South
    African Reserve Bank, 1996.
    "Annual Economic Report 1998." Johannesburg, South Africa: South
    African Reserve Bank, 1998.

Business documents

Ashanti Goldfields Company. "Annual Report 1998." 1–64. Accra, Ghana:
    Ashanti Goldfields Company, 1998.
    "Annual Report 1999." 1–63. Accra, Ghana: Ashanti Goldfields Company,
    1999.
Association of Ghana Industries. 2005. www.agighana.org/agi_info/
    about_us.htm (accessed July 2007).
    "Problems and Constraints Facing Industry in Ghana." Accra, Ghana:
    Association of Ghana Industries, undated.
Business Trust. "Business Trust: Together, We Will." 26. Johannesburg,
    South Africa: Business Trust, 2000.
Chamber of Mines of South Africa. "News, Data and Policy Information on
    the South African Mining Industry." www.bullion.org.za (accessed
    July 2007).
Chapman, T. N., and M. B. Hofmeyr. "Business Statesman of the Year
    Award." Paper presented at the Harvard Business School Club of South
    Africa, 10 August 1994.
Mauritius Chamber of Commerce and Industry. "Annual Report 1992."
    Port Louis, Mauritius, 1992.
    "Annual Report 1994." Port Louis, Mauritius: Mauritius Chamber of
    Commerce and Industry, 1994.
    "Annual Report 1995." Port Louis, Mauritius: Mauritius Chamber of
    Commerce and Industry, 1995.
    "Annual Report 1996." Port Louis, Mauritius: Mauritius Chamber of
    Commerce and Industry, 1996.
    "Annual Report 1997." Port Louis, Mauritius: Mauritius Chamber of
    Commerce and Industry, 1997.
Mauritius Employers' Federation. "The Vital Voice of Mauritius Enterprise."
    Mauritius Employers' Federation, undated.
Motlanthe, Kgalema. "Address to the Johannesburg Branch of the Black
    Management Forum." African National Congress, 2004, www.anc.
    org.za/ancdocs/speeches/2004/sp0930.html (accessed March 2007).
National Economic Development and Labour Council. "Founding Declaration
    of NEDLAC." NEDLAC, 1995, www.nedlac.org.za (accessed July 2007).

Private Enterprise Foundation. Accra, Ghana: Private Enterprise Foundation, undated pamphlet.

South African Chamber of Business. "The Voice of Business." SACOB, 2007, www.sacob.co.za/ (accessed July 2007).

South Africa Foundation. *Growth for All: An Economic Strategy for South Africa*. Johannesburg, South Africa: South Africa Foundation, 1996.

"Objectives of the Foundation." Johannesburg, South Africa: South Africa Foundation, undated.

Cited interviews

Abbey, Joseph. 2001.
Abeasi, Kwasi. 2001.
Ahwoi, Atu. 2001.
Amakye, Phillip Y. 2001.
Apea, S. K. 2001.
Armond, Peter. 2000.
Aryeetey, Ernest. 2001.
Bagbin, Alban. 2001.
Bull, Theo. 2000.
Cheeroo, Mahmood. 2001.
Coovadia, Cas. 2004.
Damali, Frank. 2001.
Dzotefe, Samuel. 2004.
Fitrell, Troy Damian. 2000.
Friedman, Steven. 2001, 2004.
Gelb, Stephen. 2001.
Godsell, Bobby. 2001.
Gyimah-Boadi, E. 2001.
Hantuba, Muna. 2000.
Lamusse, Roland. 2001.
Landman, J. P. 2001.
Lewis, David. 2004.
Mkandawire, Abel. 2000.
Mwanza, Jacob Mumbi. 2000.
Obeng, P. V. 2001.
O'Donnell, Mark. 2002, 2000.
Patel, Dipak. 2000.
Pratt, Kwesi Jr. 2000.
Roberts, Simon. 2004.
Rumney, Reg. 2004.
Scott, Guy. 2000.

Shubane, Kehla. 2001.
Simamba, Moses. 2000.
Sithanen, Ramakrishna. 2001.
Soko, Mike. 2000.
Verhoef, Grietjie. 2004.

Secondary sources

Acemoglu, Daron, Simon Johnson, and James A. Robinson. "Institutions as a Fundamental Cause of Long-Run Growth." In *Handbook of Economic Growth*, ed. Philippe Aghion and Steven N. Durlauf, 386–472. Amsterdam, The Netherlands: Elsevier North-Holland, 2005.

Adam, Heribert. "The South African Power Elite: A Survey of Ideological Commitment." In *South Africa: Sociological Perspectives*, ed. Heribert Adam, 73–102. Oxford University Press, 1971.

Adam, Heribert, Frederick van Zyl Slabbert, and Kogila Moodley. *Comrades in Business: Post-Liberation Politics in South Africa*. Cape Town, South Africa: Tafelberg Publishers, 1997.

Addison, John, and K. Hazareesingh. *A New History of Mauritius*. London: Macmillan, 1984.

Africa Private Sector Group. *Presidential Investors' Advisory Councils in Africa: Impact Assessment Study*. Washington, DC: World Bank, 2005.

African Development Bank. *Ghana: Country Strategy Paper 2005–2009*. African Development Fund, 2005.

African Peer Review Mechanism. *Country Review Report of the Republic of Ghana*. Midrand, South Africa: The New Partnership for Africa's Development, 2005.

Agyeman-Duah, Baffour. "Ghana, 1982–6: The Politics of the PNDC." *Journal of Modern African Studies* 25, no. 4 (1987): 613–42.

Allen, Richard B. *Slaves, Freedmen, and Indentured Laborers in Colonial Mauritius*. Cambridge University Press, 1999.

Amsden, Alice. *Asia's Next Giant*. Oxford University Press, 1989.

Andersson, Per-Ake, Arne Bigsten, and Hakan Persson. *Foreign Aid, Debt and Growth in Zambia*. Uppsala, Sweden: Nordiska Afrikainstitutet, 2000.

Anin, T. E. *Essays on the Political Economy of Ghana*. Ilford, Essex: Selwyn Publishers, 1991.

Anyemadu, Kwasi. "The Economic Policies of the PNDC." In *Ghana under PNDC Rule*, ed. E. Gyimah-Boadi 13–47. London: CODESRIA, 1993.

Appiah-Kubi, Kojo. "State-Owned Enterprises and Privatisation in Ghana." *Journal of Modern African Studies* 39, no. 2 (2001): 197–229.

Armah, Bartholomew K. *Reflections on the State of the Economy of Ghana in 1999*. Legislative Alert 6, no. 3, Accra, Ghana: Institute of Economic Affairs, 1999.

Arthur, Peter. "The State, Private Sector Development and Ghana's 'Golden Age of Business.'" *African Studies Review* 49, no. 1 (2006): 31–50.

Aryeetey, Ernest. "Structural Adjustment and Aid in Ghana." Accra, Ghana: Friedrich Ebert Foundation, 1996.

Austin, Gareth. *Labour, Land and Capital in Ghana: From Slavery to Free Labour in Asante, 1807–1956.* Rochester, NY: University of Rochester Press, 2005.

Ayee, Joseph, Michael Lofchie, and Caroline Wieland. *Government–Business Relations in Ghana: The Experience with Consultative Mechanisms.* Washington, DC: Private Sector Development Department, The World Bank, 1999.

Baran, Paul. *The Political Economy of Growth.* New York: Monthly Review Press, 1957.

Bates, Robert H. *Markets and States in Tropical Africa: The Political Basis of Agricultural Policies.* Berkeley, CA: University of California Press, 1981.

Bates, Robert H, and Anne O. Krueger, eds. *Political and Economic Interactions in Economic Policy Reform: Evidence from Eight Countries.* Malden, MA: Blackwell, 1993.

Bauer, P. T. *West African Trade.* New York: Augustus M. Kelley, 1967.

Bayart, Jean-Francois. "Africa in the World: A History of Extraversion." *African Affairs* 99 (2000): 217–67.

Bell, Trevor. "Should South Africa Further Liberalise its Foreign Trade?" In *State and Market in Post-Apartheid South Africa*, ed. Merle Lipton and Charles Simkins, 81–127. Johannesburg, South Africa: Witwatersrand University Press, 1993.

Bellin, Eva. "Contingent Democrats: Industrialists, Labor, and Democratization in Late-Developing Countries." *World Politics* 52 (2000): 175–205.

Bernstein, Ann. "Business and Public Policy in South Africa." Johannesburg, South Africa: The Urban Foundation, 1998.

Berry, Sara. *No Condition is Permanent: The Social Dynamics of Agrarian Change in Sub-Saharan Africa.* Madison, WI: University of Wisconsin Press, 1993.

Bienen, Henry, and John Waterbury. "The Political Economy of Privatization in Developing Countries." *World Development* 17, no. 5 (1989): 617–32.

Biermann, Werner. "The Development of Underdevelopment: The Historic Perspective." In *Development in Zambia: A Reader*, ed. Ben Turok, 128–36. London: Zed Press, 1979.

Boahen, Adu. *Ghana: Evolution and Change in the Nineteenth and Twentieth Centuries.* London: Longman, 1975.

Bond, Patrick. *Elite Transition: From Apartheid to Neo-Liberalism in South Africa.* London: Pluto Press, 2000.

Boone, Catherine. *Merchant Capital and the Roots of State Power in Senegal, 1930–1985.* Cambridge University Press, 1992.

Political Topographies of the African State: Territorial Authority and Institutional Choice. Cambridge University Press, 2003.

Brautigam, Deborah. "Institutions, Economic Reform and Democratic Consolidation in Mauritius." *Comparative Politics* 30, no. 1 (1997): 45–62.

"The People's Budget? Politics, Participation and Pro-Poor Policy." *Development Policy Review* 22, no. 6 (2004): 653–68.

"Revenue, State Capacity and Governance." *IDS Bulletin* 33, no. 3 (2002): 10–20.

Brautigam, Deborah, Lise Rakner, and Scott Duncan Taylor. "Business Associations and Growth Coalitions in Sub-Saharan Africa." *Journal of Modern African Studies* 40, no. 4 (2002): 519–47.

Brown, Andrea. *Black Economic Empowerment.* Global Equity Research, UBS Warburg South Africa Research Team. Johannesburg, South Africa: UBS Warburg, 2002.

Bundoo, Sunil Kumar, and Beealasingh Dabee. "Gradual Liberalization of Key Markets: The Road to Sustainable Growth in Mauritius." *Journal of International Development* 11 (1999): 437–64.

Burdette, Marcia. "Were the Copper Nationalisations Worth-While?" In *Beyond Political Independence: Zambia's Development Predicament in the 1980s,* ed. Klaas Woldring and Chibiwe Chibaye, 23–71. Berlin, Germany: Mouton Publishers, 1984.

Burnell, Peter. "Does Economic Reform Promote Democratisation? Evidence from Zambia's Third Republic." *New Political Economy* 6, no. 2 (2001): 191–212.

Callinicos, Alex. *South Africa between Reform and Revolution.* Reading: Bookmarks, 1988.

Carroll, Barbara Wake, and Terrance Carroll. "Accommodating Ethnic Diversity in a Modernizing Democratic State: Theory and Practice in the Case of Mauritius." *Ethnic and Racial Studies* 23, no. 1 (2000): 120–42.

"Civic Networks, Legitimacy and the Policy Process." *Governance* 12, no. 1 (1999): 1–28.

Case, William. "Malaysia: New Reforms, Old Continuities, Tense Ambiguities." *Journal of Development Studies* 41, no. 2 (2005): 284–309.

Cassim, Rashad. "The Political Economy of Trade Negotiations in Post-Apartheid South Africa." Paper presented at the ISP workshop, undated.

Center for Democracy and Development. "Elite Attitudes to Democracy and Markets in Ghana." In *CDD-Ghana Research Paper.* Accra, Ghana: Center for Democracy and Development, 2000.

"The Ghana Governance and Corruption Survey: Evidence from Households, Enterprises and Public Officials." Accra, Ghana: Center for Democracy and Development, 2000.

"Popular Attitudes to Democracy and Markets in Ghana." In *Survey Report/CDD Research Paper*. Accra, Ghana: Center for Democracy and Development, 1999.

Chabane, Neo, Johannes Machaka, Nkululeko Molaba, Simon Roberts, and Milton Taka. "Ten Year Review: Industrial Structure and Competition Policy." 81. Johannesburg, South Africa: School of Economic and Business Sciences, University of the Witwatersrand, 2003.

Chazan, Naomi. "The Political Transformation of Ghana under the PNDC." In *Ghana: The Political Economy of Recovery*, ed. Donald Rothchild, 21–47. Boulder, CO: Lynne Rienner Publishers, 1991.

Chazan-Gillig, Suzanne. "Ethnicity and Free Exchange in Mauritian Society." *Social Anthropology* 8, no. 1 (2000): 33–44.

Chikulo, Bornwell C. "Elections in a One-Party Participatory Democracy." In *Development in Zambia: A Reader*, ed. Ben Turok, 201–13. London: Zed Press, 1979.

Chileshe, Jonathan H. *Third World Countries and Development Options: Zambia*. New Delhi, India: Vikas Publishing House, 1986.

Chipungu, Samuel N. "Accumulation from Within: The Boma Class and the Native Treasury in Colonial Zambia." In *Guardians in Their Time: Experiences of Zambians under Colonial Rule 1890–1964*, ed. Samuel N. Chipungu, 74–96. London: Macmillan, 1992.

Chua, Amy. *World on Fire: How Exporting Free Market Democracy Breeds Ethnic Hatred and Global Instability*. New York: Doubleday, 2003.

Clark, Nancy L. *Manufacturing Apartheid: State Corporations in South Africa*. New Haven, CT: Yale University Press, 1994.

Collier, Paul, and Jan Willem Gunning. "Explaining African Economic Performance." *Journal of Economic Literature* 37 (1999): 64–111.

Craig, John. "Putting Privatisation into Practice: The Case of Zambia Consolidated Copper Mines Limited." *Journal of Modern African Studies* 39, no. 3 (2001): 389–410.

Dake, J. Mawuse. "Reflections on Party Politics and Impact on Democratic Development in Ghana." In *Civil Society in Ghana*, ed. F. K. Drah and M. Oquaye, 91–108. Accra, Ghana: Friedrich Ebert Foundation, 1996.

Davenport, T. R. H., and Christopher Saunders. *South Africa: A Modern History*. 5th edn. London: Macmillan, 2000.

Doner, Richard F., Bryan K. Ritchie, and Dan Slater. "Systemic Vulnerability and the Origins of Developmental States: Northeast and Southeast Asia in Comparative Perspective." *International Organization* 59 (2005): 327–61.

Doner, Richard F., Bryan K. Ritchie, and Ben Ross Schneider. "Business Associations and Economic Development: Why Some Associations Contribute More Than Others." *Business and Politics* 2, no. 3 (2000): 261–88.

Doraisami, Anita. "The Political Economy of Capital Flows and Capital Controls in Malaysia." *Journal of Contemporary Asia* 35, no. 2 (2005): 249–63.

Dubow, Saul. *The African National Congress*. Reading: Sutton Publishing, 2000.

Durand, Francisco, and Eduardo Silva, eds. *Organised Business, Economic Change and Democracy in Latin America*. Miami, FL: North-South Center Press, 1998.

Easterly, William, and Ross Levine. "Africa's Growth Tragedy: Policies and Ethnic Divisions." *Quarterly Journal of Economics* 112, no. 4 (1997): 1203–50.

Economist Intelligence Unit. *Country Report: Mauritius*. London: Economist Intelligence Unit, 1999.

"Country Report: South Africa, First Quarter 2000." Economist Intelligence Unit, 2002, www.eiu.co.uk (accessed 2002).

Ghana Country Profile 1990–91. London: Economist Group, 1990.

Mauritius Country Profile 1998–99. London: Economist Group, 1999.

Eriksen, Thomas Hylland. *Common Denominators: Ethnicity, Nation-Building and Compromise in Mauritius*. Oxford: Berg, 1998.

Evans, Peter B. *Embedded Autonomy: States and Industrial Transformation*. Princeton, NJ: Princeton University Press, 1995.

"Predatory, Developmental and Other Apparatuses: Comparative Political Economy Perspectives on the Third World State." *Sociological Forum* 4, no. 4 (1989): 561–87.

"State Structures, Government–Business Relations, and Economic Transformation." In *Business and the State in Developing Countries*, ed. Sylvia Maxfield and Ben Ross Schneider, 63–87. Ithaca, NY: Cornell University Press, 1997.

Fafchamps, Marcel. *Market Institutions in Sub-Saharan Africa: Theory and Evidence*. Cambridge, MA: The MIT Press, 2004.

Fearon, James D. "Why Ethnic Politics and 'Pork' Tend to Go Together." Paper presented at the "Ethnic Politics and Democratic Stability" conference, Wilder House, University of Chicago, 21–23 May 1999.

Fearon, James D., and David D. Laitin. "Explaining Interethnic Cooperation." *American Political Science Review* 90, no. 4 (1996): 715–35.

Fedderke, Johannes, Chandana Kularatne, and Martine Mariotti. "Mark-up Pricing in South African Industry." 50: Universities of Cape Town, British Columbia, and California at Los Angeles, 2004.

Fine, Ben. "Industrial and Energy Policy." In *The Political Economy of South Africa's Transition*, ed. Jonathan Michie and Vishnu Padayachee, 125–154. London: The Dryden Press, 1997.

Fine, Robert, and Dennis Davis. *Beyond Apartheid: Labour and Liberation in South Africa*. London: Pluto Press, 1990.

Fitch, Bob, and Mary Oppenheimer. *Ghana: End of an Illusion*. New York: Monthly Review Press, 1966.

Frieden, Jeffry A. *Debt, Development, and Democracy: Modern Political Economy and Latin America 1965–1985*. Princeton, NJ: Princeton University Press, 1991.

Frimpong-Ansah, Jonathan H. "Flexibility and Responsiveness in the Ghana Economy: Reflections on Post-Decline Atrophy Syndrome." Accra, Ghana: Ghana Academy of Arts and Sciences, 1996.

The Vampire State in Africa: The Political Economy of Decline in Ghana. London: James Currey, 1991.

Fundanga, C. "The Role of the Private Sector in Zambia's Economy." Paper presented at the Economic Policy and Development Conference, Pamodzi Hotel, Lusaka, Zambia, 27–29 October 1986.

Garlick, Peter C. *African Traders and Economic Development in Ghana*. Oxford University Press, 1971.

Geertz, Clifford. *Peddlers and Princes*. Chicago, IL: University of Chicago Press, 1963.

Gerschenkron, Alexander. *Economic Backwardness in Historical Perspective, a Book of Essays*. Cambridge, MA: Belknap Press of Harvard University Press, 1962.

Geschiere, Peter. "Imposing Capitalist Domination through the State: The Multifarious Role of the Colonial State in Africa." In *Old Modes of Production and Capitalist Encroachment: Anthropological Explorations of Africa*, ed. Wim van Binsbergen and Peter Geshiere, 99–143. London: KPI Ltd., 1985.

Godsell, Gillian. "Entrepreneurs Embattled: Barriers to Entrepreneurship in South Africa." In *The Culture of Entrepreneurship*, ed. Brigitte Berger, 85–97. San Francisco, CA: ICS Press, 1991.

Goldsmith, Arthur A. "Africa's Overgrown State Reconsidered: Bureaucracy and Economic Growth." *World Politics* 51, no. 4 (1999): 520–46.

Gomez, E. T. "The Perils of Pro-Malay Policies." *Far Eastern Economic Review* 168, no. 8 (2005): 36–9.

Gomez, E. T. and K. S. Jomo. *Malaysia's Political Economy: Politics, Patronage and Profit*. Cambridge University Press, 1999.

Granovetter, Mark. "Economic Action and Social Structure: The Problem of Embeddedness." *American Journal of Sociology* 91, no. 3 (1985): 481–510.

Greenberg, Stanley B. *Race and State in Capitalist Development: Comparative Perspectives*. Binghamton, NY: Yale University Press, 1980.

Gulhati, Ravi, and Raj Nallari. *Successful Stabilization and Recovery in Mauritius*, EDI Development Policy Case Series. Analytical Case Studies, No. 5. Washington, DC: World Bank, 1990.

Gumede, William Mervin. *Thabo Mbeki and the Battle for the Soul of the ANC*. Cape Town, South Africa: Zebra Press, 2005.

Gyimah-Boadi, E. "The Search for Economic Development and Democracy in Ghana." In *Ghana under PNDC Rule*, ed. E. Gyimah-Boadi, 1–12. London: CODESRIA, 1993.

Hamill, James. "The ANC Perspective: Meeting Expectations?" In *The New South Africa: Prospects for Domestic and International Security*, ed. F. H. Toase and E. J. Yorke, 59–102. London: Macmillan, 1998.

Hanson, Margaret, and James J. Hentz. "Neocolonialism and Neoliberalism in South Africa and Zambia." *Political Science Quarterly* 114, no. 3 (2002): 479–502.

Harris, Laurence. "The Economic Strategy and Policies of the African National Congress." In *McGregor's Economic Alternatives*, ed. Anne McGregor, 25–75. Wynberg, South Africa: Juta and Co., 1990.

Hart, Elizabeth, and E. Gyimah-Boadi. *Business Associations in Ghana's Economic and Political Transition*. Critical Perspectives, no. 3. Accra, Ghana: Centre for Democracy and Development, 2000.

Heng, Pek Koon. "The Chinese Business Elite of Malaysia." In *Southeast Asian Capitalists*, ed. Ruth McVey, 127–44. Ithaca, NY: Cornell Southeast Asia Program, 1999.

Hentz, James Jude. "The Two Faces of Privatisation: Political and Economic Logics in Transitional South Africa." *Journal of Modern African Studies* 38, no. 2 (2000): 203–23.

Herbst, Jeffrey. "Mbeki's South Africa." *Foreign Affairs* 84, no. 6 (2005): 93–105.

The Politics of Reform in Ghana, 1982–1991. Berkeley, CA: University of California Press, 1993.

"South Africa: Economic Crises and Distributional Imperative." In *South Africa: The Political Economy of Transformation*, ed. Stephen John Stedman, 29–45. Boulder, CO: Lynne Rienner Publishers, 1994.

States and Power in Africa. Princeton, NJ: Princeton University Press, 2000.

Hill, Catherine B., and Malcolm F. McPherson, eds. *Promoting and Sustaining Economic Reform in Zambia*. Cambridge, MA: Harvard University Press, 2004.

Hill, Polly. *Studies in Rural Capitalism in West Africa*. Cambridge University Press, 1970.

Hirschman, Albert O. *The Strategy of Economic Development*. New Haven, CT: Yale University Press, 1961.

Hirschmann, David. "Of Monsters and Devils, Analyses and Alternatives: Changing Black South African Perceptions of Capitalism and Socialism." *African Affairs* 89, no. 356 (1990): 341–69.

Ilophe, Dumisani, Malachia Mathoho, and Maxine Reitzes. *The Business of Blackness: The Foundation of African Business and Consumer Services, Democracy and Donor Funding*. Research Report no. 83. Johannesburg, South Africa: Centre for Policy Studies, 2001.

Hopkins, A. G. "Big Business in African Studies." *Journal of African History* 28, no. 1 (1987): 119–40.

Hutchcroft, Paul D. *Booty Capitalism: The Politics of Banking in the Philippines*. Ithaca, NY: Cornell University Press, 1998.

Hutchful, Eboe. "Why Regimes Adjust: The World Bank Ponders its 'Star Pupil.'" *Canadian Journal of African Studies* 29, no. 2 (1995): 303–17.

Hyden, Goran. *Beyond Ujamaa in Tanzania: Underdevelopment and an Uncaptured Peasantry*. London: Heinemann, 1980.

Iheduru, Okechukwu Chris. "Black Entrepreneurs in Post-Apartheid South Africa." In *African Entrepreneurship: Theory and Reality*, ed. Anita Spring and Barbara E. McDade, 69–92. Gainesville, FL: University Press of Florida, 1998.

"The Development of Black Capitalism in South Africa and the United States." In *Black Business and Economic Power*, ed. Alusine Jalloh and Toyin Falola, 572–604. Rochester, NY: University of Rochester Press, 2002.

"Social Concertation, Labour Unions and the Creation of a Black Bourgeoisie in South Africa." *Commonwealth and Comparative Politics* 40, no. 2 (2002): 47–85.

Ihonvbere, Julius O. *Economic Crisis, Civil Society, and Democratisation: The Case of Zambia*. Trenton, NJ: Africa World Press, 1996.

Iliffe, John. *The Emergence of African Capitalism*. Minneapolis, MN: University of Minneapolis Press, 1983.

Institute of Statistical Social and Economic Research. *The State of the Ghanaian Economy in 1992*. Legon, Ghana: Institute of Statistical Social and Economic Research, University of Ghana, 1993.

The State of the Ghanaian Economy in 1993. Legon, Ghana: Institute of Statistical Social and Economic Research, University of Ghana, 1994.

The State of the Ghanaian Economy in 1994. Legon, Ghana: Institute of Statistical Social and Economic Research, University of Ghana, 1995.

The State of the Ghanaian Economy in 1995. Legon, Ghana: Institute of Statistical Social and Economic Research, University of Ghana, 1996.

The State of the Ghanaian Economy in 1996. Legon, Ghana: Institute of Statistical Social and Economic Research, University of Ghana, 1997.

The State of the Ghanaian Economy in 1997. Legon, Ghana: Institute of Statistical Social and Economic Research, University of Ghana, 1998.

The State of the Ghanaian Economy in 1999. Legon, Ghana: Institute of Statistical Social and Economic Research, University of Ghana, 2000.

Jalloh, Alusine, and Toyin Falola, eds. *Black Business and Economic Power*. Rochester, NY: University of Rochester Press, 2002.

Jenkins, Carolyn. "The Politics of Economic Policy-Making in Zimbabwe." *Journal of Modern African Studies* 35, no. 4 (1997): 575–602.

Johnson, Chalmers. *Japan, Who Governs? The Rise of the Developmental State*. New York: W. W. Norton and Co., 1995.

Jung, Courtney. *Then I Was Black: South African Political Identities in Transition*. New Haven, CT: Yale University Press, 2000.

Kaplan, D. E. "The Politics of Industrial Protection in South Africa, 1910–1939." In *South African Capitalism and Black Political Opposition*, ed. Martin J. Murray, 299–326. Cambridge, MA: Schenkman, 1982.

Kaplinsky, Raphael. "Capitalist Accumulation in the Periphery – the Kenyan Case Re-Examined." *Review of African Political Economy* 7, no. 17 (1980): 83–105.

Kapur, Devesh, John P. Lewis, and Richard Webb. *The World Bank: Its First Half Century*. 2 vols. Vol. 1. Washington, DC: Brookings Institution Press, 1997.

Karl, Terry Lynn. *The Paradox of Plenty: Oil Booms and Petro-States*. Berkeley, CA: University of California Press, 1997.

Kennedy, Paul. *African Capitalism: The Struggle for Ascendancy*. Cambridge University Press, 1990.

Kentridge, Matthew. *Turning the Tanker: The Economic Debate in South Africa*. Johannesburg, South Africa: Centre for Policy Studies, 1993.

Koelble, Thomas A. "Building a New Nation: Solidarity, Democracy and Nationhood in the Age of Circulatory Capitalism." In *What Holds Us Together: Social Cohesion in South Africa*, ed. David Chidester, Phillip Dexter, and Wilmot James, 143–72. Cape Town, South Africa: Human Sciences Research Council Press, 2003.

Kohli, Atul. *State-Directed Development: Political Power and Industrialization in the Global Periphery*. Cambridge University Press, 2004.

Krasner, Stephen. "Approaches to the State: Alternative Conceptions and Historical Dynamics." *Comparative Politics* 16, no. 2 (1984): 223–46.

Kraus, Jon. "Capital, Power and Business Associations in the African Political Economy: A Tale of Two Countries, Ghana and Nigeria." *Journal of Modern African Studies* 40, no. 3 (2002): 395–436.

"The Political Economy of Stabilization and Structural Adjustment in Ghana." In *Ghana: The Political Economy of Recovery*, ed. Donald Rothchild, 119–55. Boulder, CO: Lynne Rienner Publishers, 1991.

Krog, Antjie. *Country of My Skull*. Johannesburg, South Africa: Random House, 1998.

Kurth, James R. "The Political Consequences of the Product Cycle: Industrial History and Political Outcomes." *International Organization* 33, no. 1 (1979): 1–34.

Lamusse, Roland. "The Achievements and Prospects of the Mauritius Export Processing Zone." In *Economic Planning and Performance in Indian Ocean Island States*, ed. R. T. Appleyard and R. N. Ghosh, 34–51. Canberra: National Centre for Development Studies, Australian National University, 1990.

"Adjustment to Structural Change in Manufacturing in a North–South Perspective." World Employment Programme Research, 1989.

Landman, J. P. "Labour 1: Business 0." www.jplandman.co.za (accessed 2001).

Lange, Matthew. "Embedding the Colonial State: A Comparative-Historical Analysis of State Building and Broad-Based Development in Mauritius." *Social Science History* 27, no. 3 (2003): 397–423.

Laville, Rosabelle. "In the Politics of the Rainbow: Creoles and the Civil Society in Mauritius." *Journal of Contemporary African Studies* 18, no. 2 (2000): 277–94.

Lazar, David. "Competing Economic Ideologies in South Africa's Economic Debate." *British Journal of Sociology* 47, no. 4 (1996): 599–626.

Le Vine, Victor T. *Political Corruption: The Ghana Case*. Stanford, CA: Hoover Institution Press, 1975.

Leys, Colin. "Learning from the Kenya Debate." In *Political Development and the New Realism in Sub-Saharan Africa*, ed. David E. Apter and Carl G. Rosberg, 220–43. Charlottesville, VA: University Press of Virginia, 1994.

Underdevelopment in Kenya: The Political Economy of Neo-Colonialism. Berkeley, CA: University of California Press, 1974.

Lieberman, Evan. *Race and Regionalism in the Politics of Taxation in Brazil and South Africa*. Cambridge University Press, 2003.

Lipton, Merle. *Capitalism and Apartheid: South Africa 1910–1986*. Aldershot, UK: Wildwood House, 1986.

Lodge, Tom. "The Future of South Africa's Party System." *Journal of Democracy* 17, no. 3 (2006): 152–66.

"Policy Processes within the African National Congress and the Tripartite Alliance." *Politikon* 26, no. 1 (1999): 5–32.

Lubeck, Paul M. *The African Bourgeoisie: Capitalist Development in Nigeria, Kenya and the Ivory Coast*. Boulder, CO: Lynne Rienner Publishers, 1987.

McCaskie, T. C. *State and Society in Pre-Colonial Asante*. Cambridge University Press, 1995.

McCourt, Willy, and Anita Ramgutty-Wong. "Limits to Strategic HRM: The Case of the Mauritian Civil Service." *International Journal of Human Resource Management* 14, no. 4 (2003): 600–18.

MacGaffey, Janet. *Entrepreneurs and Parasites: The Struggle for Indigenous Capitalism in Zaire.* Cambridge University Press, 1987.

McGregor BFA. *McGregor's Who Owns Whom in South Africa.* 24th edn. Florida Hills, South Africa: Carla Soares, Who Owns Whom, 2004.

McGregor, Robin, and Guy McGregor. "The Origins and Extent of the Lack of Competition in South Africa." In *McGregor's Economic Alternatives*, ed. Anne McGregor, 351–67. Cape Town, South Africa: Juta and Co., 1990.

McKinley, Dale T. *The ANC and the Liberation Struggle: A Critical Political Biography.* London: Pluto Press, 1997.

Macro-Economic Research Group. *Making Democracy Work.* Cape Town, South Africa: Centre for Development Studies, 1993.

McVey, Ruth. "The Materialization of the Southeast Asian Entrepreneur." In *Southeast Asian Capitalists*, ed. Ruth McVey, 7–33. Ithaca, NY: Cornell Southeast Asia Program, 1992.

Mamdani, Mahmoud. *Citizen and Subject: Contemporary Africa and the Legacy of Late Colonialism.* Princeton, NJ: Princeton University Press, 1996.

Mann, Michael. "The Autonomous Power of the State: Its Origins, Mechanisms and Results." In *Political Geography: A Reader*, ed. J. Agnew, 58–81. London: Arnold, 1997.

Marks, Shula, and Stanley Trapido. "The Politics of Race, Class and Nationalism." In *The Politics of Race, Class and Nationalism in Twentieth Century South Africa*, ed. Shula Marks and Stanley Trapido, 1–70. London: Longman, 1987.

Mbeki, Thabo. "Empowerment Good for the Economy and the Nation." *ANC Today* 3, no. 48 (2003), www.anc.org.za/ancdocs/anctoday.
"Questions that Demand Answers." *ANC Today* 4, no. 36 (2004), www. anc.org.za/ancdocs/anctoday.

Mbikusita-Lewanika, Akashambatwa. *Milk in a Basket! The Political Economic Malaise in Zambia.* Lusaka, Zambia: Zambian Research Foundation, 1990.

Meillassoux, Claude. *The Anthropology of Slavery: The Womb of Iron and Gold.* Trans. Alide Dasnois. Chicago, IL: University of Chicago Press, 1986.

Meisenhelder, Thomas. "The Developmental State in Mauritius." *Journal of Modern African Studies* 35, no. 2 (1997): 279–97.

Meyns, Peter. "The Political Economy of Zambia." In *Beyond Political Independence: Zambia's Development Predicament in the 1980s*, ed. Klaas Woldring and Chibiwe Chibaye, 7–22. Berlin, Germany: Mouton Publishers, 1984.

Michie, Jonathan, and Vishnu Padayachee, eds. *The Political Economy of South Africa's Transition.* London: The Dryden Press, 1997.

Migdal, Joel S., *Strong Societies and Weak States: State-Society Relations and State Capabilities in the Third World.* Princeton NJ: Princeton University Press, 1988.

Migdal, Joel S, Atul Kohli, and Vivienne Shue. *State Power and Social Forces: Domination and Transformation in the Third World.* Cambridge University Press, 1994.

Milburn, Josephine. *British Business and Ghanaian Independence.* London: C. Hurst and Company, 1977.

Miles, William F. S. "The Mauritius Enigma." *Journal of Democracy* 10, no. 2 (1999): 91–104.

Milner, Helen. *Resisting Protectionism: Global Industries and the Politics of International Trade.* Princeton, NJ: Princeton University Press, 1988.

Moore, Barrington. *Social Origins of Dictatorship and Democracy: Lord and Peasant in the Making of the Modern World.* Boston, MA: Beacon Press, 1966.

Morris, Mike. "The Development of Capitalism in South Africa." In *South African Capitalism and Black Political Opposition*, ed. Martin J. Murray, 39–64. Cambridge, MA: Schenkman, 1982.

Morrison, Minion K. C., and Jae Woo Hong. "Ghana's Political Parties: How Ethno/Regional Variations Sustain the National Two-Party System." *Journal of Modern African Studies* 44, no. 4 (2006): 623–47.

Mpuku, H. C., and I. Zyulu, eds. *Contemporary Issues in Socio-Economic Reform in Zambia.* London: Ashgate, 1997.

Mukherjee, Aditya. *Imperialism, Nationalism and the Making of the Indian Capitalist Class, 1920–1947.* New Delhi, India: Sage Publications, 2002.

Murray, Georgina. "Black Empowerment in South Africa: 'Patriotic Capitalism' or a Corporate Black Wash?" *Critical Sociology* 26, no. 3 (2000): 183–204.

Murray, Martin J. "The Consolidation of Monopoly Capital, 1910–1948: The State Apparatus, the Class Struggle and Political Opposition," in *South African Capitalism and Black Political Opposition*, ed. Martin J. Murray, 237–45. Cambridge, MA: Schenkman, 1982.

"The Development of Capitalist Production Processes: The Mining Industry, the Demand for Labour and the Transformation of the Countryside 1870–1910." In *South African Capitalism and Black Political Opposition*, ed. Martin J. Murray, 127–36. Cambridge, MA: Schenkman, 1982.

"Monopoly Capitalism in the Apartheid Era, 1948–80." In *South African Capitalism and Black Political Opposition*, ed. Martin J. Murray, 397–404. Cambridge, MA: Schenkman, 1982.

Mwenda, Kenneth Kaoma. *Zambia's Stock Exchange and Privatisation Programme: Corporate Finance Law in Emerging Markets*. Lewiston, NY: The Edwin Mellen Press, 2001.

Nafziger, E. Wayne. *African Capitalism: A Case Study in Nigerian Entrepreneurship*. Stanford, CA: Hoover Institution Press, 1977.

Nattrass, Nicoli. "The ANC's Economic Policy: A Critical Perspective." In *Wealth or Poverty: Critical Choices for South Africa*, ed. Robert Schrire, 623–34. Oxford University Press, 1992.

"Collective Action Problems and the Role of South African Business in National and Regional Accords." *South African Journal of Business Management* 29, no. 3 (1997): 105–12.

"The Truth and Reconciliation Commission on Business and Apartheid: A Critical Evaluation." *African Affairs* 93, no. 392 (1999): 373–91.

Nedelsky, Jennifer. "Reconceiving Autonomy." *Yale Journal of Law and Feminism* 1 (1989): 7–36.

Ndulo, Muna. "Domestic Participation in Mining in Zambia." In *Development in Zambia: A Reader*, ed. Ben Turok, 49–70. London: Zed Press, 1979.

Ngoasheng, Moses. "Policy Research inside the African National Congress." *Transformation* 18 (1992): 115–24.

Niane, D. T. *Sundiata: An Epic of Old Mali*. Trans. G. D. Pickett. London: Longman, 1965.

Ninsin, Kwame A. "State, Capital and Labour Relations, 1961–1987." In *The State, Development and Politics in Ghana*, ed. Emmanuel Hansen and Kwame A. Ninsen, 15–42. London: CODESRIA Book Series, 1989.

Nugent, Paul. *Big Men, Small Boys and Politics in Ghana: Power, Ideology and the Burden of History 1982–1994*. Accra, Ghana: Asempa Publishers, 1996.

OECD. "Competition Law and Policy in South Africa." 75. Paris, France: Organisation for Economic Co-operation and Development, 2003.

Okudzeto, Sam. "The Role of the Association of Recognised Professional Bodies in the Political Struggles of Ghana." In *Civil Society in Ghana*, ed. F. K. Drah and M. Oquaye, 109–28. Accra, Ghana: Friedrich Ebert Foundation, 1996.

O'Meara, Dan. *Forty Lost Years: The Apartheid State and the Politics of the National Party 1948–1994*. Athens, OH: Ohio University Press, 1996.

Volkskapitalisme: Class, Capital and Ideology in the Development of Afrikaner Nationalism, 1934–1948. Cambridge University Press, 1983.

Owusu, Francis, and Abdi Ismail Samatar. "Industrial Strategy and the African State: The Botswana Experience." *Canadian Journal of African Studies* 31, no. 2 (1997): 268–99.

Parpart, Jane L. *Labor and Capital on the African Copperbelt*. Philadelphia, PA: Temple University Press, 1983.

Parsons, Raymond. *The Mbeki Inheritance: South Africa's Economy 1990–2004*. Johannesburg, South Africa: Ravan Press, 1999.

Peil, Margaret. *The Ghanaian Factory Worker: Industrial Man in Africa*. Cambridge University Press, 1972.

Pellow, Deborah, and Naomi Chazan. *Ghana: Coping with Uncertainty*. Boulder, CO: Westview Press, 1986.

Phiri, Bizeck Jube. *A Political History of Zambia*. Trenton, NJ: Africa World Press, 2006.

Polanyi, Karl. *The Great Transformation*. Boston, MA: Beacon Press, 1944.

Posner, Daniel N. *Institutions and Ethnic Politics in Africa*. Cambridge University Press, 2005.

Rakner, Lise. "The Pluralist Paradox: The Decline of Economic Interest Groups in Zambia in the 1990s." *Development and Change* 32 (2001): 521–43.

Political and Economic Liberalisation in Zambia, 1991–2001. Uppsala, Sweden: The Nordic Africa Institute, 2003.

"Reform as a Matter of Political Survival: Political and Economic Liberalisation in Zambia 1991–1996." Dr. Polit Dissertation, Christen Michelsen Institute, 1998.

Riggs, Fred. *Thailand: The Modernisation of a Bureaucratic Polity*. Honolulu, HI: East West Center Press, 1966.

Rimmer, Douglas. *Staying Poor: Ghana's Political Economy 1950–1990*. Oxford: Pergamon Press, 1992.

Robinson, Vicki, and Stefaans Brummer. "SA Democracy Incorporated: Corporate Fronts and Political Party Funding." *ISS Paper* 129. Pretoria, South Africa: Institute for Security Studies, 2006.

Rodrik, Dani. *The New Global Economy and Developing Countries*. Baltimore, MD: Johns Hopkins University Press, 1999.

Sadie, J. L. "The Fall and Rise of the Afrikaner in the South African Economy." Stellenbosch, South Africa: Unpublished mimeo, 2001.

Sampson, Anthony. *Black and Gold: Tycoons, Revolutionaries and Apartheid*. London: Hodder and Stoughton, 1987.

Mandela: The Authorised Biography. London: HarperCollins, 1999.

Sandbrook, Richard. "Origins of the Democratic, Developmental State: Interrogating Mauritius." *Canadian Journal of African Studies* 39, no. 3 (2005): 549–81.

Sandbrook, Richard, and Judith Barker. *The Politics of Africa's Economic Stagnation*. Cambridge University Press, 1985.

Sandbrook, Richard, and Jay Oelbaum. *Reforming the Political Kingdom: Governance and Development in Ghana's Fourth Republic*. Critical Perspectives, no. 2. Accra, Ghana: Centre for Democracy and Development, 1999.

Sardanis, Andrew. *Africa: Another Side of the Coin: Northern Rhodesia's Final Years and Zambia's Nationhood*. London: I. B. Tauris, 2003.

Schatz, Sayre P. *Nigerian Capitalism*. Berkeley, CA: University of California Press, 1977.

Schneider, Ben Ross. *Business Politics and the State in Twentieth-Century Latin America*. Cambridge University Press, 2004.

"Organizing Interests and Coalitions in the Politics of Market Reform in Latin America." *World Politics* 56 (2004): 456–79.

"Why is Mexican Business so Organized?" *Latin American Research Review* 37, no. 1 (2002): 77–118.

Scott, Guy. "Zambia: Structural Adjustment, Rural Livelihoods and Sustainable Development." *Development Southern Africa* 19, no. 3 (2002): 405–18.

Seidman, Ann. "The Distorted Growth of Import-Substitution Industry: The Zambian Case." *Journal of Modern African Studies* 12, no. 4 (1974): 601–31.

Seleti, Yona Ngalaba. "Entrepreneurship in Colonial Zambia." In *Guardians in Their Time: Experiences of Zambians under Colonial Rule 1890–1964*, ed. Samuel N. Chipungu, 147–79. London: Macmillan, 1992.

Shafer, Michael D. *Winners and Losers: How Sectors Shape the Developmental Prospects of States*. Ithaca, NY: Cornell University Press, 1994.

Shenton, Robert. *The Development of Capitalism in Northern Nigeria*. London: James Currey, 1986.

Sieh, Lee Mei Ling. "The Transformation of Malaysian Business Groups." In *Southeast Asian Capitalists*, ed. Ruth McVey, 103–26. Ithaca, NY: Cornell Southeast Asia Program, 1999.

Silva, Eduardo. *The State and Capital in Chile*. Boulder, CO: Westview Press, 1996.

Simons, H. J. "Zambia's Urban Situation." In *Development in Zambia: A Reader*, ed. Ben Turok, 1–25. London: Zed Press, 1979.

Sklar, Richard L. *Corporate Power in an African State*. Berkeley, CA: University of California Press, 1975.

Skocpol, Theda. "Bringing the State Back In: Strategies of Analysis in Current Research." In *Bringing the State Back In*, ed. Peter B. Evans, Dietrich Rueschemeyer, and Theda Skocpol, 3–37. Cambridge University Press, 1985.

South African Institute of International Affairs. "Zambia: A Shining Example of Privatisation?" In *Intelligence Update*. Johannesburg, South Africa: South African Institute of International Affairs, 1999.

Southall, Roger. "The State of Party Politics: Struggles within the Tripartite Alliance and the Decline of Opposition." In *State of the Nation: South Africa 2003–2004*, ed. John Daniel, Adam Habib, and Roger Southall, 53–77. Cape Town, South Africa: HSRC Press, 2003.

Sparks, Allister. *The Mind of South Africa*. London: Heinemann, 1990.

Srebrnik, Henry. "Can an Ethnically-Based Civil Society Succeed? The Case of Mauritius." *Journal of Contemporary African Studies* 18, no. 1 (2000): 7–20.

"'Full of Sound and Fury': Three Decades of Parliamentary Politics in Mauritius." *Journal of Southern African Studies* 28, no. 2 (2002): 277–89.

Stanley, Elizabeth. "Evaluating the Truth and Reconciliation Commission." *Journal of Modern African Studies* 39, no. 3 (2001): 525–46.

Stevens, Mike, and Stefanie Teggemann. "Comparative Experience with Public Sector Reform in Ghana, Tanzania and Zambia." In *Building State Capacity in Africa*, ed. Sahr Kpundeh and Brian Levy, 43–86. Washington, DC: World Bank Publications, 2004.

Strategic African Securities. "Ghana's Economic Performance, 1990–1999: Lessons from the Analysis of Key Macro-Economic Indicators." Accra, Ghana: Strategic African Securities, 2001.

Subramanian, Arvind, and Devesh Roy. "Who Can Explain the Mauritian Miracle? Meade, Romer, Sachs or Rodrik?" In *In Search of Prosperity: Analytic Narratives on Economic Growth*, ed. Dani Rodrik, 205–43. Princeton, NJ: Princeton University Press, 2003.

Swainson, Nicola. *The Development of Corporate Capitalism in Kenya 1918–77*. Berkeley, CA: University of California Press, 1980.

"Indigenous Capitalism in Postcolonial Kenya." In *The African Bourgeoisie*, ed. Paul M. Lubeck, 137–63. Boulder, CO: Lynne Rienner, 1987.

Tangri, Roger. "The Politics of Government–Business Relations in Ghana." *Journal of Modern African Studies* 30, no. 1 (1992): 97–111.

"The Politics of State Divestiture in Ghana." *African Affairs* 90, no. 361 (1991): 523–36.

"Public Enterprise and Industrial Development: The Industrial Development Corporation of Zambia." In *Beyond Political Independence: Zambia's Development Predicament in the 1980s*, ed. Klaas Woldring and Chibiwe Chibaye, 113–28. Berlin, Germany: Mouton Publishers, 1984.

Taylor, Ian. *Stuck in Middle Gear: South Africa's Post-Apartheid Foreign Relations*. Westport, CT: Praeger, 2001.

Taylor, Scott D. "Beyond Business as Usual: Business Associations, the State and Liberalization in Zimbabwe and Zambia." Ph.D. Dissertation, Emory University, 1998.

"The Challenge of Indigenization, Affirmative Action, and Black Empowerment in Zimbabwe and South Africa." In *Black Business and Economic Power*, ed. Alusine Jalloh and Toyin Falola, 347–80. Rochester, NY: University of Rochester Press, 2002.

Terreblanche, Sampie, and Nicoli Nattrass. "A Periodization of the Political Economy from 1910." In *The Political Economy of South Africa*, ed. Nicoli Nattrass and Elisabeth Ardington, 6–23. Oxford University Press, 1990.

Thioub, Ibrahima, Momar-Coumba Diop, and Catherine Boone. "Economic Liberalization in Senegal: Shifting Politics of Indigenous Business Interests." *African Studies Review* 41, no. 2 (1998): 63–89.

Thompson, Leonard. *A History of South Africa*. Revised edn. Binghamton, NY: Yale University Press, 1995.

Turok, Ben. "The Penalties of Zambia's Mixed Economy." In *Development in Zambia: A Reader*, ed. Ben Turok, 71–86. London: Zed Press, 1979.

van de Walle, Nicolas. *African Economies and the Politics of Permanent Crisis 1979–1999*. Cambridge University Press, 2001.

van Walraven, Klaas. "The End of an Era: The Ghanaian Elections of December 2000." *Journal of Contemporary African Studies* 20, no. 2 (2002): 183–202.

Vaughan, Megan. *Creating the Creole Island: Slavery in Eighteenth-Century Mauritius*. Durham, NC: Duke University Press, 2005.

Verhoef, Grietjie. "'The Invisible Hand': The Roots of Black Economic Empowerment, Sankorp and Societal Change in South Africa, 1985–2000." *Journal for Contemporary History* 28, no. 1 (2003): 27–47.

Vickery, Kenneth P. *Black and White in Southern Tonga: The Tonga Plateau Economy and British Imperialism, 1890–1939*. New York: Greenwood Press, 1986.

Wade, Robert. *Governing the Market: Economic Theory and the Role of Government in East Asian Industrialization*. Princeton, NJ: Princeton University Press, 1990.

Waldmeir, Patti. *Anatomy of a Miracle: The End of Apartheid and the Birth of the New South Africa*. New York: W. W. Norton and Co., 1997.

Wassenaar, A. D. *Assault on Private Enterprise: The Freeway to Communism*. Cape Town, South Africa: Tafelberg, 1977.

Weber, Max. *Economy and Society: An Outline of Interpretive Sociology*. Ed. Guenther Roth and Claus Wittich. 3 vols. Vol. 1. New York: Bedminster Press, 1968.

Weiss, Linda, and John M. Hobson. *States and Economic Development: A Comparative Historical Analysis.* Cambridge: Polity Press, 1995.

Wetzel, Deborah. "Promises and Pitfalls in Public Expenditure." In *Economic Reforms in Ghana: The Miracle and the Mirage*, ed. Ernest Aryeetey, Jane Harrigan, and Machiko Nissanke, 115–31. Oxford: James Currey, 2000.

White, Nicholas J. "The Beginnings of Crony Capitalism: Business, Politics and Economic Development in Malaysia, c. 1955–70." *Modern Asian Studies* 38, no. 2 (2004): 389–417.

Wignaraja, Ganeshan. "Firm Size, Technological Capabilities and Market-Oriented Policies in Mauritius." *Oxford Development Studies* 30, no. 1 (2002): 87–104.

Wignaraja, Ganeshan, and Sue O'Neil. *SME Exports and Public Policies in Mauritius.* London: Commonwealth Secretariat, 1999.

Wilks, Ivor. *Forests of Gold: Essays on the Akan and the Kingdom of Asante.* Athens, OH: Ohio University Press, 1993.

Young, Crawford. *African Colonial State in Comparative Perspective.* New Haven, CT: Yale University Press, 1994.

Young, Roger, and John Loxley. *Zambia: An Assessment of Zambia's Structural Adjustment Experience.* Ottawa, Canada: The North–South Institute, 1990.

Index